Further Praise for

Reading Dante

"In *Reading Dante*, Prue Shaw has performed a great service. . . . In my more than 40 years reading Dante and my more than 20 years teaching him, I have never encountered a better introduction to the poet, in English or Italian, than this book. . . . [A] stunning achievement."

—Tim Redman, *Dallas Morning News*

"You might expect an introduction to *The Divine Comedy* written by one of the world's foremost Dante scholars, . . . who has spent many a year working in the dark corners of libraries decoding manuscript after manuscript, to be astute and accomplished, and perhaps even definitive. But you would not necessarily expect it to be completely enthralling, even—perhaps especially—for the non-specialist reader. But Prue Shaw's remarkable *Reading Dante* succeeds on both scores. It is a virtuoso performance . . . the finest modern companion to the great poet."   —Ambrogio Camozzi Pistoia, *Tablet*

"Scholarly, compelling and original. . . . Much of the charm of Shaw's book comes from the way she combines her personal interests and enthusiasms with scholarly accuracy and balance. If she underlines his perennial modernity, her Dante still remains the historical author. . . . [A]s interesting an introduction to Dante as one could hope to find in any language."

—David Robey, *Times Literary Supplement*

"Shaw's sharp, brilliantly engaging book delivers masterfully on its promise to fuel love for the *Comedy* precisely by dispelling readers' anxieties, and showing how the great underlying concerns of this work are not only those of every work of art but are the stuff of life itself. Moreover, she keeps us so enthralled with her compelling and fast-paced prose that the only reason one would want to put down this book is to open the one she is talking about. . . . [A] book such as Shaw's is invaluable in putting literature and language back into the central cultural place they deserve—and, more importantly, into the centre of our hearts as readers."

—Elena Lombardi, *Times Higher Education*

"Prue Shaw's brilliant new book . . . in fluent and compelling prose . . . takes on the most challenging task of all: to recover the astonishing power of the *Comedy* as literature and poetry. . . . Shaw is the opposite of pious in recovering the sheer intellectual force of Dante's theology. . . . [W]hether or not we are believers, we recognise that he is posing the fundamental questions of all human life." —Robert Gordon, *Literary Review*

"Splendid and enlightening. There couldn't be a better introduction to the language of Dante's poem for English-speaking readers." —Giulio Lepschy

"This entertaining and learned tour through *The Divine Comedy* by a noted Dante scholar blends history with criticism and sheds welcome light on some of the poem's more esoteric references. . . . Shaw is especially good at conveying the emotional and psychological aspects of Dante's journey." —*The New Yorker*

"The foremost expert on Dante in the English language, Shaw escorts us on a transcendent voyage from hell to heaven and time to eternity. It is a journey, above all, about the power of Dante's poetry—its originality, its artistic breadth, its vision of the human condition, its reaching for the stars." —Arlice Davenport, *Wichita Eagle*

"In this engaging, accessible introduction to Dante's *Divine Comedy*, Shaw offers a rich interpretation that adds historical context alongside formal analysis to rekindle our wonder. . . . The entertaining and learned Shaw succeeds in her primary objective: to send casual readers and scholars back to the poem itself." —*Publishers Weekly*

"Dante expert Shaw explains *The Divine Comedy* so easily and simply, she eliminates all trepidation in anyone daunted by his masterpiece. . . . Shaw exposes the profound depth and art of poetry that encompasses so much more than language and rhythm. . . . Read this book to discover Dante the man, the pilgrim and the poet. Then go read his greatest poem. He's well worth the exploration, and Shaw is a Virgil-like guide." —*Kirkus Reviews*, starred review

Also by Prue Shaw

Dante, *Monarchia*,
edited and translated by Prue Shaw

..

Dante, *Monarchy*, edited by Prue Shaw

..

The Letters of Giacomo Leopardi 1817–1837,
selected and translated by Prue Shaw

..

Dante Alighieri, *Commedia*,
edited by Prue Shaw

Canto decimo. doue tracta del sexto
cerchio delinferno e della pena delli
Eretici. et in forma dinduinare, in p̃.
di messer farinata predice molte cose.
et diquella che auennero a dante.
e solue una questione

Ra seruia p̃ un secreto calle
tra il muro della terra e li martyri
lomio maestro e io dopo le spalle..

O uirtu somma che p̃ liempi giri
mi uolui, incomincia come ti piace
parlami e sodisfami amici disiri.

L agente che p̃ li sepol
potrebbesi veder gi
tucti coperti e nessu

E r elli a me tutti sar
quando di josaphat
coi corpi che lasu a

S uo cimitero da que
con epicuro tucti si
che l anima col cor

P ero ala dimanda e
quincentro satisfa
e al disio ancor cheti

E t io buon duca non
ate mio cuor senor
e tu mai no puoi in

O tosco che p̃ la citta d
uiuo tennai cosi p̃
piacciati di restare

L a tua loquela tifa
diquella nobil patria natio
ala qual forse ifu troppo molesto.

S ubitamente questo suono usao
d una dellarche p̃o maccostai
temendo unpoco piu al duca mio.

Reading Dante

FROM HERE TO ETERNITY

Prue Shaw

LIVERIGHT PUBLISHING CORPORATION

A Division of

W. W. NORTON & COMPANY

NEW YORK | LONDON

First published as a Liveright paperback 2015

Since this page cannot legibly accommodate all the copyright notices,
pages 291–96 constitute an extension of the copyright page.

For information about permission to reproduce selections from this book,
write to Permissions, Liveright Publishing Corporation, a division of
W. W. Norton & Company, Inc., 500 Fifth Avenue, New York, NY 10110

For information about special discounts for bulk
purchases, please contact W. W. Norton Special Sales
at specialsales@wwnorton.com or 800-233-4830

Book design by Barbara Bachman
Production manager: Devon Zahn

LIBRARY OF CONGRESS
CATALOGING-IN-PUBLICATION DATA

Shaw, Prue, author.
Reading Dante : From Here to Eternity / Prue Shaw. — First edition.
pages cm
Includes bibliographical references and index.
ISBN 978-0-87140-742-9 (hardcover)
1. Dante Alighieri, 1265–1321—Criticism and interpretation. I. Title.
PQ4335.S54 2014
851'.1—dc23
2013041961

ISBN 978-1-63149-006-4 pbk.

Liveright Publishing Corporation,
500 Fifth Avenue, New York, N.Y. 10110
www.wwnorton.com

W. W. Norton & Company Ltd., Castle House,
75/76 Wells Street, London W1T 3QT

For Claerwen and Lucinda

A poem is made of words,
not ideas.

..

Canto decimo. Doue tracta del sexto
cerchio delinferno e della pena delli
Eretici. et i forma di(n)douinare, i(m) p(ro)...
di mess farinata predice molte cose
et di quella che auuenero a dante
e solue una questione—

Ra senza p(er) un secreto calle
tra(l) muro della terra e li martyri
lo mio maestro e io dopo le spalle
O uirtu somma che p(er) liempi giri
mi uolui, cominciar come ti piace
parlami e sodisfami a mio disiri.

li sepolcri graue
eder gia son leuati
e nessun guardia face
icu ueran ferrati
p(er)? qui tornerino
lasu anno la feriati.
di questa p(ar)te anno
tucti suoi sequaci
col corpo morti fanno.
nda che mi fari
satisfacto sann tosto
oi cheti mitaci.
iou non tegno rispofte
e se non p(er) dicei poco
pur mo accio disposto.
iauta del foco
cosi parlando honesto
restare i(n) q(ue)sto loco.
la tisu mani fosto
oiquesta nobil patria natio
al aqual forse i fu troppo molesto.
Subitamente questo suomo usrio
suua dellarche p(er)o maccostai
temendo un pro piu aldn ai mio.

CONTENTS

*M*OST ENGLISH READERS KNOW THAT DANTE IS A GREAT POET, but few of them have read him. His masterpiece, the *Divine Comedy*, is an adventure story: a journey into the mysteries of the afterlife, a pilgrimage through hell, purgatory and paradise towards a final, face-to-face meeting with God. Its broader concerns are those of any thinking person, in any time and place. What does it mean to be a human being? How are we to judge human behaviour? What matters in a life or in a death? These themes are explored in a gripping narrative, and in language that is uniquely vital and expressive.

The *Commedia*, to give it its correct title, is the greatest poem of the Middle Ages and perhaps the greatest single work of Western literature. It was a huge success in its time, quickly becoming the medieval equivalent of a best-seller. It has continued to be read by most educated people up to the present day, and has inspired poets, artists and composers for over seven hundred years. Yet to a modern reader, reading for pleasure, the idea of a poem over fourteen thousand lines long about hell, purgatory and paradise can seem vast, alien and forbidding.

This book aims to introduce the reader to Dante's poem. It is intended for the general reader who loves literature and poetry—for language lovers everywhere, whether or not they know Italian. My main concern is to communicate the power of Dante's poetry—the imaginative power, the emotional intensity, the linguistic brilliance, and the skill with which he orchestrates his themes. Dante had an exceptional capacity to evoke the visual, the visceral; to imagine a world and give it form and substance with incredible verbal economy and precision. By conjuring up the sights and sounds and smells of the familiar world with unparalleled immediacy, he was able to lead his readers through invented worlds that were utterly convincing though infinitely strange. He populated them with individuals whose emotions and moral predicaments are tangible and compelling. Those he encounters speak with eloquence and their interchanges with Dante are full of drama. He expressed the whole range of human feelings in their raw power and endless variety: hope, fear, rage, delight, remorse, nostalgia, yearning, affection, disgust, anxiety, sorrow, astonishment, melancholy, curiosity, despair.

The qualities of imagination and expression, the emotions, come to us in stories—the story of Dante's journey and the stories of those he encounters on the way. All those he meets have been judged by God: a final and absolute decision has been made about the acceptability of their behaviour during their life, and we know what it is. The counterpoint between this knowledge and the sympathy, or lack of it, we feel for them creates a space in which the ultimate meaning of human behaviour is brought into sharp relief. Anyone who has ever felt the need to think about their own behaviour or somebody else's, and to try to understand its meaning, should find the poem riveting.

The way I have chosen to introduce the poem is unorthodox. I do not offer a digest or summary of the facts of Dante's life, or the stages of his journey to the three realms of the afterlife. Such accounts can overwhelm with detail, especially if the reader is new to the poem, and make it difficult to recognise the power of its central ideas. Each chapter of the book is organised around a theme, and illustrated by key episodes from the poem. I have linked encounters and scenes that are widely spaced in the narrative in order to demonstrate their connections, rather than moving in methodical fashion from one episode to the next.

The way Dante orchestrates his themes is one of the miracles of the poem, and not easy to pick up on a first reading, any more than someone listening to Wagner's Ring cycle will immediately appreciate the intricacy and complexity of the way he handles his leitmotifs. One senses that Dante had an extraordinarily rich map of the whole *Commedia* in his head as he was writing it, and an ear highly attuned to the resonances his stories had with one another. My hope is that these seven chapters will give some sense of this. I do not aim to save you the trouble of reading the *Commedia*, as handbooks to the poem sometimes seem to do. My aim is to fire you with the desire to pick up a copy and start reading now.

Dante's life and work were shaped by two friends of his youth in Florence. Both friends were poets. One of them, who died young, he meets in purgatory. The other was not someone he *could* meet in the poem, since he was not yet dead when the journey to the afterlife supposedly takes place. But this other, "best" friend—an atheist, as it happens—left an indelible impression on the poem, and is one of its most haunting presences. The first chapter sets these two friendships against the background of the city's troubled political and social history. The theme is literary friendship and rivalry, but it is also political instability and turmoil.

These two key strands in Dante's formative experience—poetry and politics—run in parallel but are quite distinct at this stage of his life. In his thirties, for the best part of a decade, he was a politician as well as a poet, passionately involved in the public life of his city. In 1302 his political activities led to his being exiled when he wound up on the losing side of factional struggles in Florence. The Florentine years are the seedbed of his mature poetry. What brings his poetry to maturity is the experience of exile.

The opening chapter shows where Dante started, and how his failure as a politician is inseparable from his achievement as a poet. A distinguished nineteenth-century Italian said that Florence should have erected a statue not to Dante but to the obscure Florentine official who sent him into exile. Without the experience of exile Dante would not—could not—have written the *Commedia*.

The second chapter is about art and its relationship to power. Dante calls to account the great players on the world stage—popes and emperors—who have the power to change the way things are but fail to do so. The archvillain is a pope, Boniface VIII, one among many corrupt churchmen Dante attacks with startling directness. The fate of these unprincipled popes in the afterlife is a vision of Brueghel-like intensity and perversion.

The relationship between biography and art—between lived experience and its imaginative transformation into literature—is the theme of the third chapter. The poem seems richly autobiographical but resists being pinned down in these terms. It lures us towards the dramas of its author's life, but at the same time it speaks of universal concerns, leaving its author partly shrouded in mystery. Just as he is both the writer and the pilgrim making the journey, Dante is himself and everyman.

In the *Commedia* love offers a key to understanding human behaviour. The fourth and central chapter shows how Dante treated the theme of love as a young poet, and how he developed and explored it in his maturity. Dante was driven by the need to reconcile a sense of the seemingly irresistible power of love, desire and sexual attraction as forces in human life with the notion of free will—with his conviction that human beings are able to make meaningful choices about their lives and actions, and can be held accountable for the choices they make.

Hell and paradise are eternal, outside or beyond time. Time can have no part in their workings. But in purgatory time is vitally important: some of Dante's most lyrical and evocative passages mark the passing of time in the middle realm. In the course of his journey Dante encounters many people he knew when they were alive: friends and enemies, poets and public figures. Meeting them again after death stirs memory, and prompts him to rethink his own past life. Alongside personal memory, cultural memory is a rich seam in the poem, carrying us back in time to earlier stages of human history. The way time plays out in the afterlife and in the poem itself is explored in the fifth chapter.

Researchers working at CERN in Geneva using the Large Hadron Collider speak of the simplicity and beauty of the mathematical principles that underlie the variety of existence. Fractal geometry is another underlying structural principle that unifies natural phenomena from the very small to the very large. The excitement modern scientists feel at these discoveries is the excitement Dante's poem communicates about numbers and their significance. The relation of numbers to the structure and functioning of the universe and to human creativity is the subject of the sixth chapter. Dante was an independent thinker, educated about the scientific debates of his day. His concerns are cosmic; they are also parochial and intimately personal—the inner world of individual conscience. The two orders of reality connect seamlessly. Thinking about numbers helps us to understand how Dante saw the universe and human behaviour; and it enables us to appreciate both the world he has imagined and the poem that describes it.

It is sometimes said that a language is a dialect with an army. You could say that Italian is a dialect with a great poet. There was no "Italian" in Dante's time. He wrote in the dialect of his native Florence, the language we now call Italian because of him. His creation of the *Commedia* secured for Florentine the supremacy over all competing dialects. The seventh and final chapter explores this historical reality. In the *Paradiso* Dante tries to express in human language a reality that is beyond human understanding: the vision of God. Some of the most limpid, moving and radiant lines in the poem are to be found here. This last chapter tries to give a sense of the originality and poetic power of the language of the *Commedia*. Quotations throughout are in Italian, followed by my own literal prose translation, in the hope of giving the English reader some feeling for the qualities of Dante's language—its range, its rhythmic variety and its exhilarating force.

Two writers I know, liberal humanists both, on being asked if they had read Dante, answered almost in unison: why would I bother? In this book I try to show why they should bother. A nineteenth-century Italian poet, writing when evolutionary ideas had begun to permeate popular consciousness and challenge traditional religious thinking, put the point with epigrammatic neatness in the final line of his sonnet on Dante. Even if God is dead, great art survives:

Muor Giove, e l'inno del poeta resta.
(God dies, and the poet's song remains.)

Inf.	*Inferno*
Purg.	*Purgatorio*
Par.	*Paradiso*
Mon.	*Monarchia*
De v. E.	*De vulgari Eloquentia*
Conv.	*Convivio*
Questio	*Questio de aqua et terra*

THE FOLLOWING LIST INCLUDES PEOPLE WHO APPEAR AS CHARACTERS in the *Commedia* and people who are mentioned in it. The names of persons referred to in my discussion but who do not appear in the poem itself are in italics. I give the death dates of contemporary figures to show how many of the characters Dante meets in the afterlife had only recently died (just as if a contemporary of ours were to be writing about the fate in the afterlife of Ronald Reagan and Margaret Thatcher).

ADAM The progenitor of the human race and the first user of language. He is the last person Dante speaks to before he enters the Empyrean; he enlightens the poet about the natural mutability of language.

AENEAS The hero of Virgil's epic poem the *Aeneid*. The story of his travels from Troy to Italy and his adventures on the way there were often read in the Middle Ages as an allegory of human life.

ANCHISES The father of Aeneas, who visits him in the underworld in Book VI of the *Aeneid*. The episode is echoed in Dante's meeting with his great-great-grandfather Cacciaguida in *Paradiso* xv–xvii.

AQUINAS The preeminent scholastic philosopher who sought to reconcile the philosophy of Aristotle with the doctrines of the Christian faith. He is often referred to simply by his first name, Thomas.

ARISTOTLE The Greek philosopher who was, for Dante, *il maestro di color che sanno* ("the master of those who know"). His many works on every aspect of human knowledge, lost to the Christian West for many centuries, survived through Arab translations and commentaries, which were translated into Latin in the century before Dante's birth. Their interpretation and explication, and the need to reconcile their teachings with Christian doctrine, became a primary focus of scholastic philosophy.

ARNAUT DANIEL A twelfth-century Provençal poet revered by Dante; he is praised by Guido Guinizzelli in *Purgatorio* xxvi as a *miglior fabbro* ("better craftsman") of the vernacular.

Arnolfo di Cambio The great Florentine sculptor and architect who designed the façade of the new cathedral in Florence in 1300, and who sculpted the statue of Pope Boniface VIII which was to have pride of place on it for more than two centuries.

AUGUSTUS The Roman emperor at the time of the birth of Christ. Dante saw his rule as providentially ordained so that there would be peace in the world when Christ was born.

AVERROES The great Arab philosopher, who wrote a commentary on Aristotle's works; he is often referred to in the Middle Ages simply as "the Commentator." Dante, remarkably, puts him in Limbo in spite of his not being a Christian.

AVICENNA The other great philosopher of Islam who is placed by Dante among the *spiriti magni* ("great spirits") in Limbo.

BEATRICE Traditionally identified, though on somewhat scant evidence, as Beatrice Portinari, she was the Florentine girl Dante loved in his youth, who died in 1290 at the age of twenty-four. The *Vita nova* celebrates his love for her in poems with a linking prose narrative. In the *Commedia*, she is his second guide in the afterlife, accompanying him from the earthly paradise through the heavenly spheres to the Empyrean.

Bembo Renaissance author of a book on vernacular speech, *Prose della volgar lingua*, which was highly critical of some aspects of Dante's language and style.

Bernard du Poujet The cardinal who ordered Dante's *Monarchia* to be burned in Bologna in 1329 and tried to ensure that the poet's bones were disinterred and burnt with it.

Boccaccio A writer of the generation after Dante; author of the *Decameron* and many other works in prose and verse. He venerated Dante, copied and edited the *Commedia* three times, wrote a life of Dante, and initiated the practice of public readings of the poem.

BOCCA DEGLI ABATI The Florentine traitor who caused the defeat of the Florentine Guelfs at Montaperti by cutting off the hand of their standard-bearer in mid-battle so that the troops did not know where to go.

BOETHIUS The Roman statesman and philosopher (480–520) who wrote *The Consolation of Philosophy* while in prison in Pavia, where he was subsequently tortured and executed. His book became one of the most widely read and influential works of the Middle Ages.

BONAGIUNTA DA LUCCA A Tuscan vernacular poet of the generation before Dante, who in *Purgatorio* xxiv acknowledges Dante's surpassing of his precursors by referring to his *dolce stil novo* ("sweet new style").

BONCONTE DA MONTEFELTRO The leader of the Ghibellines of Arezzo, who died in the Battle of Campaldino and whose remains were never found. Dante meets him in *Purgatorio* v, where he explains how he was saved from damnation by his repentance at the moment of death. Son of Guido da Montefeltro. Died in 1289.

Botticelli The fifteenth-century Florentine painter whose exquisite drawings for the *Commedia*—one for each canto of the poem—reflect his intimate knowledge and intuitive understanding of Dante's masterpiece.

BRUNETTO LATINI The Florentine statesman who was described by the chronicler Giovanni Villani as having educated his fellow citizens in rhetoric and civic leadership; author of a number of works in the vernacular (French and Italian) and a translation from Cicero. He was in exile in France from 1260 to 1266; on his return to Florence, he held many important public offices in the city. Died in 1294.

BRUTUS The killer of Julius Caesar. A traitor to a benefactor, he is found at the bottom of hell, being chewed by one of the monstrous mouths of the three-headed Satan.

CACCIAGUIDA Dante's great-great-grandfather (c. 1091–c. 1147), who died fighting for the faith in the Holy Land during the Second Crusade.

CASELLA A friend of Dante's youth who set Dante's poems to music. We know of him only from the *Commedia*, where Dante meets him in *Purgatorio* ii.

CATO A Roman famed for his integrity and moral uprightness, Cato killed himself in Utica after the defeat of Pompey by Caesar. In spite of his suicide, a sin in Dante's moral universe, the poet chose him to be the guardian of purgatory.

CAVALCANTE DE' CAVALCANTI The father of Dante's friend Guido Cavalcanti. Dante meets him in the circle of the heretics (*Inferno* x).

CHARLES I OF ANJOU The brother of King Louis IX of France (1226–1270); his descendants, the Angevins—the name reflects the connection with Anjou, a region in western France—are a collateral branch of the French royal family, the Capetian dynasty. Charles I of Anjou became king of Sicily in 1265; he defeated Manfred at Benevento in 1266. He lost the kingdom of Sicily as a consequence of the uprising known as the Sicilian Vespers in 1282.

CHARLES II OF ANJOU The eldest son of Charles I of Anjou; king of Naples from 1285 to 1309; he secured Angevin rule in the continental part of the former kingdom of Sicily. For marrying his daughter off for a huge sum of money, he is accused by his ancestor Hugh Capet in *Purgatorio* xx of selling her to the highest bidder, just as a pirate sells a slave girl.

CHARLES OF VALOIS The third son of King Philip III (the Bold) of France; brother of King Philip IV (the Fair). Charles of Valois went to Florence in 1301, supposedly as an impartial peacemaker but in reality as a supporter of the Blacks and in collusion with Pope Boniface VIII.

CIACCO The first Florentine Dante meets in hell, in the circle of the gluttonous (*Inferno* vi). Ciacco is possibly a pejorative nickname meaning "pig" or "hog."

CICERO Latin statesman, orator and author whose *De amicitia* (*On Friendship*) was one of two works Dante studied after the death of Beatrice (the other was Boethius's *The Consolation of Philosophy*). Dante tells us that he found the books hard going to start with but immensely rewarding when he persisted, and attributes his passion for philosophy to his study of them. Cicero's distinction between crimes of violence and crimes of fraud in *De officiis* (I 13) underlies the organisation of lower hell.

CIMABUE A Florentine painter (c. 1240–c. 1302) who taught Giotto; he was preeminent in his day but was eclipsed by his pupil.

Compagni Dino Compagni was a Florentine merchant, a contemporary of Dante, who was actively involved in the political life of the city. He was the author of a chronicle of the history of Florence, which, though sometimes unreliable, is nevertheless a precious eyewitness record of events at the turn of the century.

CORSO DONATI The leader of the Black Guelfs in Florence; brother of Forese and Piccarda Donati. He worked hand in glove with Boniface VIII and Charles of Valois to seize control of Florence in the coup of October 1301 which led to Dante's exile.

Cristoforo Landino A Florentine humanist who wrote an extensive commentary on the *Commedia*, published in 1481 and embellished with engravings based on drawings by Botticelli. This was the first edition of the poem to be printed in Florence.

DANTE Author and protagonist of the *Commedia*. Born in Florence in 1265; died in exile in Ravenna in 1321. A useful distinction is that between Dante the character in the poem and Dante the poet who writes it (in Italian, between *personaggio* and *poeta*; in Latin, between *agens* and *auctor*). Dante the character is sometimes referred to as the pilgrim or (in the United States) the wayfarer. Some readers find it useful to identify a third Dante, the author who masterminds the presentation of both pilgrim and poet—and one must never lose sight of the fact that the pilgrim is, of course, a poet. The protagonist is named just once, at *Purgatorio* xxx 55, when he meets Beatrice in the earthly paradise ten years after she died, and she berates him for his betrayal of her memory. His name is the first word she utters.

DAVID The Old Testament king, prophet and author of the psalms.

FARINATA DEGLI UBERTI The Florentine Ghibelline leader who with his Sienese allies led the troops to their victory against the Florentine

Guelfs at the Battle of Montaperti in 1260. After the battle, he prevented the victors from destroying Florence, his native city.

FORESE DONATI A friend of Dante's youth with whom he exchanged rude sonnets; brother of Corso and Piccarda. Died in 1296.

FRANCESCA DA RIMINI A contemporary figure of scandal, she was murdered by her husband for having an affair with his brother. Died c. 1283–1285.

Francesco di ser Nardo da Barberino in Val di Pesa A professional copyist with his own scriptorium in Florence, reputed to have made one hundred copies of the *Commedia* in order to secure dowries for his daughters. There are two surviving copies in his exceptionally beautiful hand; we can be confident that they reflect the layout of the autograph of the poem.

FREDERICK II The last of the Holy Roman Emperors. Died in 1250.

GIOTTO The foremost Florentine painter, a contemporary of Dante; his technique radically altered the course of painting.

GUIDO CAVALCANTI A thirteenth-century Florentine poet, son of Cavalcante de' Cavalcanti; Dante's poetic mentor and friend, to whom he dedicated the *Vita nova*.

GUIDO DA MONTEFELTRO A Ghibelline statesman and warlord from the Romagna who became a friar in old age. Fatally, he was persuaded by Boniface VIII to give advice on how to defeat his enemies the Colonna and to take their stronghold, Palestrina. This led to his damnation among the counsellors of fraud, where Dante meets him in *Inferno* xxvii. Died in 1298.

Guido da Pisa A Carmelite friar who wrote one of the earliest commentaries on the *Inferno* (c. 1328–1333), in Latin.

GUIDO DEL DUCA A nobleman from Romagna, of whom we know little; in *Purgatorio* xiv he laments the passing of the good old days of virtue and honour.

GUIDO GUINIZZELLI A Bolognese poet of the preceding generation revered by Dante above all others among his Italian precursors. Died in 1276.

Henry VII of Luxembourg The figure on whom Dante pinned his hopes for the restoration of imperial authority in the Italian peninsula. Died at Benevento in 1313 before accomplishing his mission.

Hugh Capet The founding father of the Capetian line of kings of France, whose contemporary descendants (Charles of Anjou and Charles of Valois) he excoriates in *Purgatorio* xx for their destructive ambition and greed.

Jacopo di Dante Dante's son, who wrote a brief verse summary (*Capitolo*) of the *Commedia*, and a sparse commentary on it. He took a complete copy of the *Commedia* to Florence after his father's death, where it rapidly became very popular.

John the Baptist The precursor and cousin of Jesus, who lived in the wilderness and was beheaded by Herod at the request of Salome. Patron saint of Florence, whose baptistery bears his name (San Giovanni). Dante had been baptised and hoped to the end of his days to be crowned poet *nel mio bel San Giovanni*. John the Baptist's image was imprinted on one side of the Florentine gold florin.

Justinian The Roman emperor of the sixth century who codified Roman law. In *Paradiso* vi he gives a majestic account of the history of the Roman Empire as the fulfilment of a providential plan.

Leonardo Bruni The chancellor of Florence in the first half of the fifteenth century (1410–1411 and 1427–1444), who wrote a life of Dante, emphasising his civic virtues rather than his poetic talents. He saw letters in Dante's own hand which do not survive.

Levi Primo Levi was an Italian chemist and writer who survived internment in Auschwitz; he described his experience there in his book *Se questo è un uomo* (*If This Is a Man*—published in the United States as *Survival in Auschwitz*).

Mandelstam Osip Mandelstam (1891–1938) was a Russian poet arrested by Stalin and sent into internal exile. He died in a transit camp. He wrote his "Conversation about Dante" in 1933.

Manfred The illegitimate son of Emperor Frederick II, he died at the Battle of Benevento in 1266. Dante meets him among the excommunicates in *Purgatorio* iii.

MARCO LOMBARDO A courtier from Lombardy, of whom we know little; he raises the philosophical problem of free will and enlightens Dante on the relationship between papacy and empire.

MARS The Roman god of war, once the patron saint of Florence, replaced by John the Baptist. A statue of Mars that had once stood in the temple over which the baptistery was built stood in medieval times by the Ponte Vecchio, so that the medieval city could be described as lying *tra Marte e 'l Batista* ("between Mars and the Baptist"), the statue of Mars marking the southern limit of the city and the baptistery its northern limit. (See map on p. 22.)

MASTRO ADAMO A counterfeiter or forger of florins whom Dante meets in *Inferno* xxx. Burned at the stake in 1281.

MINOS The monstrous figure who stands at the entrance to the second circle of hell and judges sinners, assigning them to the appropriate circle of the abyss by wrapping his tail around himself the corresponding number of times. Minos had the same role of judge of hell in the *Aeneid*.

ODERISI DA GUBBIO A manuscript illuminator renowned for the beauty of his miniatures. Died in 1299.

Ottimo ("Best") The name given to an early commentary (1333–1340) on the *Commedia*; its author, a Florentine called Andrea Lancia, had known Dante in person.

PHILIP IV (THE FAIR) The second son of King Philip III (the Bold) of France; brother of Charles of Valois. Philip the Fair was king of France from 1285 to 1314. His reign was marked by his aggressive ambitions for territorial expansion and his energetic manoeuvres to avoid paying taxes to the pope.

PIA DE' TOLOMEI A figure of whom we know only that her husband had her murdered so that he could make an advantageous marriage with someone else. Dante meets her in *Purgatorio* v in ante-purgatory among the late repentant.

PICCARDA DONATI A nun abducted from her convent and forced to marry; sister of Corso and Forese. Her fate raises the problem of the culpability of those who fail to keep their vows because they are victims of violence. She is in the heaven of the moon (*Paradiso* iii).

Pietro di Dante Dante's second son, who became a successful lawyer and wrote a long commentary on the *Commedia* in three separate versions over a twenty-year period (1340–c. 1360).

Pluto The infernal guardian of the fourth circle in hell, who greets Dante and Virgil with garbled speech.

Pope Adrian V Pope for just over a month in 1276.

Pope Boniface VIII Pope from 1294 to 1303; Dante's archvillain. His papal bull *Unam sanctam* claimed absolute authority for the pope in spiritual and temporal affairs.

Pope Celestine V An unworldly hermit pressured into becoming pope in July 1294 and, it is thought, pressured into abdicating in December 1294 by his successor, Boniface VIII. Almost certainly the unnamed figure contemptuously dismissed in *Inferno* iii as *colui che fece per viltade il gran rifiuto* ("the one who out of cowardice made the great refusal"), though another candidate would be Pontius Pilate, who washed his hands of deciding on Jesus' fate.

Pope Clement V The French pope (1305–1314) who took the papacy to Avignon, where it remained for the next seventy years. He is described in *Inferno* xix as *un pastor sanza legge* ("a lawless shepherd").

Pope John XXI (1276–1277) Also called Peter of Spain; author of a seminal work on Aristotelian logic, the *Summule logicales*. The only contemporary pope to be found in Dante's heaven.

Pope Nicholas III The pope of Dante's adolescence (1277–1280). Dante meets him in the circle of the simoniacs (*Inferno* xix).

Ripheus A virtuous Trojan (in the *Aeneid* he is described as *iustissimus unus*, most righteous of the Trojans), placed by Dante in heaven for his devotion to justice.

Saladin (c. 1138–1193) The Muslim general who defeated the crusaders in 1187 and retook Jerusalem; famous for the magnanimity he showed to the defeated Christians. He is seen by Dante in Limbo, standing apart from the other *spiriti magni*.

Saint Augustine One of the four great Fathers of the Church (354–430).

xxviii | DRAMATIS PERSONAE

Author, among many other works, of the autobiographical *Confessions*, about his early life and conversion to Christianity, and the *De trinitate*, in which he meditated on the trinitarian structure of creation.

SAINT BERNARD The twelfth-century Cistercian, abbot of Clairvaux, famed for his devotion to the Virgin Mary and his contemplative mysticism. He is Dante's guide in the Empyrean as he approaches the Godhead in the final cantos of the poem.

SAINT FRANCIS OF ASSISI (1182–1226) Founder of the Franciscan order, authorised by Pope Innocent III when he had a dream of Francis holding up the Lateran church in Rome. Famed for the simplicity and poverty of his life. Italy's patron saint.

SAINT PAUL A Jew famously converted on the road to Damascus, after which he became an apostle for Christ, making missionary journeys to the Gentiles. Author of the Epistles to the Romans, Corinthians, Galatians, Ephesians, Colossians and Thessalonians, which form a substantial part of the New Testament, and lay the foundation for later Christian theology. At the outset of his journey to the otherworld, Dante declares to Virgil, *Io non Enëa, io non Paulo sono* ("I am not Aeneas, I am not Paul"), in so doing underlining the fact that Aeneas and Paul are the only human beings known to have had a direct experience of the afterlife, and he is following in their footsteps.

SAINT PETER Originally a fisherman, he became the first of the apostles, and ultimately the Vicar of Christ, and the bishop of Rome, having been entrusted by Christ with the keys to the kingdom of heaven. In *Paradiso* xxvii he denounces the degeneracy of the contemporary papacy, which has become a "sewer of blood and stench."

SATAN Also known as Lucifer. The leader of the angels who rebelled against God. His fall from heaven created the abyss of hell, and the mountain of purgatory. Imprisoned in the ice at the centre of the earthly globe, where his three heads chew on the bodies of the three archtraitors of benefactors: Judas, Brutus and Cassius.

SORDELLO An Italian poet from Mantua who wrote in Provençal.

STATIUS A Roman poet born in the first century A.D., whose epic poem the *Thebaid* was, alongside Virgil's *Aeneid*, a major inspiration for

Dante. In purgatory he is the only soul Dante meets who has completed the process of purgation. We do not know if his conversion to Christianity was an invention by Dante.

TRAJAN Roman emperor from 98 to 117, renowned for his integrity and devotion to justice.

UGOLINO A Pisan Ghibelline count and politician, who died horribly, immured in a tower with his children and left to starve to death, as a result of political treachery. Died in 1289.

ULYSSES The legendary Greek hero whose adventures after the fall of Troy are the subject of Homer's *Odyssey*. Dante knew of him through Ovid's *Metamorphoses*.

Vieri de' Cerchi The leader of the Florentine White Guelfs.

Villani Giovanni Villani was a Florentine contemporary of Dante who wrote an important chronicle of the city's history. Died of the Black Death in 1348.

VIRGIL The Roman poet who died in 19 B.C., just too early to be saved by the Christian message of salvation. Book VI of his epic poem the *Aeneid*, with its account of Aeneas's journey to the underworld in search of his father, Anchises, provided a model for the story of a journey to the afterlife, and a blueprint for many aspects of Dante's hell (including the infernal rivers—Acheron, Styx, Phlegethon and Cocytus—and infernal monsters and guardians, among them Minos and Cerberus). Virgil rescues Dante from the dark wood and accompanies him down into the abyss of hell and up the mountain of purgatory to the earthly paradise at its summit.

READING DANTE

The earliest known representation of Florence.

I.

Friendship

mio figlio ov'è? e perché non è teco?
(*Inf.* x 60)
(where is my son? and why isn't he with you?)

Virtue (without which friendship is impossible) is first;
but next to it, and to it alone,
the greatest of all things is friendship.
—CICERO, DE AMICITIA

ALMOST SEVEN HUNDRED YEARS AFTER IT WAS WRITTEN DANTE'S *Commedia* remains a work of compelling power to many readers, even those readers (perhaps especially those readers) who do not share its author's religious faith. Why should this be so? Dante is not just a Christian but a Catholic—and a medieval Catholic at that. His poem embodies and expresses a belief about the nature of the world and the place of human beings within it that is at once religious and scientific: the theology is antiquated, the science plain wrong.

Add to this that the poem projects a view of the moral universe—of good and bad actions, of virtue and sin—that can be described (and not unfairly) as hierarchical and judgmental: two adjectives not best designed to arouse interest or sympathy in a modern reader. The story it tells of a journey to the three realms of the afterlife—where the wicked are damned, those who repented their sins before death cleanse themselves in preparation for heaven, and the truly good enjoy beatitude—could seem simple-minded in its narrative scheme and its moral certainties. So what is its appeal?

Dante works within an orthodox religious framework. Yet the poem is absorbing and surprising in its capacity to move, to provoke and to engage the reader, of any faith or none, with the most fundamental questions about the human condition. Dante is a good Catholic but an independent thinker. He is determined to understand what it is to be a human being, and the place of the individual in society and in the cosmos—universal concerns that transcend any age or system of religious belief. Far from merely being a spokesman for medieval Catholic orthodoxy, he can reach conclusions his contemporaries found disconcerting and even dangerous.

This independence of mind is revealed early in the poem, when we find the great philosophers and poets of antiquity—Homer, Plato and Aristotle, among many others—occupying a place of special privilege on the edge of hell. Among their number, no less remarkably, are two great philosophers of Islam, Averroes and Avicenna. Unlike the damned, these thinkers and writers suffer no physical pain. Unlike the damned, they have pleasant surroundings: light, fine architecture, green grass, and good conversation—rather like the quad of an Oxbridge college, one might think. Virgil, Homer and the other classical writers assembled there often talk about poetry. Their only punishment is the knowledge of their exclusion from paradise: *sanza speme vivemo in disio* ("without hope we live in desire"). Their unrequited yearning for the divine has no hope of ever being satisfied. That is punishment enough.

Catholic theology made no such provision for the great minds and talents of the pagan past. The conventional view was that only unbaptised infants occupied Limbo, this region on the outer rim of hell (*limbo* means "edge"). The Jewish patriarchs like Abraham and Moses had been there too for a time, before they were taken up to heaven by Christ after his death. But no pagans belonged here, no matter how remarkable their lives had been for virtue or for wisdom.

One early commentator on the poem, Guido da Pisa, a Carmelite friar writing in the late 1320s, less than ten years after Dante's death, clearly admired the poet. Yet he felt it necessary to distance himself at the outset from this and similar examples of unorthodox thinking with a formula revoking in advance—*ex nunc revoco et annullo*—anything he inadvertently says in explicating the poem which is against the faith or against the holy church—*vel contra fidem vel contra sanctam ecclesiam*. (In the late 1950s at Sydney University, good Catholic girls used to take the same preemptive action by inscribing a monogram with just this meaning in the top corner of every page of their philosophy lecture notes.) Dante, explains Guido da Pisa, speaks as a poet and not as a theologian: *poetice et non theologice loquitur*. The enduring fascination of the *Commedia* lies precisely in the fact that Dante writes as a poet and not as a theologian. His view of the world was one that often alarmed his contemporaries, and it is still challenging today; but it is the way he found to express that view which makes the *Commedia* a masterpiece.

The poem tells the story of a journey to the afterlife, but it can also be seen as the story of a profound psychological crisis—and how that crisis was resolved.

Nel mezzo del cammin di nostra vita
   mi ritrovai per una selva oscura,
   ché la diritta via era smarrita.   (*Inf.* i 1–3)

(In the middle of the journey of our life, I found myself in a dark
   wood, for the straight path was lost.)

This is an experience any reader can relate to—anyone who has reached a painful point in life where the past has ceased to make sense and the way forward is unclear. Anyone facing the future with confusion, anxiety, despair. Anyone (in modern terms) who has sought counselling, seen a therapist, had a breakdown. When the American writer William Styron emerged from his first major bout of depression, he described the experience by quoting a single line from Dante, the last line of *Inferno*, saying that he "came forth and once again beheld the stars": *e quindi uscimmo a riveder le stelle.*

This making sense of his own past and coming to understand the meaning of his own life is one of the organizing principles of the narrative. The retrospective gaze that sees the pattern, discerning the true significance of events only with hindsight, operates in both the personal and the social sphere. Dante comes to understand his own disorientation and despair and how it came about; and he learns how that state connects with the state of the world around him, and what his role should henceforth be in relation to his fellow human beings.

The narrative of personal crisis unfolds against a broader backdrop of political events on the world stage. Here too it is only in retrospect, looking back from the vantage point of a new and painfully acquired insight, that everything falls into place and the outlines of the story become clear. The personal and the political prove to be indivisible. Fulfilment in one's personal life is only possible in a world ordered in accordance with the dictates of justice and peace. To bring about such a state in the world becomes the poet's mission, his instrument the poem he writes.

All the great themes of literature are here. Desire, time, memory. Revenge, forgiveness, atonement. Love and hate, loyalty and betrayal. Destructiveness and self-destructiveness. Exile and homecoming. Human diversity and resourcefulness, and the conditions necessary for human flourishing. Human weakness, and the ways in which people deceive themselves and project their distorted perceptions through the stories they tell about their lives. Money and power, and the damaging effects of an obsession with them on individual lives and the social fabric. War and peace, and the way the world should best be ordered. Intellectual ambition and the thirst for knowledge. The struggles of the artist with his medium. All this is embedded in a narrative framework that is intensely personal and evocative in its concrete detail, but universal in its insight into human behaviour and its concern for human happiness.

The narrative framework is simple: a journey to the three realms of the afterlife, where the protagonist meets and talks to the souls of the dead. He is accompanied on the journey first by the Roman poet Virgil, down into the cone-shaped pit of hell and up the mountain of purgatory. Then the girl he had loved in the Florence of his youth, Beatrice, takes him from the top of the mountain up through the heavens to the Empyrean (paradise), which lies outside the created world of time and space. Here, in the final lines of the poem, he sees God. The choice of guides is singular. A more pedestrian expectation might have been for a guide with religious street cred: a saint, perhaps, or an angel or a theologian.

Equally original is the geography of hell and purgatory, which only becomes clear as Dante travels and as we read. Hell takes the form of a series of nine concentric circles around a vast funnel-shaped underground abyss that goes all the way to the centre of the earth, where Lucifer is trapped. The distribution of sins in these nine circles is based not on biblical or Christian sources, but on Aristotelian and Ciceronian ideas of wrongdoing and evil behaviour. It is a scheme invented by Dante.

Fig. 1   Botticelli's plan of Dante's hell.

The mountain of purgatory, which rises in the southern ocean at the antipodes of Jerusalem, is likewise original in its conception, but the hierarchy of sinful dispositions it corrects is more orthodox. Each terrace on the mountain corresponds to one of the seven deadly sins as they are described by the Fathers of the Church. There is a holding area at the bottom of the mountain (ante-purgatory) for those who delayed repenting and who must therefore now delay starting on their journey up the mountain. This is Dante's invention; as is the placing of the Garden of Eden or earthly paradise, the original home of Adam and Eve before they sinned, at the top of the mountain. This last detail is especially significant. Dante has imagined an otherworld whose geography links the two key episodes of Christian world history. Adam's sin, which caused his expulsion from the Garden of Eden, and Christ's crucifixion, which redeems that sin—the earthly paradise and Jerusalem—are on the same axis, which passes through the centre of the earthly globe.

Dante's physical journey through this strange terrain is matched by a mental and psychological journey, a journey in knowledge and understanding. The protagonist learns as he goes. By the end, he has not just resolved his spiritual crisis; he has become the person who is capable of writing the poem which records that experience. Spiritual and artistic progress prove to follow the same trajectory. The poem could not have been written had the state of confusion and despair in which the poet found himself at the outset not been confronted and triumphed over. The trajectory is both linear and circular: in our end is our beginning. The story of the journey is, among other things, the story of becoming capable of writing the poem about the journey.

Two themes which emerge in the course of the narrative and are played out over much of its length enable us to chart his progress. Those themes are Dante's own history as a poet and his ambitions in public life. The two come together in the story of his relationship with Guido Cavalcanti, the first of the two friendships of his young manhood that this chapter considers. That friendship was essentially a friendship between writers, but it played out against the turbulent politics of the city in which the two young men lived. We will, in due course, need to consider that political background in some detail in order to understand the tensions in the friendship, and why, eventually, the friends fell out.

Cavalcanti, some ten years older than Dante, was one of the most

brilliant figures in Florentine culture in the closing decades of the thirteenth century. He was famous for his intelligence, his wit and his rather
withdrawn aristocratic manner. The contemporary chronicler Dino
Compagni describes him as "courteous and bold but haughty and solitary
and intent on studying." His reputation for these qualities outlived him.
Some fifty years later Boccaccio tells a story about him in the *Decameron*,
showing his insouciance in extricating himself from a potentially tricky
encounter with a gang of high-spirited revellers who want him to join
their group. (An exact modern equivalent would be the Oxford Bulling-

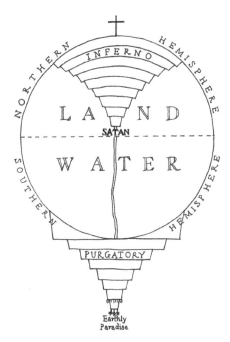

Fig. 2 In Dante's cosmos the mountain of purgatory, with the earthly
paradise at its summit, is at the antipodes of Jerusalem, so that the place
of mankind's fall (the Garden of Eden) is on the same axis as the site of
his redemption through the crucifixion. The fall from heaven of Lucifer
(Satan), imprisoned at the centre of the earth, caused the creation of both
hell and purgatory: the earth displaced from the vast cavity of hell with its
nine circles formed the huge mountain of purgatory with its seven terraces.

don Club, baffled that Bertrand Russell doesn't want to be a member, needling him and putting pressure on him to have a rethink.)

The story is told on the sixth day, devoted to tales of those who get themselves out of an awkward situation with a clever remark. The revellers, who are on horseback, come upon Cavalcanti walking pensively through the cemetery by the baptistery in Florence, completely absorbed in his thoughts. They back him up against a tomb and taunt him: you refuse to mix with us, but when you've proved God doesn't exist, so what? Cornered, Cavalcanti replies: Gentlemen, you can say what you like to me in your own home. He then leaps swiftly and with surprising agility over the tomb and escapes, while his bemused tormentors wonder: what could he possibly mean? he must be out of his mind. Only one of them understands the put-down and explains it to his dim-witted companions. Tombs are the home of the dead: this cemetery is our home because mentally and spiritually *we* are dead.

Like Dante, Guido Cavalcanti was a poet. The youthful Dante, not

Fig. 3   Guido Cavalcanti cornered by revellers
outside the baptistery.

yet twenty, and anxious to make his mark, had sent a sonnet to a number of poets. In it he described a disturbing (and actually rather grotesque) dream, and invited them to comment on its meaning. Cavalcanti's response, also in the form of a sonnet, marked the beginning of their friendship. The older poet became a mentor to the younger one and in time his *primo amico*, his best friend. When Dante later collected his early lyric poems to Beatrice, in a *libello* ("little book") called the *Vita nova*, linking them with a narrative commentary in prose, he dedicated the book to Cavalcanti.

Cavalcanti was a love poet, author of some exquisite sonnets on the effect of his lady's mere presence on those who see her:

Chi è questa che vèn, ch'ogn'om la mira,
    che fa tremar di chiaritate l'âre
e mena seco Amor, sì che parlare
    null'omo pote, ma ciascun sospira?

(Who is she that comes, whom every man gazes at, who makes
    the air tremble with brightness and brings Love with her, so
    that no man can speak, but each one sighs?)

He also wrote poems in a more earthy vein, though with equal delicacy and linguistic finesse. One tells of a chance meeting with an obliging shepherdess in the woods—in effect, a casual sexual encounter. Yet nothing about it seems coarse or even, truth to tell, very physical: *In un boschetto trova' pasturella / più che la stella—bella, al mi' parere* ("in a small wood I found a shepherdess, more beautiful than the stars, to my mind").

Cavalcanti's most ambitious and difficult poem, both intellectually demanding and technically dazzling, was a philosophical ode on the nature of love (*Donna me prega*: "A lady asks me"). In it love is analysed as a dark and destructive force beyond the control of the rational faculties—an essentially negative aspect of human experience. In effect, he says, if you love, you are doomed to suffering and mental disarray. One way of viewing the *Commedia* is to see it as Dante's mature response to the bleak view of love so compellingly expressed in his best friend's masterpiece.

The friendship with Cavalcanti must have been a difficult one. Guido was an unbeliever—not an uncommon position for an intellectual in Florence at the time. Boccaccio notes in passing that Cavalcanti spent much of his time trying to think up proofs that God does not exist. Benvenuto da Imola, a contemporary of Boccaccio who wrote an important commentary on the *Commedia*, rich in explanatory detail on every aspect of the poem, catches the quality of these two gifted young men in the city of their birth when he calls them Florence's two eyes: *erant duo oculi Florentiae*. They alone, he seems to imply, see the city as it truly is.

Guido Cavalcanti is the great absent figure in the *Commedia*. Though long dead by the time Dante came to write the poem, he was still alive in the spring of 1300, the fictional date of the journey to the afterlife. Dante is thus able to evade the question of whether his friend is destined for damnation (as his atheism would require) or for salvation (the possibility of a change of heart in extremis can never be ruled out). He was to die just a few months later in the summer of 1300, as a direct result of the political turmoil and urban violence that had engulfed Florence.

The year 1300 was a momentous one both for Dante and for Florence. It started with Pope Boniface VIII declaring a Jubilee—the first ever Jubilee, of which the millennium Jubilee celebrated in 2000 was the seven-hundredth anniversary. In the Jubilee proclamation, Boniface promised absolution from their sins to all believers who made a pilgrimage to Rome and visited the basilicas of St. Peter and St. Paul a certain number of times. Dante may himself have gone to Rome during the Jubilee. A simile in the *Inferno* describes with eyewitness precision the arrangements made to deal with the huge influx of pilgrims to the city. The pilgrimage churches were on opposite sides of the Tiber. There was only one bridge spanning the river. In a primitive form of traffic control, the pilgrims moving in one direction were kept on one side of the bridge, and those moving in the opposite direction were kept on the other. The two streams of sinners moving in opposite directions around the narrow circle of the seducers and pandars in hell are just like those pilgrims crossing the bridge in Rome, Dante tells us. Difficult not to suspect a hint of irony here in the comparison between damned souls and devout pilgrims.

Florence in 1300 was a vibrant and prosperous city, an international mercantile and banking centre with trade and financial dealings right across Europe, from London to the Levant. Because of its commercial success and entrepreneurial energy, the city had become the banking capital of the continent. Florentine families like the Peruzzi and the Bardi were bankers to the pope and to various crowned heads of state, including several English kings. Florentine merchants travelled everywhere, often setting up substantial expatriate business colonies in other countries. The Florentine influence was so pervasive that the pope famously declared that Florentines were the fifth element in the world, alongside earth, air, fire and water.

The city's wealth and prosperity were generated by the flourishing textile trade. Wool and silk were imported raw, worked by skilled artisans, and re-exported as luxury goods. This had led to an influx of immigrants into the city from the surrounding countryside. By 1300 there were over 100,000 inhabitants—a huge metropolis in medieval terms. Only Venice and Milan equalled Florence in size; only Paris was larger. Some thirty thousand of these inhabitants earned their living by the manufacture of woollen cloth. Just a few generations earlier the city had been one fifth the size. To accommodate this increase in the population the city walls were twice rebuilt in the course of the thirteenth century, once in 1258, and again between 1284 and 1334. This second expansion, which largely occurred during Dante's lifetime, enclosed an area almost six times that of the previous walls of just a generation earlier. Florence was living through a massive population boom.

In the closing years of the century there was an ambitious programme of urban renewal, reflecting the city's pride in its status and prosperity. Buildings at the heart of the medieval city that have become iconic for today's visitors were begun or underwent major restructuring

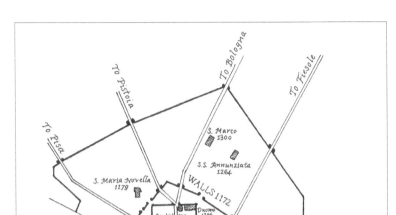

Fig. 4 The two new sets of city walls constructed in the thirteenth century (1258 and 1284–1333) show the massive expansion in the size of Florence. The medieval walls of c. 1087 enclosed an area only slightly bigger than the original Roman walls.

and expansion. Construction of the cathedral began in the mid-1290s, and it changed its name from Santa Reparata to Santa Maria del Fiore ("of the Flower") in honour of the lily which was Florence's emblem. Work on its new façade began in 1298, based on a design by the great Florentine architect Arnolfo di Cambio. Arnolfo also planned the Franciscan church of Santa Croce, with its vast, spacious nave in pale stone. In the same year, building started on what was to become Palazzo Vecchio, with its fortresslike rustication, its battlements and its imposing tower, designed (again probably by Arnolfo) as a suitable residence for the highest elected officials in city government. A sense of the city's pride and confidence in its own destiny is reflected in an inscription placed on the walls of the Bargello (the seat of government for the early commune, now a museum) as early as 1255, and still visible there today. The inscription refers to the city *que mare, que terram, que totam possidet orbem*: "which possesses the sea, the land and the whole globe." Florentines were thrilled by what their city was becoming.

But in parallel with—and undoubtedly caused by—its growth and entrepreneurial success as the mercantile and banking capital of Europe, Florence had had a troubled political history for many decades. A recapitulation of that recent history will help us to understand the complexities of Dante's position and the strains of his friendship with Cavalcanti. Like all the cities of Tuscany, Florence was a commune: an independent, self-governing city-state. This was a time of ferocious political debate and bold constitutional innovation. By the turbulent closing years of the century, the city had evolved a system of democratic government that saw power shared on a rotating basis. A group of six elected *priori* or priors served for a two-month period as the chief executive body (a kind of Cabinet), and when their brief term of office expired, they were replaced by a new group of six. The priorate had been instituted in 1282 to curb the arrogance and abuse of power of the old aristocratic families. It was on the industriousness and enterprise of the rising middle and lower classes—the bankers, merchants, cloth workers and dyers—that the prosperity of the city depended.

The system, designed to ensure that there could be no monopoly of power in the hands of a small number of influential families or individuals, helped prevent the formation of an entrenched power base; but it had the fatal drawback of instability. In a famous invective in *Purgatorio*, Dante laments the constant changes to every aspect of civic life entailed by this system. Addressing Florence directly, he notes:

> Quante volte, del tempo che rimembre,
>   legge, moneta, ufficio e costume,
>   hai tu mutato, e rinovate membre!   (*Purg.* vi 145–47)

(How many times, within your memory, have you changed laws,
  coinage, offices and customs, and renewed your members!)

The "renewing of members" (that is, changes in the makeup of the citizen body) was the result of banishment imposed on one group of citizens or another by their political rivals when they were in the ascendancy. As one group went into exile, the rival faction returned to the city. In the decade of Dante's birth the struggle had been between Ghibellines and Guelfs.

The names Ghibelline and Guelf, first attested in Florence around 1242, derive from the German words Waiblingen (the name of a Hohenstaufen castle in Swabia) and Welf, the family name of an imperial opponent of Frederick II, the last Holy Roman Emperor (1220–1250). Transliterated into Italian and adapted to Italian speech patterns, Waiblingen and Welf became the Ghibellines and the Guelfs, associated respectively with the imperial and the anti-imperial (or pro-papal) cause. The origins of the Holy Roman Empire went back to the crowning of Charlemagne in 800, but it had become fatally weakened in more recent times. The struggle between empire and popes had dominated European political life for more than a hundred years. It was waged with particular ferocity in northern Italy in the middle years of the thirteenth century as the empire tried to regain control of the wealthy city-states that had once lain within its territory. In Florence the Ghibellines came to power in 1260, ousting the Guelfs, but were in their turn expelled from the city in 1266, the year after Dante was born. By 1300 the Guelfs had been in power in Florence for more than three decades.

But with the consolidation of their power, the Guelfs within the city had split into two factions, the Blacks and the Whites, and the power struggles between these factions were to prove as damaging and divisive as those between the Guelfs and Ghibellines a generation earlier. Whereas the split between Guelfs and Ghibellines broadly reflected that between pro-papal and pro-imperial supporters and policies, the split within Florence into Blacks and Whites was not based on ideological principles at all, but simply reflected violent rivalries among coalitions of powerful families for control of the city. The names Blacks and Whites were imported from neighbouring Pistoia, where two brothers had ended up on opposing factions within the city's Guelf party. One was fair-haired, the other dark: their supporters became known as Whites and Blacks.

The contemporary chronicler Dino Compagni, himself an active participant in the city's political life, gives an account of the split in terms of a spurned marriage alliance and wounded family honour. His narrative uncannily echoes the story told of the original split into Guelfs and Ghibellines many years earlier. That had likewise involved a marriage alliance between two powerful families, which was jeopardised when the groom changed his mind at the last minute. On both occasions, the outraged relatives of the jilted bride took violent exception to the dishonouring of their family name and swore revenge.

But it is more useful to think of the split into Blacks and Whites not as a consequence of an isolated scandalous episode but in terms of what held powerful families together. This was a patriarchal society. Inheritance was through male descendants in the male line only; property so inherited could not be divided. It was thus in the interests of all male members of the same extended family to defend the houses and property they held in common. These strong family or clan loyalties overrode any sense of civic duty or wider responsibility to the common good. Powerful families sought support among the lower orders, and their power and prestige could be measured in terms of the loyalty they commanded among their less prominent and less wealthy fellow citizens.

In the closing decades of the century, in tandem with the consolidation of Guelf power in the city, the system of government in Florence had evolved. As part of the process by which the political life of the commune had become more democratic, the power of the elite wealthy families had been gradually curtailed, and the right to political representation had been extended first to the greater and then to the lesser guilds—in effect, to the middle and working classes. Many (though not all) of the elite families were of noble ancestry, their wealth and power based on holdings of land in the surrounding countryside and ownership of substantial property within the city. Characteristically this property took the form of a fortified house with a high tower, which served as a stronghold when fighting broke out with rival families. Civic and domestic architecture allowed public spaces to transform easily into a war zone, with arrows and other missiles being launched from the towers onto the streets below. There were perhaps 150 such fortified tower houses in Florence at this time, though they were constantly being pulled down and rebuilt as the political fortunes of different families changed.

The guilds were associations of members of the same profession or trade, whose interests (and standards) they protected. The greater guilds represented the professions: lawyers, bankers, doctors, merchants. The lesser guilds represented craftsmen and tradesmen, especially labourers in the woollen industry, whose vast expansion in the course of the century lay behind Florence's now preeminent position as the financial hub of Europe. Together the greater and lesser guilds constituted the *popolo*, a term almost always used to mean not the whole of the city's population but that part of it in opposition to the interests of the powerful families—often called the magnates or simply the *grandi*, the big guys. The conflict between *popolo* and *grandi* was at the heart of the city's turbulent political life. Attempts to curtail the power of the *grandi* lay behind the legislative innovations in these closing decades of the century. The institution of the priorate in 1282, when Dante was an adolescent, was a game-changing step.

Priors had to be a member of a guild. Each one of the six priors at any given time was from a different guild, and from a different area of the city. They were elected by guild members. The city's burgeoning prosperity as a flourishing centre of banking and the textile industry depended on the entrepreneurial flair and industriousness of the members of both the greater and lesser guilds. A key piece of legislation known as the Ordinances of Justice reflected the mercantile reality that underpinned the city's prosperity, and enshrined it in a new electoral law. These ordinances, which came into force in 1293, extended the right to political representation to a significant proportion of the lesser guilds hitherto excluded from any role in the governance of the city, and, conversely, excluded from eligibility for office a large number of powerful families—more than seventy of them. Around three thousand citizens were disenfranchised. But the ordinances were not uncontested. Attempts to overturn them or subvert them were a constant feature of civic life in the last years of the century. These tensions led to explosive conflicts of interest: between elite families, between the elite and the *popolo*, and between the two sections of the *popolo* represented by the greater and lesser guilds, whose interests were far from identical.

Membership in a guild was now an indispensable qualification for participating in the political life of the city. Such membership was open to professionally nonactive members, but not, crucially, to aristocratic or upper-class citizens. Dante, aspiring to an active role in political life, had joined the Guild of Physicians and Apothecaries in order to become eligible for public office. This composite guild represented doctors who treated the sick and importers of herbs, spices, drugs and specialty goods. It was not an unusual choice for an intellectual, perhaps because of the connections between the practice of medicine and the study of philosophy and natural science. By contrast, Dante's friend Cavalcanti, who belonged to an old and noble family, was for that very reason excluded from participation in the political process. This key change in the law marked a turning point in the city's political life. It may also have marked the point at which Dante and his "best friend" began to go their separate ways, after the fruitful literary collaboration and shared poetic interests of more than a decade. But Cavalcanti was there at the beginning of Dante's career as a poet; he had encouraged and supported the younger writer, and Dante never forgot that.

Dante was a politically ambitious man, a full and passionate participant in the unfolding story of Florentine politics. In the mid-1290s, as his political ambitions began to take concrete shape, he served on various councils concerned with the city's affairs, through whose operation the business of running the city was conducted. There were five different councils, ranging in size from thirty-six to three hundred members, all elected by guild members, from an eligible electorate of around thirty thousand. Dante served on a Special Council of the *Capitano del Popolo* (literally, "Captain of the People"; roughly, the commune's head of military operations). The Special Council was reconsidering the procedure for electing priors. He served on the Council of One Hundred. In the spring of 1300, he represented Florence as ambassador on a mission to the neighbouring town of San Gimignano, where he sought to persuade the inhabitants to cooperate with the Florentines in electing a new military leader for the Tuscan Guelfs. He was in the thick of things. His political career was flourishing.

That career reached its apex in the summer of 1300. From mid-June to mid-August he served for the statutory two-month period as a prior, one of the six elected representatives on the highest decision-making body which governed the city. His term of service coincided with the coming to a head of factional tensions in the city that had been developing for almost a decade. Those tensions worked themselves out within the city as conflicts between different families among the *grandi*, and between different sections of the *popolo*. But they also connected with the broader political scene beyond the city walls and the wider conflict between papacy and empire that engulfed much of Italy.

Like the other large Tuscan cities (Siena, Pisa, Lucca, Arezzo, Pistoia), Florence was an autonomous, self-governing political entity. To protect its liberty—freedom from either papal or imperial control—was an over-riding goal shared by all fellow citizens. The relationships between any two Tuscan cities might at a given moment be of hostility or of wary cooperation, depending on which families were dominant in a particular city and what policies were favoured by it in relation to the competing claims for its allegiance of church and empire. Rome and the papal territories were close to hand. The pope's increasingly open ambition for political domination in the area was potentially a threat to the survival of the Tuscan city-states as independent communes. As a Guelf city, Florence was in theory an ally of the pope, but the split into Blacks and Whites reflected and exacerbated the problematic nature of that alliance. In fact, as events unfolded, it became increasingly clear that the pope, while professing disinterested concern and a desire for peace, in reality

their own safety, protected from contact with their fellow citizens—both from physical violence and from intimidation. The law required them to live, eat and sleep in the tower. Going home to sleep was tantamount to resigning from office.

The leader of the Whites was Vieri de' Cerchi. The Cerchi family also lived in the Porta di San Piero district, though they owned property all over the city. They were sworn enemies of the Donati, who feared and resented the increasing wealth and political presence of a family whose roots were not aristocratic but mercantile. Compagni describes the Cerchi as "men of low birth, but good merchants and very rich; they dressed well and had many retainers and horses, and they put on a fine display."

Fig. 6   The baptistery in a fourteenth-century fresco (detail).

If we track the deteriorating relationship between these two powerful families, and the descent of the city into a state of civil war, a few incidents stand out. In 1280 the Cerchi family had acquired a particularly grand house, the biggest in the city, almost next door to the Donati. Compagni specifically refers to this ostentatious real estate acquisition and the envy it aroused as a prime cause of the hatred between the two families. In 1289 Vieri de' Cerchi and Corso Donati led the Florentine troops and their allies against the Ghibellines of Arezzo at the Battle of Campaldino, where Dante did active military service for his city. This

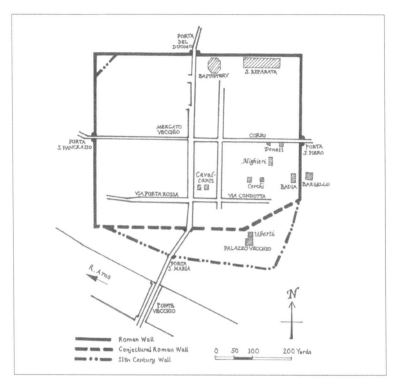

Fig. 7   Central Florence, showing the principal streets and
public buildings and the houses and towers of the Alighieri,
Cavalcanti, Donati and Cerchi families.

battle, which effectively put an end to the hopes of the Ghibelline cause
in Tuscany, was a triumph for the Florentines. At Campaldino both Corso
and Vieri distinguished themselves for their bravery. But soon they were
once again violently and dangerously at loggerheads.

The tensions between the two factions crystallised in 1300, for reasons that remain difficult to fathom. The civic unrest came to a head
with the popular May Day festivities that celebrated the arrival of spring.
Traditionally, groups of young Florentines, men and women, would play
musical instruments and sing in the streets, moving between houses with
their semienclosed courtyards. Two of these groups met and clashed.
There was a violent brawl, during which a man's nose was cut off. Com-

pagni described the fateful blow as "the destruction of our city, because it caused great hatred among the citizens." A member of the Donati family was the perpetrator; the man who lost his nose was a Cerchi. The incident served to clarify factional loyalties, and led to open rioting in the streets between warring powerful families and their followers. The endemic urban violence and disorder had become a state of civil war.

Less than two months later, on June 23, there was another violent clash when the elected guild leaders went in procession to the baptistery to make offerings to John the Baptist, the city's patron saint, to mark the city's feast day on the twenty-fourth. On the way there, they were waylaid, manhandled and beaten up by some *grandi*, who complained that, in spite of their military service at Campaldino in the city's defence, they were now barred by law from holding political office and participating in civic celebrations. The rancour and ill feeling that had been simmering for years between guild members and *grandi* had again come to the boil.

The six newly elected priors, appointed just a week before, met the following day. Faced with the breakdown of civil order, and the disturbances that were raging in the streets, they voted to banish the ringleaders on both sides whose behaviour was stirring up political unrest in the city. Three of the Cerchi were banished, though not Vieri himself. Corso Donati, who had been banished the previous year but had worked in exile to foment the unrest, had his sentence confirmed.

Dante was one of the priors. Among those the new priors banished was his friend Guido Cavalcanti. While in exile in Tuscany Guido caught malaria. Before the summer was over Dante's *primo amico* was dead.

Cavalcanti, though not the leader of the Whites, was a prominent figure who had been actively involved in the unrest as the warring families skirmished in the streets. As an intellectual, he was a particular target of Corso Donati's contempt. Corso's nickname for him was "Cavicchia," meaning "bolt" or "peg." The nickname manages to suggest both that Cavalcanti is stupid, deluded in his philosophical pretentions, and that he is sexually deviant, possibly even effeminate. Compagni singles out the hatred between these two larger-than-life figures—the writer and intellectual on the one hand, and the charismatic but violent thug on the other—as another of the principal causes of the split into Blacks and Whites. He tells us that Corso had tried to have Cavalcanti murdered while he was on a pilgrimage to Santiago de Compostela in Spain. On his return, Cavalcanti had openly tried to kill Corso in a public square in Florence. Dante's best friend, the poet and intellectual renowned for his aloofness and fastidiousness and exquisitely crafted poems, was also, in effect, an urban guerrilla.

GUIDO CAVALCANTI IS the great absent figure in the *Commedia*. But he is a powerful presence in the poem, in spirit if not in person. The most haunting of the episodes in which he is a ghostly presence is the one where Dante meets Guido's father, Cavalcante de' Cavalcanti, in the circle of the heretics in hell. We are in canto x of the *Inferno*. (Each of the one hundred sections into which the poem is divided is called a canto.) We are in that part of the circle of the heretics reserved for those who deny the immortality of the soul and the possibility of a life after death. Like his son, Guido's father was an atheist. One early commentator remarks that the father erred through ignorance, but the son strove to defend his error with knowledge. The heretics are punished in a vast cemetery strewn with sarcophagi containing the sinners. Those who thought life ended in the grave are destined to spend eternity in a tomb.

In this circle Dante meets and talks to two sinners who share a tomb, one of them his friend's father. The other is a figure of almost legendary stature from recent Florentine history: Farinata degli Uberti. Farinata, who had died in 1264, the year before Dante was born, was the great leader of the Florentine Ghibellines who had joined forces with the Sienese at the battle of Montaperti in 1260 to defeat the Florentine Guelfs, leading to the expulsion of the Guelfs from the city. But when after the battle the victors proposed razing Florence to the ground, Farinata alone had spoken up at the council of Empoli and saved the city from annihilation. He had saved Florence when its old enemies the Sienese were bent on destroying it. In Dante's eyes this made him a hero and patriot, although as a Ghibelline he was of necessity an enemy.

The two sinners who share a tomb are, as it happens, not only Florentines, atheists, and both from powerful families; they are also related by marriage. Guido Cavalcanti was married to Farinata's daughter. The wedding had been arranged, as such marriage alliances often were, in an attempt to build bridges between opposing political factions within the city by creating family links that would foster stability and peace. Cavalcanti had been not much more than twelve years old when the betrothal took place. Dante does not tell us about this family connection, though contemporary readers would have been aware of it.

As they pick their way between the tombs, Dante asks his guide Virgil whether it might be possible to talk to any of the sinners. Without warning, a voice booms out, addressing him. He has been recognised as a Tuscan, indeed as a Florentine, by his speech. The Florentine accent was evidently as distinctive then as it is now.

> O Tosco che per la città del fuoco
>   vivo ten vai così parlando onesto,
>   piacciati di restare in questo loco.
> La tua loquela ti fa manifesto
>   di quella nobil patrïa natio,
>   a la qual forse fui troppo molesto.   (*Inf.* x 22–27)

> (O Tuscan who, still living, goes through the city of fire, speaking so courteously, please stay in this place. The way you speak shows that you come from that noble birthplace to which perhaps I caused too much harm.)

Dante instinctively draws closer to Virgil out of fear, but Virgil encourages him to respond: *Volgiti! Che fai?* ("Turn around! What are you doing?") Dante turns, to see Farinata standing erect in the sarcophagus. He is visible from the waist up, a heroically proud and unbowed figure:

> ed el s'ergea col petto e con la fronte
>   com'avesse l'inferno a gran dispitto.   (*Inf.* x 35–36)

(and he stood tall with his chest and with his brow as though he
held hell in great scorn.)

As Dante approaches, Farinata has just one question for him: *Chi fuor
li maggior tui?* ("Who were your ancestors?") By identifying his forebears
Dante reveals his Guelf allegiance. Farinata's response is to underline the
implacable hostility between the two opposing sides:

> Fieramente furo avversi
> a me e a miei primi e a mia parte,
> sì che per due fiate li dispersi.   (*Inf.* x 46–48)

(They were fiercely hostile to me and to my ancestors and to my
party, so that twice I scattered them.)

The triumphalist mention of the two Ghibelline victories which
saw the Guelfs expelled from Florence, first in 1248 and then in 1260,
prompts a taunt from Dante. They may have been chased out, but they
came back both times: your people didn't master that art. The Guelfs
ousted the Ghibellines in 1251 and again in 1266; since then, they had
held sway in the city. The conversation, which had started so cour-
teously in the name of their shared citizenship, has degenerated into
boastful animosity.

It is now interrupted by the appearance of a second figure, whose
head, visible only to his chin, emerges from the open sarcophagus. He
looks anxiously around, as though searching for someone, and when he
fails to find what he is looking for, he says, weeping:

> Se per questo cieco
> carcere vai per altezza d'ingegno,
> mio figlio ov'è? e perché non è teco?   (*Inf.* x 58–60)

(If you go through this blind prison because of high genius,
where is my son? and why isn't he with you?)

It is Guido's father, Cavalcante de' Cavalcanti. His words and his punishment have revealed his identity to Dante, who replies:

> Da me stesso non vegno;
> colui ch'attende là, per qui mi mena
> forse cui Guido vostro ebbe a disdegno.   (*Inf.* x 61–63)

> (I do not come on my own; the man who is waiting there is taking
> me to someone whom your Guido perhaps held in contempt.)

These gnomic words, with their veiled reference to his friend's unbelief, hint at their ideological falling-out over the matter of religious faith.
Virgil is taking Dante to Beatrice, and Beatrice will in due course take
him to heaven. But what causes Cavalcante to despair is a simpler matter
of syntax. He shouts:

> Come
> dicesti? elli ebbe? non viv'elli ancora?
> non fiere li occhi suoi lo dolce lume?   (*Inf.* x 67–69)

> (What did you say? he *held*? isn't he still alive? doesn't the sweet
> light strike his eyes?)

Dante's innocent use of the past tense *ebbe* seems to imply that
Guido is dead. His father's distraught questioning seeks reassurance
that this is not so, but Dante's hesitation before responding seems to
confirm the worst. Cavalcante falls back into the tomb and no more is
seen of him.

Farinata continues talking to Dante as if this anguished interlude had
not taken place, picking up exactly where they had broken off. If they
haven't mastered that art, he says, that causes me more torment than
this punishment in hell: *ciò mi tormenta più che questo letto.* But not much
time will pass before Dante himself will learn how difficult it is to master
the art of returning to the city. This—a glancing reference to his future

exile—is a second puzzle for Dante, who is already perplexed by the fact that Cavalcante does not know if his son is alive or dead.

Why, Farinata goes on, are the Florentines so pitiless against the Uberti family in their laws? Their banishment had never been revoked, even when other Ghibelline families had been allowed to return. The Uberti houses in the centre of the city had been demolished as a lasting punishment for the humiliating defeat Farinata had inflicted on his birthplace at the hands of its old enemy Siena. The space thus cleared was never built on again. To this day, it forms part of what became Piazza Signoria—specifically, the space to the side of Palazzo Vecchio, just a few hundred yards from the Bargello. The building of Palazzo Vecchio on this site to house the priors at the turn of the century meant that the Uberti family would never be able to reclaim their land and rebuild their houses. Nineteen years after his death, when Dante was an impressionable eighteen years old, Farinata had been posthumously condemned for heresy.

Dante explains that it is the memory of the great slaughter of Florentine troops at the battle of Montaperti which causes this harshness. The river Arbia ran red with Florentine blood, as contemporary chroniclers reported and as Dante may have learnt firsthand from an uncle who fought in the battle. It has been estimated that four thousand Florentine Guelfs died. (Italians have a long memory. Sienese fans at football matches today still taunt the Florentines by chanting, 'Montaperti! Montaperti!') Farinata reminds Dante that he was not alone in the fighting but that he alone defended the city and saved it from destruction when the Tuscan Ghibellines and their imperial allies met after the battle to determine Florence's fate.

The mood has changed, and Dante seeks clarification of something that is puzzling him. Is he right in thinking that the shades of the dead can foresee the future but do not know what is happening now in the world of the living? (Farinata has confidently alluded to something that lies in store for Dante, but he is unaware of the current misfortunes of the Ghibellines; Cavalcante does not know if his son is alive or dead.) Farinata confirms that this is so: they know events that are a long way off, but as these events get closer or actually happen, this knowledge is extinguished. This is one of the most cruel and refined aspects of the punishment of the damned, punishing them as it does not in their bodies but in their minds. Their state seems like the experience of dementia, but more painful because they are fully aware of what they do not know. Guido was to die just a few months later in the summer of 1300, close enough to the fictional date of the journey in the spring of that year for this law to be operational.

This bald account of the sequence of events in canto x of *Inferno* barely begins to suggest its power. The density of historical reference—fifty years of bloody Florentine history evoked in a few lines, in a few sharp questions and sharper answers exchanged between fellow citizens who love their birthplace with equal passion—is matched by the complexity of the more personal strand in the narrative. Cavalcante's opening words manage to suggest both rivalry (the two young poets are equally gifted, are they not?) and abandonment or even betrayal by Dante (so why isn't he with you?).

The scene unfolds rapidly. Nothing is explained or glossed. Everything is done through direct speech. The exchanges are intensely dramatic, one encounter erupting into the next. The contrast between the protagonists is established as much by their words and manner of speaking as by their physical bearing and movements.

Our first impression is of the difference between Dante's two interlocutors: Farinata's aloof, almost motionless watchfulness, Cavalcante's agitated mobility; fierce self-control in the reaction to distressing news versus openly distraught display; blunt assertion versus broken questioning. But in reality what they have in common is far more significant: a continuing obsession with the world of the living, the shared urgency of their desire to know the fate of what had been the sole focus of their energies and interests when they were alive. Whether that was the fate of a political party or of a gifted son is ultimately insignificant. That passionate involvement in the world of the living caused them to be blind to the possibility of a life after death. They share the same destiny in the stony landscape of hell.

Structurally the canto is satisfyingly symmetrical. In the first and final sections Dante and Virgil are alone; in the second and fourth sections Dante talks to Farinata; in the centre is the encounter with Cavalcante. Cavalcante's anguished question about Guido (isn't he still alive?) is at the exact centre (line 68 of 136). The pace is so fast that there is an interlocking series of misunderstandings and partial clarifications. In an act of charitable concern for his friend's father, Dante asks Farinata to tell him that Guido is not dead and to explain the reason for his hesitation in replying.

But in other respects Dante's behaviour is more questionable. He has been swiftly drawn into a rancorous exchange that perfectly exemplifies the divisiveness of partisan allegiances. This is a man still deeply embroiled in local politics. If the physical journey through the realms of the afterlife has its mental counterpart in a journey in knowledge and understanding, one strand in that mental journey is the political education the protagonist receives. By the end of the journey Dante's political vision will be radically different from his starting point. This political theme will unfold and evolve over the length of the whole poem.

The veiled allusion to his own future suffering touches on a related theme, which will be explored later. He will learn how hard it is to return to the city of his birth, Farinata tells him. Dante was to be exiled from Florence less than two years later, in 1302, when factional intrigues in the city escalated as a result of the pope's intervention. For the moment, the gnomic words leave him as troubled by the encounter with Farinata as Farinata is by the encounter with him. Both have learned distressing news they are powerless to change.

All the themes encapsulated in this justly famous canto—the state of Florence, torn by partisan wrangling and political infighting; the city's warring relations with neighbouring communes; poetic talent and poetic rivalry, and the use to be made of a vocation for poetry; loyalty and treachery in the personal and the public sphere—will recur and be developed over the length of the poem. Like the motifs in Wagner's Ring Cycle, they are never absent for long, and even a line or two is enough to bring them hauntingly to the surface. Dante's orchestration of these themes and others is one of the glories of the poem.

THESE SAME POWERFUL THEMES—friendship, poetry, the ruinous state of Florence—come together again in an episode much later in the journey. On the terrace of the gluttonous near the top of mount purgatory Dante meets his old friend Forese Donati. Forese was the brother of Corso, the ruthless Black Guelf leader whose flagrant infraction of the antimagnate legislation had more than once led to his banishment from Florence. But unlike Guido Cavalcanti, Corso returned from exile and continued to play an active role in the affairs of the city, with disastrous consequences. The Donati family, as we have seen, was an old and powerful one—one of those families whose control over the city the Ordinances of Justice were precisely designed to curb. But Forese was not a public figure; nor was the third sibling, their sister Piccarda, whom Dante will meet in the *Paradiso*.

The punishment of the gluttons in purgatory is to be in a state of acute hunger and thirst, a corrective to their excessive intake of food and drink while they were alive. In appearance they are a ghostly premonition of concentration camp victims. Their extreme emaciation, skeletal features and hollow eye sockets make it impossible to recognise people by their appearance. So Forese is not immediately recognised by Dante when the two old friends meet. But when Forese exclaims with astonishment and pleasure on seeing his old friend, Dante recognises his voice. The spontaneous affection each then expresses at coming upon the other in these unlikely circumstances makes this one of the most touching recognition scenes in the whole poem.

Forese explains the paradox that the shades of the dead, with their insubstantial shadow bodies, can nonetheless suffer extreme hunger and thirst. He offers a striking definition of the nature of punishment in purgatory, a key to understanding what penitential suffering really is: *io dico pena, e dovria dir sollazzo* ("I say punishment, and I should say pleasure"). The punishments here are willingly, indeed joyfully, endured by the shades as the necessary precondition for their reaching paradise. They are a temporary, if painful, stage on the way to beatitude. In hell, the punishments are eternal and immutable. The spirit in which they are suffered by the damned is one of obstinate persistence in the mental state that caused them to sin in the first place, so perfectly embodied in Farinata and Cavalcante. The physical punishment is almost less important than the mental obduracy—the wilful rejection of the divine—that their behaviour enacts.

Dante asks how it is that Forese, who died less than five years earlier, has made so much progress up the mountain. Why is he not much lower down in ante-purgatory, the holding area at the foot of the mountain reserved for those who turned to God only at the end of their lives? The procrastination and spiritual slackness reflected in repentance postponed until one's deathbed are punished by delay, an enforced wait before the climb up the mountain can begin. Forese explains that the prayers of his dear wife, Nella, are the cause of his rapid advancement. Her goodness and piety set her apart from her female compatriots, with their shameless pursuit of luxury and their immodest fashions. The women of Barbagia in Sardinia (the region was a byword for wildness) are more civilized than the *sfacciate donne fiorentine*, the "shameless Florentine women."

Forese asks Dante to explain how it is that a living man can be visiting the afterlife (the shadow Dante's solid body casts has caught the attention of other souls as well). Dante's reply refers allusively and rather mysteriously to their shared past:

> Se tu riduci a mente
> qual fosti meco, e qual io teco fui,
> ancor fia grave il memorar presente.   (*Purg.* xxiii 115–17)

(If you recall to mind how you were with me, and how I was
    with you, remembering it now will still be painful.)

He was rescued from that life of dissoluteness by Virgil, who is leading him to Beatrice. Forese is the only person in the poem to whom

Dante uses Beatrice's name with this easy familiarity, as a name that will be recognised by someone who knew her. It requires no explanatory periphrasis (*donna del ciel*, "lady from heaven" or suchlike) of the kind invariably provided for others.

The reference to a shared past of which they both have cause to be ashamed is both specific and nonspecific. It is explicitly identified with *quella vita*, "that life," the dark wood from which Dante was rescued by Virgil—a state of moral and spiritual aberration so grave that only direct help from heaven could save him. But the exact nature of the going astray is not spelled out. Some modern readers take the allusive *qual fosti meco, e qual io teco fui* to refer to a homosexual episode in the youth of the two young men (though none of the early commentators on the poem interprets the line in this way). Like some of Dante's most haunting lines, it raises possibilities without resolving them. We take away only the certainty that for all their affection and delight in seeing each other, the memory of some aspects of their shared past is—and should be—painful and a source of shame to both of them.

We *can* be sure that there was a literary dimension to their misconduct. Forese and Dante had exchanged sonnets, three sonnets each, making a sequence of six: a kind of correspondence in verse known as a *tenzone*, a poetic argument or dispute. The sonnets are very different in kind from the earlier exchange with Cavalcanti, where the subject was love. Here the tone is combative and jocularly abusive. The poets trade insults, each seeking to outdo the other in the extravagance and outrageousness of their claims. Dante accuses Forese of gluttony, and of thieving to feed his gluttony. He will surely end up in prison. Forese alludes to a dishonourable incident involving Dante's father (now dead), perhaps involving usury. Dante may end up in the poorhouse.

Dante gets the better of the exchange, both in the inventiveness of his insults and in the verbal élan which they are delivered. Forese's wife suffers from a cold in midsummer because of her inadequate bedcovering (the clear implication is that Forese is either unfaithful or impotent). Forese is a bastard, and short of asking his mother, it is impossible to know who his real father is. The jocular exchange between friends, perhaps initially no more than a lively reworking of the traditional genre of the *improperium*, or poem of insult, here becomes something more morally questionable. The casual extension of the offensiveness to innocent third parties unable to speak for themselves (Forese's wife and mother) is more troubling than a spirited if tasteless exchange between young poets displaying a talent for verbal exuberance.

Even worse, the lines calling Forese's paternity into question make an insouciantly irreverent reference to religion: Forese's father has as little to do with him as Joseph has with Christ. To compound the offence, the word *Christ* falls in the rhyme position. In the *Commedia*, the word *Christ* never rhymes with another word. When it falls in the rhyme position, as it does on four occasions in the *Paradiso*, it is always repeated so that it rhymes with itself. This, it has often been suggested, is one of the ways in which the *Commedia* makes amends for the youthful misuse of poetic gifts in the *tenzone*. The purgatorial encounter clearly makes amends for other aspects of the sonnet exchange: the tenderly loving words for Forese's wife (*la vedovella mia, che molto amai*, "my dear widow, whom I greatly loved"), the tribute to her goodness and her affection, which have so benefited him now in the afterlife by speeding his progress up the mountain.

Forese's scathing words about Florentine female fashions, with their vertiginous décolletage—they go around *mostrando con le poppe il petto*: "showing their chest with their breasts"—remind us of the city's preeminent position as a centre for the production of luxury textiles. The Florentines had devised techniques and methods for the handling and working of wool and silk that were secrets jealously guarded from commercial rivals and competitors in other cities. The city's favoured geographical position meant that it was ideally placed to import wool from England and Spain and silk from Asia, and then re-export the finished luxury fabrics at great profit, as well as supplying the local market with the materials for the extravagant fashions that Forese here denounces. Those Florentine fashions are so lewd, he says, that there will come a time in the near future when they are denounced by preachers from the pulpit. And in fact we know that in 1310 laws were introduced by the bishop of Florence forbidding women to wear clothes that exposed any part of their torso, on pain of excommunication.

The city's wealth, and the influx of new citizens from the hinterland which that wealth attracted, were in Dante's eyes a principal source of its instability. There were other explanations for the Florentines' natural (and notorious) quarrelsomeness, their inability to live peaceably alongside one another. One such explanation draws on foundation stories about the city, reputedly founded by noble Romans in opposition to uncouth Fiesolans. On this view, the descendants of Caesar (the Florentines) and the descendants of Catiline (the Fiesolans) are now fatally mixed in the citizen body. They can never live at peace with one another. Another explanation of civic strife sees its cause in a different dimension of the city's history. Originally Florence's patron had been Mars, the god of war. The remains of a statue of Mars still stood on the Ponte Vecchio in Dante's time. With the building of the baptistery, Mars had been discarded in favour of John the Baptist. Discord and combativeness associated with a disgruntled god of war were, it was said, built into the very fabric of the city and its monuments.

An urgent desire to know what lies in store for his birthplace is one of the driving forces of the narrative in the poem. Dante's anxious questioning of Ciacco, the first Florentine he meets in hell, encompasses both the city's future: *a che verranno / li cittadin de la città partita?* ("what will become of the citizens of the divided city?") and the great figures from its recent past: *dimmi ove sono* ("tell me where they are"), in heaven or in hell? When he meets Farinata, he already knows that these leaders of an earlier generation whose fate intrigues him came to a bad end. He will meet several more of them lower down in hell.

The theme of Florence is painful whenever it arises, as it always does when he meets a Florentine in hell. In canto xvi the causes of the city's instability are firmly located in the economic boom of recent decades and the influx of migrants to the city: *la gente nova e i sùbiti guadagni* ("the new people and the quick profits"), as he scornfully refers to them. By canto xxvi Dante can congratulate his city on the vast territorial expansion of her banking and trading interests. Her influence extends not just over land and sea, as she herself proudly boasts, but throughout hell itself.

Godi, Fiorenza, poi che se' sì grande
   che per mare e per terra batti l'ali,
   e per lo 'nferno tuo nome si spande!   (*Inf.* xxvi 1–3)

(Rejoice, Florence, since you are so great that you beat your wings
   over sea and land, and your fame spreads throughout hell!)

The phrase ironically extends the Bargello inscription which boasted of Florence's preeminent trading position in the world to include new territory. Dante has just met no fewer than five Florentines among the thieves in hell. No reader can fail to note how well represented the city is in the underworld. Dante meets more than thirty of his fellow citizens in hell, just four in purgatory and only two—one of them his own great-great-grandfather—in paradise.

This is the only time in hell Dante addresses his native city directly. He will do so again in purgatory, in the painfully intimate, angry, fiercely ironical words that include the lines quoted earlier about the city's fatal instability. This apostrophe itself comes at the end of an impassioned invective calling to account the warring factions and families that divide the cities of Italy (with the Montagues and Capulets of Verona making their first appearance on the European literary stage). Dante turns to Florence and sardonically congratulates his city that none of his strictures apply to her:

Fiorenza mia, ben puoi esser contenta
   di questa digression che non ti tocca . . .
   tu ricca, tu con pace e tu con senno!   (*Purg.* vi 127–28, 137)

(My Florence, you can be well pleased with this digression,
   which does not touch you . . . you are rich, you are at peace
   and you are wise!)

Florence, with its never-ending series of changes in legislation, political institutions and even the makeup of the body politics, is like a sick woman tossing and turning on her bed, whose constant restless motion seeks to assuage her pain but is itself the expression of her malaise. The struggle to institute, fine-tune and protect the fledgling institutions of democratic accountability and the rule of law against the vested interests of the *grandi* would seem to be incompatible with peaceful and healthy civic flourishing.

By contrast with the highly charged and intensely dramatic encounter with Farinata and Cavalcante, the meeting with Forese seems almost low-key, framed as it is by the artless questions "How come you're here?" (xxiii 42) and "When will I see you again?" (xxiv 76). Two friends who have not seen each other for years and who unexpectedly run into each other catch up on what has happened in the interim. But their interaction—utterly natural, in spite of the fact that the circumstances are so strange and one of them is grossly disfigured—accommodates the same density of themes.

Once again Dante uses the dramatic technique by which one encounter interrupts another, though this time the scene unfolds on a broader canvas. Forese points out and names many other sinners on the terrace of gluttony. One of them is an earlier vernacular poet, Bonagiunta da Lucca, who seems eager to talk to Dante. Bonaguinta offers the famous definition of the *dolce stil novo* ("sweet new style"), the innovative poetic manner of Dante's youth. His words acknowledge and celebrate Dante's originality and distinction as a lyric poet—the emergence of his unique poetic voice. This is embedded in an episode where the misuse of those gifts in the *tenzone* with Forese is, by clear implication, recognised and deplored. These two dimensions of Dante's poetic past—the exquisite lyricism of the *Vita nova* in the footsteps of Cavalcanti and the coarseness of the Forese *tenzone* at its polar opposite—together form the indispensable stylistic apprenticeship, without which he could not have gone on to write the *Commedia*. In the Florentine friendships of his young manhood is forged the stylistic mastery of the high style and the low style, which will in the fullness of time enable him to write his masterpiece.

When the conversation with his old friend resumes, inevitably the talk comes back to Florence, and back to Forese's brother, Corso, and his role in the city's future. Earlier, Dante had asked after their sister, Piccarda, and been told that she is already in heaven. The meeting with her will be his first encounter with a blessed soul in paradise, an exquisitely courteous and gentle episode that sets the tone for the third realm of the afterlife, and lays out one of its organising principles. Piccarda was a nun, but she had been abducted from her convent and forced to marry. It was her brother Corso, needless to say, who had organised her abduction. No considerations of family feeling or brotherly concern could hold in check his violence, his arrogance, his ambition, his thuggery.

Piccarda's fate raises a theological conundrum. How blameworthy are those forced by violence to break their religious vows? And there is a related question, which underlies the organisation of paradise and the *Paradiso*: how can there be degrees of blessedness? Dante meets Piccarda in the first and lowest heavenly sphere. She is there because of her broken vows, which are an imperfection in her earthly existence reflected in her position in paradise. Her explanation, in response to a question from a puzzled Dante, is that all souls in paradise accept the station to which they have been allotted. She encapsulates this in one of the most famous, and famously simple, lines in the poem: *E 'n la sua volontade è nostra pace* ("And in His will is our peace"). For the nineteenth-century English poet Matthew Arnold this line, with its poetic limpidity and profundity, was one of his touchstones for true poetry, against which other lines could be measured and judged. T. S. Eliot, equally an admirer, said that these were "words which even those who know no Dante know."

Corso was to die not many years later, in 1308, after a period of three years in control of Florence. He shamelessly ransacked and plundered the city and was eventually expelled from it. Fleeing on horseback, he was assassinated by Catalan mercenaries employed by his political opponents. Forese, with the sure knowledge of the future shared by souls in the afterlife, predicts in macabre and apocalyptic detail that Corso will be dragged down to hell by the very horse on which he was riding at the time of his death. So these three siblings from the Florence of Dante's youth, his close neighbours in the medieval heart of the old city, illustrate the different destinies that await human beings in the afterlife.

The encounter with Forese, like the encounter with Cavalcante, takes us back to the years of Dante's youth and young manhood: his friendships, his ambitions, his close sense of commitment to and deep love of his native city—to a time when it still seemed possible that it might be set on the right path. But those themes are touched and deepened also by his despairing knowledge at the time of writing that its fate was out of control, and that terrible things lay in store for it and for him.

The falling-out with Guido Cavalcanti, who had been his best friend, was ideological, but it was also political and literary. Just as Cavalcanti's unbelief must have come to constitute an unbridgeable chasm between them, so too must his aristocratic detachment from the political fortunes of the city to which Dante was so passionately committed in an active role. And so too, it seems safe to assume, must the direction in which Dante's talent as a poet was taking him. Ten years of fruitful, stimulating, creative collaboration and companionship came to what must have been a painful end. The best friend of his youth—the disenfranchised atheist, the incomparable love poet in the rarefied high style—is left behind.

In the estrangement from Cavalcanti lie the seeds of the future. Dante will go on to explore and express with unparalleled power the religious faith that fires him. His political commitment will come to transcend local issues and to engage with fundamental questions about the conditions necessary for human beings to flourish wherever they live. And he will go on to conceive an almost unthinkably ambitious poem of encyclopedic aspirations, which will use the vernacular speech of his native Florence in all its rich multifariousness of linguistic register to create a poetic masterpiece that can stand alongside the epics of the great classical poets—and in so doing prove himself one of the greatest poets of all time.

2.

Power

. . . poetry makes nothing happen
—W. H. Auden,
"In Memory of W. B. Yeats"

What is poetry that does not save
Nations or people?
—Czeslaw Milosz,
"Dedication"

WHAT IS POETRY FOR? DANTE'S LIFE AS A WRITER CAN BE CHARTED
in terms of his response to this question. In his youth he writes love poems,
as young men often do, to express his feelings and to impress the girl he
is dazzled by. But at least as important, probably more so, Dante writes to
impress his friends with his poetic technique. The *Vita nova* is the story of
his love for Beatrice, the young Florentine girl whom he first saw when
he was nine, who much later greeted him in the street, but then later still
cut him dead, to his great sorrow. To compound his tragedy, Beatrice died
when she was twenty-four. In the *Vita nova*, the love poems he wrote for
her are introduced and linked by a narrative and commentary in prose
written after she had died, when he was in his late twenties.

But the *Vita nova* is not just the story of his love for Beatrice. It is also,
crucially, the story of his development as a poet who expresses that love and

tries to understand its meaning. The turning point in the story comes not when she dies, but when the young man realises that exalting her beauty and virtue is an end in itself. That is what his poetry is for. Its proper end is divorced from any sense of it as a means to winning her favour. His understanding of that truth has the force of a revelation. It is enough simply to celebrate Beatrice for her numinous value as an embodiment of what is best in the world and a reflection of the goodness of her creator.

In the poems written between the *Vita nova* and the *Commedia*, the function of poetry has changed. This is the period when Dante was actively involved in the political life of the Florentine commune, followed by the early years of his exile. Poetry has become an instrument of exploration. On the one hand, there is intellectually rigorous exploration of complex philosophical ideas like nobility and justice. On the other, there is exploration of more earthy aspects of reality the younger man might have shied away from writing about (as reflected in the sonnet exchange with Forese, and the poems for a *donna petrosa*, a "woman of stone," who is indifferent to his passion). There is a linguistic dimension to the exploration. These poems use language in ways that are outside and even at odds with the experience of the *Vita nova*, as the opening lines of one of them clearly states: *Così nel mio parlar voglio esser aspro / com'è ne li atti questa bella petra* ("I want to be as harsh in my speech as this fair stone is in her behaviour"). In the *Commedia*, poetry is for something else again. Celebration and exploration remain a part of the picture, but they are subsumed into a greater and more urgent goal.

Auden, writing in memory of Yeats on the eve of World War II, famously said that "poetry makes nothing happen." Dante thought that it could, and hoped that it would. He did not share our modern sense of the impotence and marginality of the poet faced with the horrors of the contemporary world. Poetry in the *Commedia* is, precisely, for changing the world. The poet writes—he is instructed by Beatrice in the course of his journey to write—*in pro del mondo che mal vive* ("for the benefit of the world which lives badly").

To bring about a change he must call to account not just misguided Florentine leaders but the major political players on the European stage of his time. Their shamelessly self-serving misconduct lies at the root of the world's ills. The popes fail in their role as spiritual guides; the secular rulers are motivated by naked ambition and greed. Any failure of nerve he might suffer in criticizing the famous and powerful is preempted when he meets his ancestor Cacciaguida in paradise. Cacciaguida tells him that his words, when they are digested, will provide vital nourishment for his readers. The *Commedia* is unabashedly a text that sets out to change things for the better.

FOR DANTE'S CONTEMPORARY READERS, canto xix of the *Inferno* must have been profoundly shocking—perhaps it still is shocking for good Catholics today. In it Dante shows how the papacy of his time, driven by greed and political ambition, has abandoned its true role as spiritual leader of the human race. The damning portrayal is presented in language of great eloquence, and through arresting visual imagery. The case against the papacy is not rationally argued. Everything is dramatic and dynamic. The episode centres on a misunderstanding, which sparks off a dialogue through which the theme of papal corruption emerges. The dialogue is as remarkable for its revelation of character as for its brazen admission of papal wrongdoing by a recent incumbent of the papal throne.

Dante and Virgil are picking their way down from one section to another in the area of lower hell known as the Malebolge (literally, "evil pouches"). There are ten such circular pouches or ditches in this eighth circle, devoted to ten different kinds of fraudulent behaviour. The vast hole at their centre plunges down to the bottom of hell and the centre of the earth. The travellers cross the ditches over stone bridges, from which they can look down on the sinners punished within them. In canto xix they have reached the circle of simony. Those guilty of this sin are men of the church (priests, friars, cardinals, popes) who buy and sell things of the spirit (church sacraments and ministries), perverting their true meaning and value by treating them as an opportunity for personal material enrichment.

As Dante and Virgil cross a bridge over the third ditch, an extraordinary spectacle greets their eyes. They look down on a rocky landscape riddled with round holes. From each hole protrude the naked legs of a sinner whose upper body is hidden from view inside the rock. As flames lick over the sinners' feet, they kick out to alleviate the pain. The scene is as surreal and disturbing as any Dante has yet encountered.

His attention is caught by a pair of legs kicking out more wildly than the others, and he asks who the sinner is. Virgil says that if they climb down into the ditch he can hear it from the man himself. When they have clambered down, Dante stands by the legs of the upturned sinner in his hole, like a friar hearing the confession of a murderer about to be put to death. (The Florentine statutes stipulated that the punishment for murderers was to be buried alive, placed head down in a hole.) Dante's physical bearing as he bends forward to catch the words that emerge from the hole exactly reflects this gruesome ritual of capital punishment. But there is an ironic inversion of roles: Dante, a layman, is about to hear the confession not just of a cleric but of a pope. He does not know this as the conversation begins.

The voice that emerges from the hole is irascible, modulating from tetchy incredulity, to disgruntled aside, to sarcastic rhetorical question:

Ed el gridò: "Se tu già costì ritto,
  se tu già costì ritto, Bonifazio?
  Di parecchi anni mi mentì lo scritto.
Se' tu sì tosto di quell'aver sazio
  per lo qual non temesti tòrre a 'nganno
  la bella donna, e poi di farne strazio?"   (*Inf.* xix 52–57)

(And he shouted: "Is that you standing there already, Boniface,
  is that you standing there already? The prediction lied to me
  by several years. Are you so soon sated with that wealth for
  which, without fear, you took the fair woman by deception,
  and then defiled her?")

Dante is nonplussed at this outburst. Virgil tells him to say: I'm not who you think I am.

On hearing this the sinner's mood and manner change. In a voice that has become querulous, he asks: What do you want from me? if it matters so much to you to know who I am, then *sappi ch'i' fui vestito del gran manto*: "know that I was clothed in the great mantle"—that is, I was a pope. Almost casually he admits to nepotism (offering plum ecclesiastical appointments to members of his own family) and simony (selling church offices for personal profit). He plays with laconic wit both on his family name—the Orsini were one of the greatest Roman families; the family emblem was a bear, *orsa*—and on the word *borsa*, purse, used both for the bag in which he stored his money while he was alive and now, metaphorically, for the hole in hell in which he finds himself as a consequence. Thus we and Dante learn his identity. He is Giovanni Gaetano Orsini, or Pope Nicholas III:

> e veramente fui figliuol de l'orsa,
>> cupido sì per avanzar li orsatti,
>> che sù l'avere e qui me misi in borsa.   (*Inf.* xix 70–72)

> (and truly I was a son of the bear [i.e., an Orsini], so eager to
>> advance the bear cubs, that up there I put money and down
>> here, myself, into a purse.)

He explains that beneath him in the rock are earlier popes who were guilty of simony. As soon as the next one arrives, he will be displaced downwards by the incoming occupant—that Boniface whom he had mistakenly believed Dante to be. An even more wicked, lawless pope will follow Boniface, who will in his turn be pushed down farther into the rock.

Nicholas III was pope from 1277 to 1280, the years of Dante's adolescence. He was notorious for his nepotism and simony. Contemporary observers and modern historians concur in their harsh judgment. No problem in putting him in hell, then, as the journey to the afterlife takes place in 1300. What is striking is the sense of a strong character that emerges from the few words Dante gives him: sharp, peevish, a clever talker, utterly untroubled by moral scruples.

Much more difficult for Dante to deal with were the popes of his maturity. The loathed and reviled Boniface VIII was pope from 1294 to 1303 and was directly responsible for the disastrous turn of events in Florence in those years. His successor, Clement V (1305–1314), compounded the offence by moving the papacy to Avignon, where it was even more directly under the control of the French king. (There had been a strong and divisive French presence in the College of Cardinals for many years.)

By a stroke of dramatic genius Dante has established that both these popes are expected in hell. The person who confidently predicts this not only has the sure knowledge of the future shared by all the dead, but is himself a pope. With startling nonchalance, he has indicted not just himself and a long line of nameless predecessors but also two popes whose wrongdoing is not a thing of the past, but of the present (spring 1300), and of the years to follow, in which Dante will write the poem.

Conscious that perhaps he is being foolhardy, Dante asks Nicholas a question, then answers it himself. How much money did Jesus want when he gave the keys to Peter?

> Certo non chiese se non "Viemmi retro."   (*Inf.* xix 93)

> (Certainly he asked nothing, except "Follow me.")

The apostles took no money when they chose Matthias to take the place of Judas after his betrayal. Simony perverts the ideal of apostolic poverty: Nicholas's punishment is just (*tu se' ben punito*: "you are rightly punished"). A layman pronounces a verdict on a pope. Only Dante's reverence for the pope's office prevents him from using even harsher words:

> ché la vostra avarizia il mondo attrista,
>   calcando i buoni e sollevando i pravi.   (*Inf.* xix 104–5)

> (for your greed makes the world a sorry place, trampling on the
>   good and raising up the wicked.)

The Italian word *avarizia* is wider in significance than the English *avarice*. It means the same thing as *cupidigia*, "greed," an insatiable desire for money and material possessions and the power that goes with them. The second-person-singular *tu* has now become a more inclusive plural *voi*. The charge is no longer just against Nicholas, but against all the corrupt popes whose conduct is in conflict with the ideals and aspirations of the church's origins.

> Fatto v'avete dio d'oro e d'argento;
>> e che altro è da voi a l'idolatre,
>> se non ch'elli uno, e voi ne orate cento?   (*Inf.* xix 112–114)

> (You have made yourselves a god of gold and silver; and what
>> difference is there between you and idolaters, except that they
>> worship one god, and you worship a hundred?)

In contrast with Nicholas's contorted, witty, punning formulations, Dante's appeal to the example of the apostles is biblical in its simplicity and directness.

There is a second, very different, strain of biblical language in the canto: the highly wrought sexual imagery of the Apocalypse, with its talk of adultery, fornication and the great harlot. Traditionally, the church is the bride of Christ. The pope is Christ's vicar. By selling church sacraments and offices, the pope is prostituting the bride. When Dante expresses his outrage at papal simony and the perverse relationship between a pope hungry for power and corrupt secular rulers who conspire with him for their own ends, he draws on this tradition, using the verbs for whoring (*puttaneggiar*) and committing adultery (*avolterare*).

More than a century and a half after Dante wrote these lines, Botticelli illustrated the whole poem with a series of marvellously subtle and detailed drawings, one for each canto. When he came to draw this scene, he distilled the shock value of this highly sexualised language into pictorial form. Dante's sinners are visible only to the thighs. Botticelli shows them exposed to the groin, so that the sight which greets Dante and Virgil as they descend into this circle—and us as we gaze at Botticelli's drawing—is a rich panorama of naked splayed legs, buttocks and testicles.

Fig. 8 Botticelli: Dante talks to Pope Nicholas III (detail).

Canto xix offers us a startling vision of a corrupt papacy in gloriously concrete symbolic form. Every aspect of the punishment of the simoniacs is a parodic inversion of ecclesiastical dignity and attributes. Their grotesque upside-down position has them looking not to heaven, as they ought, but downwards; they delve into the earth, as though burrowing for the gold and silver that was the object of their earthly desires. The fire licking their feet is a parody of the pentecostal tongues of fire that played on the heads of the apostles (Acts 2.3–4). The rock of Peter—"You are rock [*petrus*], and upon this rock [*petram*] I will build my church" (Matthew 16.18)—is as it were riddled by termites, eaten away from within by degenerate priests. The hole reserved for popes, with each new arrival taking the place of his predecessor, who is pushed farther down into the rock, constitutes a sinister and perverted apostolic succession.

When Nicholas accuses Boniface of having "taken the fair lady by deception"—that is, of having tricked his way into becoming pope—he is reporting a widely circulated story. Whether there is any truth in it, or it is a malicious invention of rival factions in the papal court, is difficult to say. Certainly, Boniface was renowned not just for his sharp intelligence but for his guile, his ambition, his unscrupulousness. His predecessor had been a compromise candidate. He was an unworldly hermit from Abruzzo who had never been to Rome, and who had accepted the position with great reluctance, taking the name Celestine V. After only a few months in office, he had been pressured (some said duped) into abdicating—an event almost unprecedented in the history of the church. The question of whether a pope *could* abdicate became a subject of intense legal scrutiny and debate.

The story went that Boniface had engineered the abdication. As Celestine lay in bed at night, he heard a spectral voice urging him to renounce his office. The voice belonged to Boniface or one of his henchmen, speaking through a tube, hidden behind hangings in the papal bedroom. Or he heard the voices of children claiming to be angels, telling him to abdicate. Again the scenario was engineered by Boniface. Or Boniface himself dressed up as an angel, with luminous wings and mask and hands, and then woke Celestine at night in the dark and urged him to renounce the papal throne. All these various versions of the story are reported in early commentaries on the poem. What is certain is that only months after abdicating, Celestine died. There were those who said that Boniface had had him murdered for good measure.

Dante clearly thought of Celestine's abdication as an act of moral cowardice. He is almost certainly the unnamed sinner who is damningly referred to in the famous words *colui / che fece per viltade il gran rifiuto* ("the one who out of cowardliness made the great refusal") in the first circle of hell, just inside the gate. Here those who did not make a stand for right or wrong are passed by in contemptuous silence: *non ragioniam di lor, ma guarda e passa* ("let's not speak of them, but look and pass on"), Virgil instructs Dante.

History does not concur with Dante in his judgment of Celestine, who was and still is the patron saint of L'Aquila in Abruzzo, where his coronation as pope took place in 1294 and where pilgrims still venerate him to this day. In July 2010, in a public audience at Sulmona, Pope Benedict XVI praised Celestine as a role model for his humility. Celestine's mortal remains were rescued from the late-thirteenth-century church of

Santa Maria di Collemaggio in L'Aquila on April 9, 2009, after the disastrous earthquake that hit the town a few days earlier.

The stroke of dramatic genius by which Dante contrived to put Boniface in hell before his time must have caused him some satisfaction. But to understand why Boniface was the archenemy we must go beyond the gossip and backbiting of the papal court and return to Florence to look at papal involvement in the city's destiny in these decades. That involvement culminated in a bloodbath in the streets of Florence.

The cities of Tuscany—Florence, Pisa, Lucca, Siena, Arezzo, Pistoia—had always been vulnerable to papal interference. Their favoured geographical position in the centre of Italy made them highly desirable potential acquisitions or allies for the pope. The papal states lay close to hand to the south and east. (See Fig. 5 on p. 19.) Control of these towns would help protect Rome from potential encroachments of imperial forces from the north. The Holy Roman Empire, centred in the German principalities, had in effect been moribund since the death of Frederick II in 1250, but his various descendants from time to time spearheaded sporadic uprisings of imperial fervour. Even when the Tuscan cities were riven by internal factions and family animosities, as they always were, guarding their independence as autonomous political entities—self-governing city-states—was an overriding political aspiration shared by all citizens. Paradoxically, the dispute between papacy and empire for political dominance in Italy worked to the advantage of the communes. The relentless squabble between the two powers which sought to control them was one of the things that enabled them to reinforce their liberty.

When the pope was thwarted he could impose an interdict, as happened to Florence more than once in the course of the thirteenth century. An interdict was a powerful weapon. Supposedly a spiritual punishment, debarring the city from ecclesiastical functions and privileges, in reality it severely affected the city's prosperity by attacking its business interests. While the city was under interdict, its citizens—the rich bankers and merchants, whose clientele was international, or the tradesmen and artisans whose sphere of operation was local and regional—were in effect excommunicated. To deal with them was to flout ecclesiastical authority. This was a trade embargo: the medieval equivalent of UN sanctions. It was important therefore not to displease the pope too often or too irrevocably. In fact the interdicts on Florence had never lasted long. An accommodation of some kind was always reached.

IN THE CLOSING DECADES of the century a third force had come into play alongside papacy and empire. The royal house of France had become an increasingly powerful player in Europe, with disastrous consequences. Anti-imperial ambitions made the French royals natural allies of a beleaguered papacy, but their thirst for dominance and power sometimes threatened the interests of the very ally with whom they conspired. Two Frenchmen of different generations, both called Charles and both the brothers of kings, were to play a decisive role in the history of Italy and Florence in these years.

The first was Charles of Anjou, the brother of King Louis IX (who became Saint Louis in 1297, when he was canonised by Boniface VIII). Charles came to Italy as the pope's ally and at his invitation the year Dante was born. A year later (1266), he inflicted a historic defeat on imperial forces at the Battle of Benevento. This was the death blow to the imperial cause in Italy for many decades. He became king of Sicily and Naples by papal concession as a reward for supplying and leading troops to fight the pope's cause. His territorial ambitions in the peninsula were later aided and abetted by Pope Nicholas III. He was still in power at the time of the rebellion known as the Sicilian Vespers (1282), when the Sicilians rose up against French overlordship of the island.

In the aftermath of Benevento, when imperial forces were vanquished in the south and the Guelfs were once again in control of Florence, Charles of Anjou had been sent by the pope as peacemaker (*paciarius*) to the city. The regime he installed there under a series of lieutenants lasted for ten years, during which time the power of the newer merchant families and the guilds that represented them steadily increased. Several of the great Florentine banking families had not only underwritten the cost of Charles's expedition with a huge loan but were also bankers to the pope. This financial connection gave Florence unrivalled status in the world of international finance, but it also meant that the pope was always keenly well informed about what was going on in the city. The Florentine *popolo* valued the commercial benefits of contact with the Angevins and the markets they opened up in the south of Italy, but at the same time it maintained a consistently wary opposition to papal interference in the affairs of the city—a delicate balancing act.

A generation later another Frenchman called Charles—Charles of Valois, brother of King Philip the Fair—was sent to Florence by Boniface VIII with the same title his compatriot had had more than three decades earlier: *paciarius*—peacemaker in Tuscany. In the light of his behaviour, the title must have seemed bitterly ironic to many Florentines. The pretence was that he would act as impartial intermediary between the warring factions when the city was close to civil war. In fact, on Boniface's orders, he secretly favoured the Blacks and Corso Donati, and his actions were directly responsible for the coup that saw the White Guelfs, including Dante, expelled from the city.

Boniface had been complicit with Corso for some time. Corso had obliged one of his sisters, Ravenna, to leave the cloister so that he could obtain her inheritance for himself. The inheritance came from her deceased husband. Corso had no claim on it, but Boniface ruled in his favour. Corso had carried off a Cerchi who was about to become a nun and forced her to marry him (his second marriage) in order to secure *her* inheritance. Boniface ratified the union after the event. Compagni lists this as one of the main reasons for the split into Blacks and Whites. Expediency, not principle, always dictated Boniface's actions. When Corso was banished from Florence in 1299, Boniface made him *podestà* ("chief magistrate") at Orvieto, enabling him to bide his time and plot his return. In 1300 Boniface encouraged Corso, from Orvieto, to exacerbate the tensions within Florence to provide a pretext for papal intervention in the commune's affairs.

And when the fate of Florence hung in the balance in late 1301, just two months before Dante was sentenced to exile, Boniface's connivance ensured the victory of the Black Guelfs over the Whites. Charles of Valois—the supposed peacemaker sent by the pope, who was granted entry to the city only on giving the commune a guarantee of his impartiality—entered the city accompanied by his men. With Boniface's covert support, Corso and a small band of his followers were able to reenter the city shortly afterwards. Corso took control, threw open the prison, and encouraged the released felons and his own followers to ransack and pillage the property of the Whites for six days. In his chronicle Compagni, who was a prior at the time, gives a dramatic account of the mayhem. A new priorate was established, all of them Blacks. A few weeks later (January 1302), the White Guelphs, Dante included, were sent into exile. The city remained in Corso's control for three years. There was no doubt that this coup d'état and its outcome was Boniface's intention and Boniface's doing.

On the circle of avarice in purgatory Dante finds the penitent sinners lying facedown on the ground. Their posture enacts the excessive attachment to earthly goods which is the essence of their sin. Their hands and feet are tied, leaving them restrained and powerless, reflecting the inhibiting effect of avarice on their ability to do good works. Keeping close to the inner wall of the mountain in order not to step on them, Dante comes upon the man from whom both Charles of Anjou and Charles of Valois were directly descended. He is Hugh Capet, the founding father of the Capetian dynasty in France some two hundred years earlier. The dynasty's success and longevity, and thus its increasingly powerful role in the Europe of Dante's time, was due to an unbroken run of eleven successive male heirs who outlived their fathers—a remarkable achievement for the time. But Capet's own bitter words to Dante invite us to see that long line of heirs from a very different perspective.

Dante's *dimmi chi fosti* ("tell me who you were") provokes an impassioned speech. In an outburst of pent-up grief and shame which allows no conversational give-and-take, the French king rails against his descendants and their role in causing the evils that bedevil Europe. After explaining who he is, he tells the story of his unexpected accession to the throne in lines of vibrant energy:

Io fui radice de la mala pianta
    che la terra cristiana tutta aduggia . . .
Chiamato fui di là Ugo Ciappetta;
    di me son nati i Filippi e i Luigi
    per cui novellamente è Francia retta.
Figliuol fu' io d'un beccaio di Parigi. . .   (*Purg.* xx 43–52)

(I was the root of the evil plant which casts a gloomy shadow on
    Christian lands . . . On earth I was called Hugh Capet; the
    Philips and the Louis by whom France has been ruled in recent
    times are my descendants. I was the son of a Parisian butcher . . .)

(Dante is inaccurate on this last point—it was another Hugh Capet
who was a butcher's son.) Then Capet moves on to excoriate his descendants, three Frenchmen called Charles whose intervention in Italian
affairs has had, and is to have, disastrous consequences. Before them, the
royal line was undistinguished, but not actively engaged in wrongdoing:
poco valea, ma pur non facea male ("it wasn't worth much, but it wasn't
actually doing wrong." This is one of those incisive throwaway lines
Dante delights us with when he isn't even trying). Capet summarises
the career of Charles I of Anjou with biting sarcasm. (Charles of Anjou
was the brother of King Louis IX of France. From him were descended
the Angevins, a collateral branch of the French royal family.) Capet ends
with the fiercely ironical statement that, to make amends for previous
misdeeds—military depredations in Provence, Normandy and Gascony,
and the execution in a public square in Naples of the sixteen-year-old
imperial pretender, Conradin—Charles "pushed Thomas back up to
heaven" (*ripinse al ciel Tommaso*). That is to say, he had Thomas Aquinas murdered—Aquinas, the great scholastic philosopher. The turn of
phrase suggests that Charles might have thought he was doing Thomas
a favour by killing him, as though the future saint (who died in 1274 and
was canonised forty-nine years later) would have been grateful for the
early leg-up to heaven he was given by being summarily dispatched.
    But worse is to come. The behaviour of Charles of Valois towards

Florence will be even more shameful, not a matter of military might and deception, but of treachery, the weapon of Judas ("the lance Judas jousted with"). This is the Charles, the son of King Philip III of France and brother of King Philip IV, who was Boniface's accomplice in the coup of 1301, which led to the expulsion of the White Guelfs and to Dante's own exile. A third Charles, Charles II of Anjou, will sell his own daughter in marriage for political advantage and financial gain, as a pirate might sell a slave girl. *Avarizia* is the driving force behind these shameful careers. All these royal figures descended from their troubled ancestor are motivated only by insatiable greed—for territory, for money, for power.

The final outrage in the series of shaming events linked to Hugh Capet's line lies just a little further in the future (1303). By this time the pope and the French royal family will be openly at loggerheads. The French will conspire with the powerful Colonna family in Rome, Boniface's most dangerous local enemies and rivals, who themselves had papal ambitions and a strong position in the curia. Boniface was a native of Anagni, now a small hilltop town about forty miles southeast of Rome. But at this time it was an important power base. With a population of around twenty thousand, it was a big place in medieval terms. Boniface was the fourth pope from Anagni in less than two hundred years, and, like his three predecessors, he chose to spend much time there during his pontificate. (The Vatican became the fixed seat of the papacy only much later in its history.)

The Colonna family stronghold was at Palestrina, another small (but impregnable) hilltop town halfway between Rome and Anagni. Palestrina was strategically important for Boniface's military control of the area. In 1297 Boniface had declared a crusade against the Colonna, calling on all Christians to rally in his support. The outrageous claim was that fighting the Colonnas was a sacred duty like fighting the infidel, and that death in battle fighting for Boniface would be viewed as martyrdom.

The final violation in Hugh Capet's long charge sheet against his descendants is the incident known as the *schiaffo di Anagni*. A minister of the French king Philip the Fair, a man called William of Nogaret, acted on the king's instructions in this matter, in collusion with the Colonna family. They manhandled and intimidated Boniface, who was held prisoner and humiliated in the papal quarters at Anagni. A *schiaffo* is literally a slap or blow struck to the face with an open hand. Whether this was in reality a physical assault, or merely a psychological assault on the pope's dignity, we cannot be certain. The two eyewitness accounts we have differ on this point in their report of the incident.

This humiliating episode (which caused scandal all over Europe when it became known) is described by Capet in language which sees it as a reenactment of the crucifixion:

> veggio in Alagna intrar lo fiordaliso,
> e nel vicario suo Cristo esser catto.
> Veggiolo un'altra volta esser deriso;
> veggio rinovellar l'aceto e 'l fiele,
> e tra vivi ladroni esser anciso.   (*Purg.* xx 86–90)

(I see the fleur-de-lis enter Anagni, and Christ made prisoner in
  the person of his vicar. I see him being derided once again; I
  see the vinegar and gall renewed, and I see him killed among
  thieves who remain alive.)

This is Boniface, the archvillain, but his manhandling and humiliation at the hands of the agents of the French monarchy, far from giving Dante any satisfaction, is the worst crime of all. Boniface died just a few months later as a direct result of his maltreatment.

The energy of this sustained denunciation by the founding father of the French dynasty makes it unmatched as political invective. This is as close as Dante ever comes to using a character in the afterlife simply as a mouthpiece for his own views. The energy of the moral revulsion is Dante's own, but here, unexpectedly, the eloquence is in defence of Boniface, the man he so loathed. The distinction between office and incumbent is fundamental. Boniface is a despicable and evil man, but the office of pope commands respect. Once again Dante has structured the narrative in dramatic terms; once again we are witnessing self-recrimination. Just as it is a pope who condemns other popes in *Inferno* xix, so here it is their own ancestor who condemns the degenerate descendants of the Capetian dynasty for their shameful crimes, crimes that have had such catastrophic consequences for Italy and Florence.

THE PAPACY AND the French royal family had for a long time had a common enemy in the claimants to the imperial throne, and a common cause in seeking to ensure that those claimants never achieved their goal of regaining political dominance in Italy. Successive Holy Roman Emperors had attempted to bring under control the wealthy city-states of north and central Italy that lay within the boundaries of the old empire. After the death of Frederick II in 1250, his son Manfred failed to follow through on the promise of his early successes. Manfred sent troops to help the Sienese and the Florentine Ghibellines at the Battle of Montaperti in 1260, and briefly the Ghibelline cause was in the ascendancy. Just six years later, he suffered the catastrophic defeat against papal forces and French troops led by Charles of Anjou at Benevento, south of Rome—the battle in which he died.

Dante meets Manfred, the failed imperial claimant, in a landmark encounter early in purgatory. Manfred's story of his death in battle and its aftermath makes audaciously polemical points about the limitations on the pope's power to excommunicate and the ease with which that power can be misused for political purposes. It also makes the fundamental theological point that turning to God even at the moment of death is enough for salvation. This meeting is one of the earliest encounters in purgatory, and it sets the tone for much of what is to follow.

Dante and Virgil are on the shore at the foot of the mountain, uncertain which way to go, when they encounter a group of souls who are coming hesitantly towards them, equally unsure of the way. These souls are still a good stone's throw away when they stop in a huddle against the inner wall of the mountain. Those at the front notice the shadow cast by Dante's body. The insubstantial bodies of the dead, by contrast, have no solidity and do not cast shadows. The souls hesitate and draw back in wonderment. Virgil reassures them that this visit by a living man to the afterlife is willed in heaven.

One of the souls asks Dante if he recognises him. Dante takes a good long look:

Io mi volsi ver' lui e guardail fiso:
> biondo era e bello e di gentile aspetto,
> ma l'un de' cigli un colpo avea diviso.
Quand'io mi fui umilmente disdetto
> d'averlo visto mai, el disse: "Or vedi";
> e mostrommi una piaga a sommo 'l petto.
Poi sorridendo disse: "Io son Manfredi,
> nepote di Costanza imperatrice . . ."   (*Purg.* iii 106–13)

(I turned towards him and looked steadily at him: fair-haired he
> was, and handsome and noble-looking, but a blow had split
> one of his eyebrows. When I had respectfully declared that I
> had never seen him, he said: "Now look," and showed me a
> wound high on his chest. Then smiling he said: "I am Man-
> fred, grandson of the empress Constance . . .")

Although the striking good looks of the young man are disfigured by
two wounds, one on his face and one on his torso, the wounds cause him
no pain, and he smiles as he speaks. He is anxious that Dante should take
back news to his daughter, another Constance, to reassure her that he is
here *s'altro si dice* ("if people are saying different")—if people are saying,
as well they might be, that he must be in hell. His fate in the afterlife
might have seemed a foregone conclusion. He was reputed to have murdered several close relatives to advance his career, and to be guilty of a
host of other sins, including drunkenness and debauchery, possibly even
patricide. One pope had declared him a Muslim and a heretic. Two other
popes had excommunicated him.

But in lines of sublime simplicity he explains what happened as he
died, after receiving his two mortal wounds on the battlefield:

Poscia ch'io ebbi rotta la persona
> di due punte mortali, io mi rendei,
> piangendo, a quei che volontier perdona.

Orribil furon li peccati miei;
    ma la bontà infinita ha sì gran braccia,
    che prende ciò che si rivolge a lei.   (*Purg.* iii 118–23)

(After I had broken my body with two mortal wounds, I gave
    myself up, weeping, to Him who willingly pardons. My sins
    were horrible; but infinite goodness has such wide arms that
    it takes what turns to it.)

God's mercy is infinite. The sinner has only to turn towards it with
heartfelt repentance to be accepted with open arms, even at the moment
of death. This is a fundamental principle which governs one's destiny in
the afterlife.

Manfred describes the fate of his mortal remains after his death in
battle, where (contemporary chroniclers tell us, though he does not say
this himself) he had acquitted himself with great bravery. The soldiers
who found his body on the battlefield had buried it, and as a sign of their
respect, each soldier had placed a stone over the grave, creating a cairn
to mark the spot. But on the orders of the vengeful Pope Clement IV, the
archbishop of Cosenza disinterred the remains and scattered the bones
outside hallowed ground after declaring him excommunicated. If the
archbishop had understood God's infinite mercy,

l'ossa del corpo mio sarieno ancora
    in co del ponte presso a Benevento,
    sotto la guardia de la grave mora.
Or le bagna la pioggia e move il vento
    di fuor dal regno, quasi lungo 'l Verde,
    dov' e' le trasmutò a lume spento.   (*Purg.* iii 127–32)

(the bones of my body would still be buried at the end of
    the bridge near Benevento, under the guardianship of
    the heavy pile of stones. Now the rain wets them and

the wind stirs them outside the kingdom, almost along
the river Verde, where he transported them with light
extinguished.)

The kingdom outside which he is buried is the kingdom of Sicily,
whose boundary with the papal state was marked by the river Verde.
Manfred's body is vengefully removed in death from the kingdom he
had gained in life at the church's expense. The *lume spento* which caught
Ezra Pound's imagination—the evocative phrase *A lume spento* was the
title he gave his first volume of poems—is the sign of his excommunication. The excommunicated were buried with no ceremony and with
candles extinguished in order to mark their estrangement from the com-
forts of religion.

And yet in spite of the brutal ritual of disinterment and excommunication, in spite of papal power and vindictiveness, Manfred is saved. The
difference between salvation and damnation can be a single instant of
genuine repentance and turning from sin, even at the moment of death.
It is not in the pope's power to stand between the creature and his creator, just as it is not in his power to guarantee absolution in advance for a
sin about to be committed even at his own urging. The distance between
what should be the pope's true spiritual role and the brutal reality of
his active engagement in the skullduggery of politics could not be more
pointedly or more poignantly underlined.

The last attack on Boniface's wickedness is delivered by Saint Peter
in canto xxvii of the *Paradiso*. The condemnation of Boniface that had
emerged by implication in the canto of the corrupt popes in hell is now
spelled out, and by the founder of the church himself, the first *vicar-
ius Christi* or representative of Christ on earth. Saint Peter lambasts
his degenerate successor and the moral squalor of the papal court over
which he presides.

Quelli ch'usurpa in terra il luogo mio,
il luogo mio, il luogo mio che vaca
ne la presenza del Figliuol di Dio,

fatt' ha del cimitero mio cloaca
>del sangue e de la puzza; onde 'l perverso
>che cadde di qua sù, là giù si placa.   (*Par.* xxvii 22–27)

(He who usurps on earth my place, my place, my place which is
>vacant in the eyes of the Son of God, has made of my cemetery
>a sewer of blood and stench; wherefor the perverse spirit who
>fell from on high [Satan] feels satisfaction down there [in hell].)

Boniface's occupation of the papal throne is a usurpation. The papal court in Rome is a stinking sewer. Satan himself takes satisfaction in Boniface's evildoing. And, in case by this time we had forgotten, Beatrice's final words in the poem, near the very end, in *Paradiso* xxx, remind us that Boniface will end up in the hole in hell reserved for simoniac popes. Her words remind us that his successor, Pope Clement V, will push Boniface farther down into the hole: *e farà quel d'Alagna intrar più guiso*, "and he'll make that man from Anagni go farther down" (*Par.* xxx 148).

DANTE IS AS "ENGAGED" a political writer as there has ever been, and as brave a one. A modern parallel would be Russian writers exiled under Stalin for speaking out: Osip Mandelstam comes to mind. Dante wanted a better world for the poor and the powerless, whose lives are made wretched by the greed and corruption of the powerful, and by the endemic warfare and civic unrest entailed by their ruthless pursuit of personal ambition. His calling to account of those responsible for the sorry state of the world—religious and secular leaders who fail in their duties because of naked self-interest and greed—is as powerful a political statement as any ever penned. The underlying aspiration is always clear: peace, so that human beings can lead productive and fulfilling lives; justice, so that wrongdoers are punished.

Dante's mature understanding of how peace and justice could be achieved seems unrealistic to modern eyes, and was unrealisable even in the late Middle Ages. He thought that there should be an emperor, a single supreme secular ruler over the whole of mankind, to function in parallel with but be independent of the pope, its spiritual leader. He formulated this theory in his prose treatise on ideal government (*Monarchia*). It will strike readers today as highly abstract and theoretical, quite divorced from the practicalities of politics in the real world.

But Dante was no armchair theoretician. His views were born of direct and painful experience in the real world of politics. His own political career, so promising in its early stages, had gone disastrously wrong. He lived his last two decades in exile, dependent on the charity and good-will of others, eking out his existence by performing duties as secretary or ambassador in the courts of rulers.

It is the poem, not the prose treatise, which gives the truest sense of his political vision, and expresses the full force of his passionate idealism. The *Commedia* is not a political tract, just as it is not a sermon. The power with which Dante projects his vision of a world gone wrong was the only power he could call on: the power of words. One need know very little medieval history (none at all, in fact, when one starts reading the poem) in order to appreciate the force of his vision. One merely needs to be alive to the power of his shaping imagination and his language.

One thing Boniface VIII was cannily aware of was the power of art for political propaganda. In an age where opportunities for visual propaganda were restricted, he seems to have had a natural talent for self-promotion and self-aggrandisement through the visual arts. He made a point of being painted and sculpted by the outstanding artists of his time. Giotto depicted him proclaiming the Jubilee in a mural that is still visible in part in the Basilica of St. John Lateran in Rome. When the great Florentine sculptor and architect Arnolfo di Cambio was commissioned in 1296 to design Florence's new and vastly enlarged cathedral on the site of the much smaller church of Santa Reparata, he made a portrait bust of Boniface in marble. The bust was to have pride of place high on the cathedral's façade, gazing down on the baptistery, the heart of the city's spiritual and social life—the place where Dante had been baptised, and where he hoped in vain to the end of his days to be crowned with the poet's laurel wreath.

The statue of Boniface remained in this commanding position on the cathedral façade for two centuries. (It can now be seen in the Museo dell'Opera del Duomo in Florence. Today's cathedral façade dates from the late nineteenth century.) Other statues of Boniface, always in full regalia with all the symbols of his status and power—papal throne, papal tiara, keys and robes—were placed in equally elevated positions in other important cities. In Anagni he still gazes out over the town from a loggia high up on the cathedral wall. In Orvieto statues were installed over the two main gates into the city (their weathered remains are now in the church of San Francesco). The face is always recognizable. He is said to be the first pope of whom we have a realistic likeness. Indeed, his face quickly came to signify "pope," even when it was a different pope. No fewer than three other popes in the frescoes in the Basilica of St. Francis in Assisi, painted around 1300, have been given his recognisable facial features. The self-aggrandisement reflected in these artistic ventures attracted much adverse comment at the time.

Fig. 9   Giotto: Boniface proclaims the Jubilee.

Fig. 10   Arnolfo di Cambio: Pope
Boniface VIII.

In 1310, just seven years after Boniface's death, the French king
Philip the Fair mounted a posthumous trial against him. The aim was to
declare his papacy illegitimate, as a way of invalidating the many anti-
French bulls promulgated during his tenure, bulls affecting both rights
and taxes payable to the church. The charges were familiar ones. The
ousting and murder of his predecessor Celestine V, who was now canonised and would become a saint in 1313—but not, significantly, with
the name he had held as pope. Sexual misdemeanours. Simony and nepotism. Usury, at rates of interest as high as 60 percent. Sorcery. Heresy.

Atheism. There was also a charge of idolatry, directly related to his habit of placing statues of himself in prominent positions. By a neat trick, he was accused both of associating himself with images of Christ in triumph, and of reviving the ancient pagan practice of placing statues of idols over city gates. After years of taking evidence from those who had had dealings with him, the trial was abandoned inconclusively.

Well ahead of time, indeed as soon as he became pope, Boniface commissioned Arnolfo di Cambio to design his tomb in St. Peter's in Rome, one of the most splendid funeral monuments of any medieval pope. It includes a mosaic panel that shows Boniface being presented by Saint Peter himself to the Virgin Mary in heaven. Boniface was preemptively protecting his posthumous reputation. He is said to have taken great pleasure in gazing at this magnificent structure, which seemed to offer a guarantee of a kind of immortality. (The tomb was dismantled two centuries later, when St. Peter's was restructured; parts of it can now be seen in the crypt of the basilica. The mosaic is in Saint Petersburg.) But Boniface cannot have imagined that alongside the imposing monuments he had taken such care to leave as his lasting memorial on earth there would be an equally powerful and far less flattering image of him passed down to posterity, evoked through the imagination and words of a great poet: a grotesque, naked, upside-down figure whose legs would kick out wildly for a few years, and who would then disappear from view, forever locked inside the dark rock in hell.

Political power is transient, but art endures; the poet trumps the pope. In New York recently as I passed the Lincoln Center for the Performing Arts in a taxi, I was startled to catch a glimpse of an oddly familiar figure half-hidden among the trees in the small patch of green park that stands opposite the entrance. On investigation, it proved to be a larger-than-life-size bronze sculpture of Dante, erected in the early twentieth century in homage to the power of art—the power of the written word in its highest, poetic form, to reflect and immortalize human destiny. While Boniface's sculptured representations languish in museums, of interest to a few antiquarians, the poet stands tall and proud, book in hand, confidently addressing the New World and the new millennium.

Dante's death warrant.

3.

Life

La Commedia è anche la storia,
stavo per dire l'autobiografia, di un poeta.
(The *Commedia* is also the story,
I was going to say the autobiography, of a poet.)
—GIANFRANCO CONTINI

We all know that Art is not truth.
Art is a lie that makes us realize the truth . . .
—PABLO PICASSO

IN 1300 DANTE WAS THIRTY-FIVE YEARS OLD, *NEL MEZZO DEL CAMMIN*—exactly halfway through our allotted biblical span of threescore years and ten. He was born in 1265, the biographies tell us. Yet we have no documentary evidence for this date of birth: no register of births, no birth certificate. We deduce it from a poetic text.

We have very little evidence about Dante's life outside the texts he wrote. Of course the construction of a narrative, even an autobiographical one, will be shaped by artistic, and perhaps ideological, imperatives. Lived experience or historical fact may be altered or elaborated in the interests of aesthetic and emotional truth and to satisfy structural demands. To reconstruct Dante's biography is mostly a process of speculation and supposition. Much of the documentary evidence that survives is tangential, with little bearing on the intimate personal experience of the poet or even the basic facts of his life.

That surviving evidence, collected in a modest modern printed volume called the *Codice diplomatico dantesco*, tells us a little about his family circumstances. His mother died when he was a boy (there was a younger sister, whose name we do not know). His father remarried, and this second marriage produced two half siblings, one of whom, Francesco, seems to have been close and to have helped Dante in adulthood in times of financial difficulty. There are documents relating to the paying of debts and the securing of loans.

On his public role we have a little more. The State Archive in Florence preserves the minutes of meetings of the various councils that governed the city around the turn of the century. From 1295 on Dante served on several of these councils. We can see his political allegiances, and get a sense of his increasing identification with the White cause in its more intransigent form. Several times the fact of his having expressed an opinion for or against a proposal is noted. The issue of the election procedure for choosing priors is a recurring matter of debate.

One minute is particularly revealing. On this occasion, when he alone spoke against a proposal, his opposition to it is noted as a matter of record. The Council of One Hundred was considering a request from the pope: *Dante Alagherii consuluit quod de servitio faciendo d[omino] pape nichil fiat* ("Dante Alighieri advised that, on the matter of assisting the pope, nothing be done"). Boniface had asked that the services of one hundred Florentine knights granted to him earlier be extended for a further period. Dante's opposition is a firm piece of evidence, were it needed, of his distrust of Boniface, and his belief in the need to make a stand against his encroachments on Tuscan independence. The vote did not go Dante's way. Boniface got his cavalry.

We do not know whether Dante and Boniface ever met face-to-face. It seems certain that Dante was part of a diplomatic mission to Rome in late 1301 sent by the White Guelphs to try to influence the pope's behaviour toward Florence as events in the city got out of hand. Our source for this is again Dino Compagni, the contemporary chronicler of the city's history, who was actively involved in its political life and who himself became a prior a little more than a year after Dante, just as the situation in Florence reached a crisis point. As a White Guelph and a member of the *popolo*, his take on events is arguably partisan, but his knowledge of this fact seems secure. He does not tell us if the two actually met.

Also in the archives in Florence are the key documents that tell the stark facts of Dante's banishment. A first one records the exile imposed on him, along with other White Guelfs, on January 27, 1302. There were three charges against him: financial corruption and extortion in public office; opposition to the pope's requests for aid; connivance in the expulsion of the Black Guelphs from Pistoia. There were three punishments: a fine of five thousand florins; exclusion from public office for the rest of his life; and banishment from Florentine territory for two years. If the fine was not paid within the space of three days, his property would be destroyed. Dante was probably on the return journey from Rome when the news reached him. He never reentered the city.

Another document records the death sentence imposed on him in absentia on March 10 of that same year. He was condemned to be burnt at the stake should he fall into the hands of the authorities, and his property was confiscated. A third document dates from 1315, when the death sentence was reconfirmed and extended to his children, after he had rejected the offer of an amnesty made by the commune to the exiled White Guelfs. This time execution was to be by decapitation.

Copies of a dozen or so letters he wrote survive. Some of these he wrote on behalf of patrons at the courts where he found refuge after his exile. They reflect the circumstances of his existence as a writer dependent for his livelihood on his hosts, but they throw no light on his own feelings or experiences. Other letters are in effect political manifestos in which he publicly calls to account powerful figures whose conduct can influence the course of events on the world stage: the cardinals who are to elect the new pope; the princes who can welcome the new emperor; the Florentines within the city who can change the city's policy of implacable opposition to that new emperor. There is one letter addressed to the emperor himself, encouraging him in his Italian enterprise. These are highly wrought

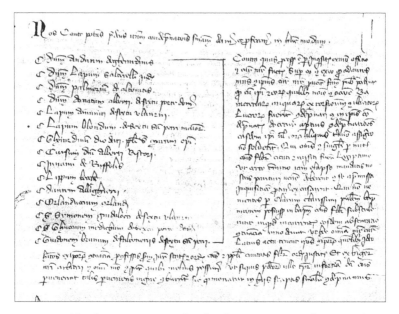

Fig. 12 The document preserved in the Florentine State Archive recording the death sentence imposed on Dante and other White Guelfs in
March 1302. Dante's name (*dantem allighierij*) is eleventh on the list. The
final lines condemn those on the list to exile in perpetuity and death by
burning should they return to Florentine territory (*talis perveniens ingne
comburatur sic quod moriatur*).

rhetorical compositions. They are eloquent and forthright in their take on
contemporary events, but they throw little light on Dante's personal circumstances. He identifies himself in these letters as *Florentinus exul inmer-
itus* ("a Florentine undeservedly in exile"). In a later letter he is *Florentinus
natione non moribus* ("a Florentine by birth, not in his conduct").

Only one letter gives a powerful sense of a precise moment in his
own life and his perception of his own history. It is the letter he wrote to
an unidentified "Florentine friend" (possibly a man of the church: he is
addressed as "my father"). In it he explains his refusal to accept the amnesty
offered to the White Guelf exiles in 1315 on what he judged to be humiliating terms. To benefit from the amnesty, he would have had to plead

guilty to the trumped-up charge which had been the pretext for his exile. That charge—that he had used his political position for personal gain: that he was guilty, that is, of corruption in office—was a particularly offensive one for a man who believed that he was acting for the public good. He would in addition have had to pay a substantial fine, and to take part in a public ceremony of ritual mortification called the oblation, staged before the assembled Florentine citizenry in front of the baptistery. The same ceremony was used for common criminals. Here is his response to this offer:

> . . . I learn that, by a decree recently passed in Florence about the pardon of the exiles, if I were prepared to pay a fine, and suffer the stigma of the oblation, I could be pardoned and return at once. . . .

> Is this the gracious recall of Dante Alighieri to his native city, after close on fifteen wretched years of exile? Is this the reward for innocence manifest to all the world . . .

> No thinking person could perform such a foolhardy act of self-abasement as submitting himself to be presented at the oblation like a felon in chains. . . . Nor could a man who preaches justice, after suffering wrong, pay money out of his own pocket to those who wronged him, as though they deserved it.

> No, father, this is not the path to a homecoming. If some other way can be found . . . which does not detract from my good name and honour, I will accept it without dragging my feet. But if Florence is not to be entered in such a way, then I shall never enter Florence.
>
> (Epistle xii)

The angry rejection of the humiliating terms on offer, so at odds with any notion of justice or integrity or a true sense of the meaning of events, reflects a fierce sense of wounded personal honour. The same fiery and uncompromising temperament is often on display in the *Commedia*.

Leonardo Bruni, the chancellor of Florence who lived a hundred years after Dante and wrote a brief life of the poet, had access to autograph letters which do not survive. We have his reliable description and partial translation into Italian of one such Latin letter. It pinpoints the period Dante served as prior as marking the turning point in his life: "All my misfortunes and all my troubles were caused by and started with the ill-fated assemblies of my priorate. . . ." The point at which he achieved the highest office possible in the commune, the summit of his political ambition, was the very point at which things started to go disastrously wrong.

Dante's parallel career and reputation as a poet can be charted with a handful of documents that survive from his own lifetime. In 1287, when he was just twenty-two years old, a sonnet of his describing a Bolognese landmark, the Garisenda Tower, was copied at the end of a legal document in Bologna to fill up the remaining space on the page. We deduce that Dante had visited Bologna, an ancient university city with a rich cultural and literary heritage. Clearly this poem was in circulation, and not just among his friends.

Lawyers at the time took pains to avoid leaving any blank space in legal documents, in order to prevent the amending of the documents by the addition of codicils. Fragments of poetic text, probably cited from memory, were often used as a space filler. In 1317 and again in 1319, while Dante was still alive and well before he had finished writing the *Paradiso*, we find lines from the *Inferno* quoted for this purpose in Bolognese documents. We can safely conclude that the *Inferno* had been released to the public before the poem was complete, and that it was widely popular.

These tantalising snippets testify to widespread knowledge of his poems during his lifetime. They must be counterbalanced by the fact that no manuscript of any of his works in his own hand has survived. We do not even have a signature. (By contrast, Boccaccio and Petrarch, writers of just a generation later, left extensive autograph copies of many of their works.) Leonardo Bruni describes the handwriting in the autograph letters he saw as *magra e lunga e molto corretta* ("thin and long and very correct"). The earliest surviving manuscript of the *Commedia* dates from 1336, fifteen years after its author's death in 1321. But we have a good idea of what the autograph probably looked like. Scholars have

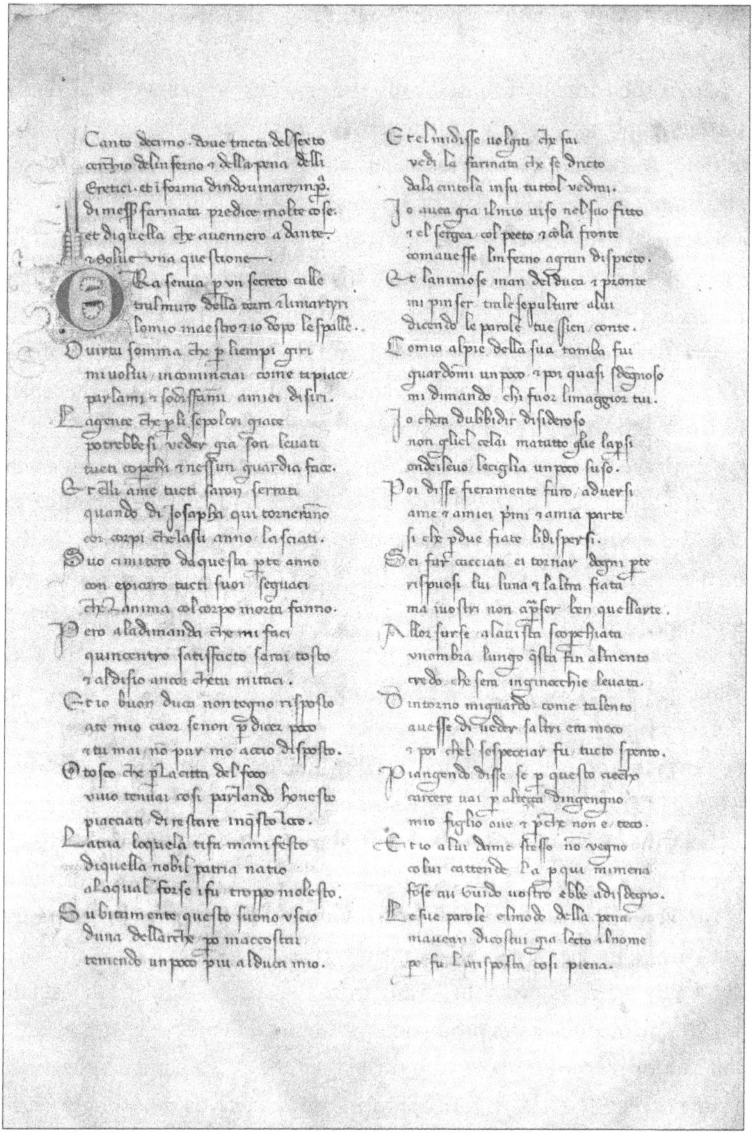

Fig. 12 A page of ms. Triv. 1080 containing the opening of *Inferno* x, very close in layout to what the autograph of the *Commedia* would have looked like. The beautiful hand is that of a professional scribe, Francesco di ser Nardo.

been able to reconstruct a plausible "virtual" exemplar on the basis of early surviving copies.

Since the content of so many of Dante's works appears to be directly autobiographical, arguing from text to life might seem the obvious thing to do. But it would be a naïve reader who took the *Vita nova*, for example, simply at face value. The prose narrative which links and expounds a selection of his early love poems is clearly shaped to an artistic end to form the *libello*, the "little book" in praise of Beatrice. Only those poems which fit the chosen shape of the story are used. There are poems written for Beatrice that are not included, and it seems clear that some of the poems which are included were originally written for women other than Beatrice and adapted to this new narrative purpose.

With the *Commedia* these problems are compounded. One of the most moving encounters in the *Inferno* is the one with Brunetto Latini that so inspired T. S. Eliot in the "Little Gidding" section of *Four Quartets*: "In the uncertain hour before the morning / Near the ending of interminable night . . ." Yet we simply do not know the nature of Dante's relationship with Brunetto, an eminent Florentine statesman and writer of the previous generation. Dante meets him among the sinners against nature in *Inferno* xv.

The landscape evoked so memorably by Eliot is London at dawn after a bombing raid during the war. Dante and Virgil are in the seventh circle of hell, the circle of violence, and they are in its third subcircle, which contains the violent against God, nature and art. They are crossing a wasteland of burning sand on which are falling flakes of fire. They are walking along the raised stone bank of a river of blood that flows through the sandy plain. The vapours rising from the stream extinguish the falling fire, providing some protection for the travellers on the stone bank, but not for the sinners below on the plain. One of the sinners recognises Dante and pulls at the hem of his garment. Dante would willingly pause to talk, but the sinners must not stop moving. So they walk along in tandem, Dante bending his face down towards Brunetto as they go. He does not dare to leave the higher ground and walk along with him on the sand.

Brunetto Latini's stature in Florentine culture is a matter of historical record. He wrote influential books and translated key classical texts into the vernacular, including part of Cicero's *De inventione*, all with the aim of instilling civic virtues in his fellow citizens. The chronicler Giovanni Villani celebrates him for the educative effect of his teaching on uncouth Florentines. He was, Villani says, "the one who began to teach the Florentines to be less coarse, to make them capable of speaking well and of knowing how to guide and rule our republic according to the art of politics."

Before Dante was born, Brunetto had been chancellor of the commune at the time of the first popular government (1250–1260). On his return from exile in France, where he remained during the six years of Ghibelline supremacy (1260–1266), he was again at the heart of the city's cultural life. He continued to be so for decades, until his death in 1295. He championed the idea of an urban society grounded in law and justice. He was determined to bring the *grandi* to accept these ideas. He was, in other words, both a writer and a high-profile public figure, the two areas in which Dante himself hoped to excel: a double role model of enormous distinction. Was he a teacher of Dante's? a more informal mentor? an older friend? We simply do not know. Our only evidence of their relationship is the poetic text itself.

Certainly, Dante is surprised to find Brunetto in this section of hell: *Siete voi qui, ser Brunetto?* ("Are you here, ser Brunetto?") he exclaims with astonishment. We may infer that Brunetto's homosexuality was not a matter of common knowledge. Dante's poem has in effect "outed" him. Certainly, Dante's words express affection and indebtedness:

> ché 'n la mente m'è fitta, e or m'accora,
>> la cara e buona imagine paterna
>> di voi quando nel mondo ad ora ad ora
> m'insegnavate come l'uom s'etterna: (*Inf.* xv 82–85)

> (for in my mind is fixed, and it now saddens me, the dear, good,
>> fatherly image of you when in the world from time to time
>> you taught me how man becomes eternal:)

As an acknowledgement of lasting gratitude for a formative, shaping influence on his life these words are as direct and touching as any in the poem. That Dante nowhere in his writings mentions his own father seems significant. The "paternal" image of Brunetto could be seen as a father substitute. When later in the poem Dante meets a forebear in paradise, the words of Virgil's Anchises to his son Aeneas in the Elysian Fields of the afterlife are explicitly quoted—*O sanguis meus* (*Aeneid* vi 835, *Par.* xv 28): "O my bloodline." But it is not his father who utters them; it is his great-great-grandfather.

The words in which the value of Brunetto's teaching is asserted—"you taught me how man becomes eternal"—sit oddly with the fact of his damnation. This is the only time in the poem that the verb *etternarsi* is used; and it is used here of a human teaching by an evidently flawed human being. Elsewhere in the poem, the adjective *etterno* is always used in a context linked to God and things created by God, never by human beings. Thus we read over the gate of hell *io etterna duro*, "I last for eternity." Our sense that an acknowledegment of intellectual and psychological indebtedness is a key moral obligation in Dante's ethical universe, and ingratitude a particularly heinous moral failing, will be confirmed when we find that at the very bottom of hell, among the traitors, the very worst of them are those who betrayed benefactors.

We cannot even be sure that Brunetto is condemned for homosexuality, though most of those in this circle of hell certainly are. Reputable Dante scholars have argued—though without convincing most readers—that the sin against nature for which he is damned was, variously, writing in French rather than in his native Italian (his most important work, the *Trésor*, was written while he was in exile in France); or embracing the wrong political philosophy; or subscribing to the Patarine heresy, a deviant form of religious belief.

The relationship between what really happened and what the poem tells us remains elusive. The art is all the more compelling for that reason. Time and again as we read the *Commedia*, we confront the paradox that the power of Dante's poetry comes from its strong autobiographical element—lived experience, firmly rooted in time and place and circumstance—but that this experience is transmuted and transformed by the power of the poet's imagination and his command of language, so that often it becomes almost impossible to assert anything with confidence as a fact, except that this is a great poet writing at the height of his powers.

The problem is even more complicated in the *Commedia* than in the *Vita nova*, for two very precise reasons. The narrative framework of the *Commedia* has its own independent logic and momentum, shaped to an end that is larger and more all-encompassing than the merely personal; and that narrative framework takes the form of an allegory.

Long narrative poems in the Middle Ages were often allegories. The events they recount are entertaining, but behind those events lies a deeper meaning. The long French poem the *Roman de la Rose*, written in the thirteenth century, was the first-ever European vernacular best-seller. The *Roman* tells the story of a young man who attempts to enter an enclosed and heavily guarded garden in order to pluck a beautiful rose. We understand that this is an account of a seduction, the wooing and winning of a lady by a passionate lover, whose courtship is for a long time thwarted by those aspects of her personality that counsel caution and circumspection. Thus we have characters called Jealousy, Shame, Honour and Ill Repute. The story works at two levels, the surface or literal level (breaking into the garden to steal the rose), and the deeper or allegorical level (courting, breaking down the defences of and ultimately possessing an initially reluctant loved one). The common human experience of sexual attraction and pursuit in the face of obstacles is given narrative form. A psychological experience becomes a plot.

Even texts which were not created by their authors to carry an allegorical meaning can lend themselves to this kind of interpretation. The *Aeneid* was often so read and understood in the Middle Ages. The surface meaning of Virgil's poem is the travels and travails of Aeneas between the time he leaves Troy and arrives in Latium, where he will found the city that is to become Rome. But the poem also yields a second meaning—the trials and tribulations any man will face in the course of his life, which test his mettle as a moral agent. Aeneas resists the attractions of Dido, demonstrating great self-control. He persists in his mission despite many obstacles, demonstrating courage and fortitude. Medieval readers evidently found this habit of reading for an underlying uplifting meaning second nature. Dante himself read the *Aeneid* in this way, as we learn from the *Convivio*.

The *Commedia* can be read in a similar way to the *Roman de la Rose* or the moralised *Aeneid*. Dante the pilgrim can be taken to represent any Christian. His guides Virgil and Beatrice can be seen as representing the two sources of help and comfort offered to all human beings in their dealings with the vicissitudes of earthly existence: human reason and divine grace. The opening line of the poem encourages us to recognise a representative function in the protagonist and his predicament: *Nel mezzo del cammin di nostra vita* ("In the middle of the journey of our life"). It is *our* life too, not just his.

But to read the *Commedia* in this way as a simple two-level allegory like the *Roman de la Rose* leaves out of account almost everything about the poem that is most vital and original. Allegory in this sense can seem, in Benedetto Croce's dismissive phrase, little more than cryptography—a sometimes tiresome game of hiding simple messages behind codes. Once the code has been cracked (*a* stands for *b*), the meaning of the text is exhausted. "He plucks the rose" decodes as "he deflowers the girl." Much of the most interesting thinking about the *Commedia* in the last seventy years has focused on exploring these issues, and on trying to determine and describe exactly how allegory works in the poem. There are some important aspects of the question about which all thoughtful readers can agree.

Virgil undoubtedly does represent human reason, but he is first and foremost the historical Virgil, the great poet of antiquity whom Dante revered above all others. (Dante had no direct knowledge of Homer, whose reputation he took on trust.) Beatrice does indeed represent divine grace or revelation (or whatever is necessary for salvation in a Christian world that human beings cannot supply for themselves), but she is first and foremost the historical Beatrice, the girl Dante knew and loved in the Florence of his youth. Virgil and Beatrice are not ciphers invented to carry a moral or spiritual meaning. To attach a label to them is to diminish them. They are real individuals who once were alive. They have names, identities and histories that are theirs and theirs alone.

Equally, Dante is not a generic Christian like the hero of *The Pilgrim's*

Progress. He is himself, an individual with a unique identity, which includes his nationality, his profession, his appearance and his way of speaking. Time and again it is these distinctive identifying characteristics that spark off the encounters with the shades of the dead. Often their interest is aroused simply by virtue of his being a living man. He casts a shadow; his body has weight; he breathes. But equally often, perhaps more often, he is recognised—as an Italian, as a Tuscan, as a Florentine, as a man with family and political allegiances, as a friend, as an enemy, as a poet. He is recognised by his face, by his clothes, by his accent, by his skill with words.

And he has a name. Like Marcel in Proust's *À la recherche du temps perdu* he is named just once in the text. At the climactic moment when he is reunited with Beatrice in the earthly paradise and she speaks to him for the first time, his name, Dante, is the first word she utters. (Botticelli, who knew the *Commedia* intimately, seems deliberately to echo this by signing his own name just once to his series of drawings for the poem. It is visible on a placard carried by one of the angels in the sheet devoted to *Paradiso* xxviii.) Like Marcel, Dante becomes in the course of the work the writer who is capable of writing the work of which he is the protagonist. The story recounted in the work is, among other things, the story of how he becomes that writer. The historical reality of the protagonists in the poem, the uniqueness of their characters and experience grounded in their personal histories and identities, is not at odds with their exemplary value. On the contrary, it deepens and enriches it. If Dante represents everyman, as in some sense he undoubtedly does, he is nonetheless first and foremost himself.

This kind of allegory is sometimes called "historical" allegory because the people in it really lived. But even this is not an adequate account of what is going on in the poem. Writing in the *Convivio*, Dante touches on another tradition of allegory. The allegorical sense, he tells us there, can be understood in two different ways. There is allegory as it is understood by poets and allegory as it is understood by theologians. As an illustrative example of poets' allegory he cites the story of Orpheus, who with his lyre tamed the wild animals and moved the trees and stones. The deeper significance of this tale is that the wise man, by using the instrument of his voice—that is, by speaking eloquently—can tame hard hearts and persuade the uneducated to do his will.

This is just the kind of two-level allegory we find in the *Roman de la Rose*. Dante defines it as a *veritade ascosa sotto bella menzogna*, a "truth hidden beneath a beautiful lie." The poet invents a fiction—makes up a story—in order to convey a truth. Poets' allegory differs from allegory as understood by theologians precisely in this respect—that is, in the relationship of the literal meaning to truth or fact. The distinction is a crucial one.

Allegory as understood by theologians is more usually called "typology" or "figuralism." This is a technique of biblical interpretation which establishes a network of significant links between episodes in the Old and New Testaments. Thus Jonah's three days in the belly of the whale prefigure the three days between Christ's crucifixion and resurrection. A mosaic in Ravello cathedral dating from 1272 illustrates the point beautifully. It shows Jonah swallowed by and then emerging from the whale or sea monster. As he emerges, he is clearly depicted as Christ Pantocrator, or "Ruler of All." The image shows the economy and compression of meaning figuralism allows (the significance of the Jonah story and its connection with the story of Christ, in a single image). Figuralism establishes meaningful links across time and human history.

Here are some other examples of theological allegory. Abraham's willingness to sacrifice his son Isaac prefigures God's willingness to sacrifice his son Christ for the benefit of humanity. The exodus of the Israelites from Egypt in the time of Moses prefigures the saving of Christians from a life of sin and their leading to eternal life by Christ. These episodes in the life of Christ are the fulfilment of the Old Testament episodes. The Old Testament episodes are figures or types of those in the New Testament. They become more meaningful as a consequence of this relationship. Their meaning is not only historical but also allegorical (figural, typological)—a foreshadowing of revelation. The Old Testament episodes are for Dante, as for any medieval Christian, historically true. They are emphatically *not* a fiction invented to convey a truth—not a *bella menzogna*, or "beautiful lie."

Dante's historical allegory is in some ways analogous to figuralism. Virgil and Beatrice really lived. Dante didn't invent them to represent human reason or divine grace. The same is true of almost all the people he meets on his journey. The life they lived on earth can be seen as the figure or foreshadowing, the state of the soul in the afterlife as the fulfilment. Although these are two different phases in the existence of a single individual, rather than two different people related in history, as happens in biblical figuralism, the analogy is an illuminating one.

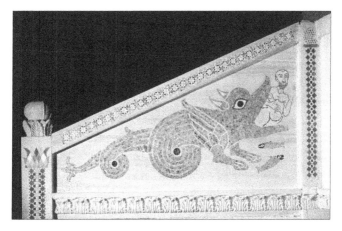

Fig. 13   Jonah emerges from the whale as Christ Pantocrator.

The crucial point is that nothing is an invention. In the circle of the lustful in hell Dante meets Francesca da Rimini, a victim of a crime of passion, murdered by her husband when he discovered her adulterous affair with his brother Paolo. Francesca's earthly existence prefigures her eternal destiny. Her story speaks to the reader far more powerfully than any abstract personification of Lust could do—just as it is all the more troubling for not being about a character who is obviously licentious or promiscuous. Dante's poem does not give us personified abstractions of moral qualities, nor does it give us characters the author invented. It presents us rather with the richness and complexity and specificity of individual cases anchored in history and concrete circumstance. Its originality and its power, as critics have always recognised, come from this.

But what of the narrative in which these figures are embedded? One of the most striking things about the *Commedia* is that it is not, as one might have expected it to be, a dream vision. Allegories in medieval literature often are. By introducing the story as an account of a dream, an author ensures that the fictional status of the literal meaning—the fact that it is a *bella menzogna*, something he made up, not something that really happened—is established at the outset. Thus the *Roman de la Rose* begins by telling us that the poet will recount a dream he had: "In the twentieth year of my life . . . I lay down one night, as usual, and slept very soundly. . . . During my sleep I saw a very beautiful and pleasing dream . . . Now I wish to tell this dream in rhyme . . ." And more than 21,000 lines later, the poet-lover wakes from his dream: "Before I stirred from that place where I should wish to remain forever, I plucked, with great delight, the flower from the leaves of the rosebush, and thus I have my red rose. Straightway it was day, and I awoke." Langland's *Piers Plowman* opens and closes in much the same way, as do several works by Chaucer and Boccaccio.

Dante's narrative strategy is exactly the opposite. The poem begins not with a moment of falling asleep but of awakening: *mi ritrovai per una selva oscura* (I found myself again, I came to myself, in a dark wood). By contrast, he had been *pieno di sonno*, "full of sleep," when he went astray, when he abandoned the true path and got lost in the wood. The medieval reader's comfortable narrative expectations have been turned upside down. This is not an account of a dream, but of something that happened when the poet woke up.

This truth claim made by the poem is neatly echoed in a story recounted by Boccaccio in his life of the poet. Boccaccio tells how some women sitting chatting in a doorway in Verona saw Dante walk past and agreed that you could tell he'd been to hell because of his dark complexion and frizzy black hair ("on account of the smoke and fire down there"). In Boccaccio's account, Dante overheard this conversation and smiled a little to himself as he walked on. We may be less naïve than the women of Verona—presumably no reader today thinks that Dante actually went to hell—but there is no gainsaying the fact that the poem is asking to be accepted as literally true. In Charles Singleton's thought-provoking formulation: "The fiction of the *Divine Comedy* is that it is not fiction."

The poem ends, to be sure, with a moment of rapt absorption as

Dante is caught up in the beatific vision. A visionary experience is the goal of the journey and the outcome of the journey, but not the mode of the journey. There are dreams and visions within the poem which are an important part of the protagonist's experience on the way. There are three dreams in purgatory, one for each night he spends on the mountain. There are ecstatic visions of examples of envy and of anger punished, again in purgatory. But the journey itself is not presented as experienced in a dream or vision.

Early commentators on the poem felt uneasy with this claim, and no less uneasy with the notion that the experience recounted might be genuinely visionary. The rich fourteenth-century commentary tradition on the *Commedia* begins just a few years after Dante's death. Two of its earliest practitioners are his own sons Jacopo and Pietro. Jacopo, on this evidence, was singularly ill-equipped to understand his father's literary genius, but he deserves our gratitude for the crucial role he played in assembling a complete text of the poem after his father's death. Neither Jacopo nor Pietro, nor their fellow practitioners, seem to be alive to the profound originality of Dante's literary practice—or if they are, they prefer to disguise it, tending to insist that the poem is indeed a fiction, the story it recounts something that Dante made up, not something he really experienced (only the naïve ladies of Verona would think that), or even really experienced in a vision (which would make his book a dangerously subversive text if it was indeed directly inspired by or dictated by God).

This controversial issue is sometimes referred to in the dry scholarly phrase "the ontological status of the text." A fascinating light is thrown on the question by the images used in manuscripts to illustrate the opening pages of the poem. These illustrations often seem designed to offer a key with which to approach the text that follows. Just one manuscript (ms. Egerton 943 in the British Library) opens with a miniature which clearly implies that the poem is the record of a dream. This (very misleading) image echoes the one regularly used for the opening page of manuscripts of the *Roman de la Rose* (where it is entirely appropriate). We have a sleeper in bed on the left, and the same figure setting out on his adventures on the right, this second segment representing the content of the dreamer's dream.

Fig. 14 The poet dreaming.

This is a standard way of portraying a dreamer and his dream. A fresco in the Basilica of St. Francis in Assisi, dating from c. 1300 and traditionally attributed to Giotto, shows Innocent III dreaming of Francis holding up the Lateran church.

Fig. 15 Pope Innocent dreams of Saint Francis.

The Egerton image might almost be thought of as a way of preemptively censoring the poem or taming it, implying: what you are about to read is only a dream.

Many manuscripts open with an image of the seated poet, apparently lost in a trance. This echoes another standard image, one associated with biblical illustrations of the prophets. These images might suggest that the poem records a vision, or that the poet has prophetic insight into the state of the world and perhaps into the future. We see this, for example, in the opening images of manuscripts in the Budapest University Library and Oxford's Bodleian Library.

Figs. 16 and 17   **The poet in a trance.**

It is difficult to be sure where images like these shade into images of a poet lost in the throes of artistic inspiration, imagining the created world he portrays in his poem. Manuscripts which open with an image of the poet seated at his desk, pen in hand, sometimes show the dark wood rising behind him. Thus the illustration in a manuscript in the Biblioteca Apostolica Vaticana might be taken to imply, as we post-Romantics would be inclined to say, that the dark wood is a product of the poet's creative imagination.

Fig. 18
The poet as
creative writer.

Many opening illustrations simply circumvent the question of the text's status by showing Dante and Virgil as they set out on the journey together, sometimes walking through the initial capital letter of the first line (**ɴ** in medieval script) as though through an arched doorway, leading us into the world of the poem.

Fig. 19   Dante and Virgil enter the world of the poem.

The terms *dream, vision, fiction* are of course not rigorously exclusive one of another. There are ambiguities and overlappings inherent in their meanings. And there is an important distinction to be made between a dream vision (a literary genre, a narrative mode with recognised conventions) and a vision. A vision is a religious experience of the divine by people—mystics—who have access to an aspect of reality denied most mortals. A work that tells the story of a dream is avowedly a *bella menzogna*—not something that happened in real life, but something the author made up, a fiction (with its paradoxical and potentially troubling twin aspects of inventiveness and falsehood). A vision, by contrast, is an experience of something which exists independently of the writer and to which he may exceptionally be given privileged access. And of course the fiction a writer invents may be that he had visions, as our early commentator Guido da Pisa suggests when he says that Dante *fingit . . . suas visiones* ("shapes . . . his visions").

Having started so confidently with an assertion of realism in the opening of the poem, Dante does much later use the word *vision* to refer to the experience it recounts. His ancestor Cacciaguida instructs him *tutta tua visïon fa manifesta* ("reveal your whole vision," or—more simply, and perhaps more accurately—"tell all that you have seen"). By the middle of *Paradiso*, where this encounter takes place, the ground may have shifted somewhat. As Dante's sense of his prophetic mission kicks in, he seems more willing to blur the boundaries between realistic account and vision. The title he uses for the poem in the course of writing it changes. The word *comedìa* ("comedy") is used twice in the *Inferno*, where the contrast is explicitly with Virgil's *tragedìa* ("tragedy"), the *Aeneid*. But in the *Paradiso* the terms used to refer to the poem are *poema sacro* and *sacrato poema* ("sacred poem"), suggesting that Dante has come to believe that the truth-telling power of his verse is a gift from God. The *Commedia* has become the poem *al quale ha posto mano e cielo e terra* ("to which both heaven and earth have put their hand"). But there is also a clear acknowledgement, in the closing lines of the poem, that this is a work of the creative imagination: *a l'alta fantasia qui mancò possa* ("here the power of my lofty imagination failed"). Realistic account? vision? poetic and imaginative fiction? As always, it is impossible to pin Dante down. He operates with such creative freedom that it defies our capacity to analyse and define.

Some readers, particularly modern ones, think Dante had real visions or mystical experience, which he is reporting in the poem. Thus William Anderson in his book *Dante the Maker* claims that Dante had three great mystical visions, one for each section of the poem. (Anderson was himself a Sufi, which may account for his interpretative bias.) But there is no documentary evidence of any kind to support this claim, and other texts Dante wrote suggest a temperament of a precisely opposite kind.

The little-read *Questio de aqua et terra*, a short prose work in Latin, shows him at the end of his life, anxious to establish his intellectual credentials by delivering a lecture on a thorny scientific issue to a quasi–academic audience (think Seamus Heaney giving a lecture on tectonic plates to the British Academy). The question at issue: why does land emerge above the surface of the oceans when scientific theory suggests that the sphere of earth at the centre of the globe should be completely covered by an enveloping sphere of water? Dante's answer is that the emerging land is drawn upwards by the attraction of the stars in the eighth sphere. The stars function like a magnet attracting the earth upwards, and at the same time release underground vapours that press upwards from below.

The *Monarchia*, another late work in Latin, reflects a logical, rationalist approach to political philosophy, arguing from first principles (though always on a bedrock of faith) that human flourishing is dependent on a system of world government in which a universal emperor is set over the human race in secular matters, in parallel with, but independent of, the pope, their spiritual leader. Neither the *Questio* nor the *Monarchia* suggests the temperament or experience of a mystic.

Medieval commentators, uneasy at Dante's challenge to their certainties, sometimes deal with the problematic nature of the experience recounted in the *Commedia* by treating the poem as an encyclopedia of sin and virtue. They downplay the narrative aspect of the text—what Dante did on the journey, an experience that profoundly changed him. They emphasise instead the reporting aspect—what Dante saw on the journey. What he saw is an orderly hierarchy of sins and punishments, reflecting an intellectual system which commands our understanding, rather than a psychological experience which engages our emotions. As though to emphasise the point, in many manuscript illustrations Dante and Virgil are a pair of observers who stand passively to the side of the picture and gaze at the spectacle before them, as in the miniatures in the Chantilly manuscript or the Holkham Hall manuscript now in the Bodleian Library. A modern analogy might be a journalist who visits a foreign country merely as an observer to report on what he sees, as compared with one who is profoundly changed by his experience.

Fig. 20   Metamorphoses of the thieves.

Fig. 21   The simoniacs.

Dante and Virgil are distinguished in manuscript illustrations by their hats, with Dante's medieval headgear quickly becoming iconic. Often Virgil has a beard, to denote seniority. Only with Botticelli do we get a sense of the poet as a participant in the action (now a recognisable individual with a profile as distinctive as his hat). His difficulties en route are themselves a focus of interest, a source of inventiveness and delicious detail in the drawings—further evidence, if it were needed, of Botticelli's genius and his profound knowledge and intuitive understanding of Dante's text. Thus we have Dante scrambling up rocks to escape from danger ; Dante reacting with amazement as he feels for the missing letter

Fig. 22   Botticelli: Dante scrambles up the rocks (detail).

Fig. 23   Botticelli: Dante feels his forehead (detail).

P on his forehead, which has been brushed away by the wing of the angel guarding the entrance to the second terrace of purgatory; Dante and Virgil deep in conversation as they climb up to the first terrace of purgatory.

Dante scholars argue with passion about the kinds of allegory Dante uses in the *Commedia* and how best to describe and understand their interrelationships. There is a vast scholarly literature devoted to the subject.

Fig. 24   Botticelli: Dante and Virgil in
conversation (detail).

But no first-time reader will feel the need to agonise over these questions
(the medieval version of literary theory or hermeneutics). No unified-field
theory of the way allegory works in the poem is ever likely to emerge.

For much of the time the allegorical or symbolic dimension of the
poem speaks for itself. No reader will miss the significance of the dark
wood, or the threatening presence of the three wild animals that block
Dante's attempt to climb the sunlit hill. Even a child reading a fairy story
can decode these elemental symbols as signifying lostness, confusion,
danger. No reader will miss the relationship between the life lived on
earth and the fate of the individual in the afterlife, nor the way the punishments of the souls in hell and purgatory relate to the nature of their
moral failing. Those punishments are not just punitive, a matter of sin
and retribution. They show the behaviour in its essence for what it really
is. The parallel between Dante's physical journey and his journey in
knowledge and understanding will be apparent to any attentive reader.
Where there is a figural connection with the life of Christ—as there is
when Manfred, displaying the wound on his chest, reenacts the story

of Christ and doubting Thomas—recognising the figural connection enriches the encounter but is not crucial to understanding it.

Virgil and Beatrice are the two supremely meaningful figures in Dante's own poetic and emotional life, the one a literary passion, the other an enigmatic, elusive real-life relationship. Their choice as guides to the afterlife links autobiography to allegory in a powerfully original way. Dante reinvents and transcends a medieval genre, inspired in part by the account in *Aeneid* vi of Aeneas's visit to the underworld but also by biblical narratives and their ways of signifying. In so doing he created a poem that is in every way a match for the great classical epics of antiquity.

OF DANTE'S LIFE AFTER EXILE we can say with certainty that he travelled widely throughout Italy, and in circumstances that he found humiliating. He tells us so himself in the *Convivio*: "I have travelled through almost all the regions to which this language extends, a wanderer, almost a beggar . . ." This experience introduced him to Italian in its many dialectal varieties. It shaped his thinking about the nature of language and the question of what form of language a writer aspiring to write well should use.

If we try to track these travels after his banishment from Florence with more precision, we know some secure facts, but not many. We know that he was at San Godenzo, in the Mugello region north of Florence, in 1302, with the exiled Whites and the Ghibellines with whom they had now made a makeshift alliance. He may have been with them at other places. We know that later in the decade he was at various times in Forlì, in Verona, in the Lunigiana area of northern Tuscany as a guest of the Malaspina family, in the Casentino area in the east of Tuscany, perhaps also at Lucca and in the Veneto. There are documents recording his role in 1306 as special envoy sent to resolve a dispute between the Malaspina cousins and the bishop of Luni. He successfully negotiated a peace treaty between them.

He may have been present in Milan when Henry VII was crowned in Sant'Ambrogio, just as he may have been at Pisa when the emperor passed through on his way to his coronation in Rome. Then again he

may not. He certainly saw the emperor on one occasion, as the one letter he addressed to him makes clear, but we do not know where. We
know that in the last decade of his life he spent six years in Verona at the
court of Can Grande della Scala, and then four in Ravenna at the court
of Guido Novello, where he was a respected literary figure with a certain
reputation who exchanged eclogues in Latin with the professor of rhetoric at Bologna university, Giovanni del Virgilio. We even know the exact
date on which he delivered his lecture on the *Questio de aqua et terra* in
Verona in the little church of Sant'Elena: January 20, 1320.

What of his love life? The *Vita nova* tells us that in his ninth year he
met Beatrice, that he met her again at eighteen, that on a later occasion
she cut him dead in the street, causing him great pain, that he resorted
to a subterfuge in order not to appear to be gazing at her in church by
seeming to gaze at an intermediate figure (the so-called screen lady), that
he had disturbing dreams, that her father died, and that her own death at
twenty-four was deeply distressing to him.

But the *libello* which tells of his love of Beatrice is not a confessional
outpouring. It is rather a carefully structured work (poems and linking
prose narrative) designed to illustrate a crucial turning point in his own
artistic development as a love poet. Even a cursory glance shows that
Dante is talking as much about his poems as about his feelings. Sometimes what he says about a poem can seem curiously reductive, a primitive form of practical criticism, more concerned with the way the parts
of the poem fit together than with emotional insights or linguistic sub-
tleties. Even early biographers of Dante, much closer than we are to the
source material, had a difficult task drawing any firm conclusions about
Beatrice, beyond the fact that she was a profoundly meaningful figure
for his artistic and creative life. The little book ends with a promise that
he will write of her what has never been written of any woman, a promise he fulfilled in the *Commedia*.

We know that Dante was betrothed at the age of eleven to Gemma
Donati, who belonged to a minor branch of the powerful Donati family.
Such childhood betrothals were the normal custom at the time. We know
the couple had three, possibly four, children, all born before he went into
exile. Just as Dante never mentions his father in his writing, so too he

never mentions his wife. Boccaccio's *Trattatello in laude di Dante* (*A Short Treatise in Praise of Dante*), whose title reflects the reverence in which the author held his subject, describes rather touchingly how Dante's wife was initially put out by her husband's long hours at his desk but made her peace with them and learned not to mind them. We do not know if at some point she joined Dante in exile; she may have done. Boccaccio tells us that Dante was lustful, and not only in his youth but in his middle age as well. Here we may suspect a bias on the part of the biographer, never bashful in talking of his own sexual appetites. Or he could just be extrapolating from two poems Dante wrote probably around 1307, in the early years of exile. These poems describe intense sexual desire and the difficulty of controlling it with one's willpower. Whether the passion described is real or fictitious we have no way of knowing. We do know that Dante's daughter Antonia became a nun in Ravenna and took the name Beatrice.

Boccaccio tells two stories about the composition of the *Commedia* which may be fanciful but may contain a germ of truth. One is that the first seven cantos of *Inferno* were composed before the exile, an idea that scholars now dismiss as very unlikely. The other is that on Dante's death the final thirteen cantos of *Paradiso* could not be found but that they were eventually located in a secret hiding place behind a hanging on the wall after his son Jacopo had a dream which revealed their whereabouts to him. Jacopo was responsible for assembling a complete text of the poem (*Inferno* and *Purgatorio* had been in circulation for some years) and, a few years after his father's death, taking it with him to Florence. The ban on the children's returning to the city had at last been lifted. In the decades which followed, Florence, with its professional scriptoria, soon became a productive centre for the copying of the poem. The *Commedia* rapidly became very popular. It was a controversial and unsettling text, far from pious orthodoxy or sanctimonious sermonising. That undoubtedly was part of its appeal.

Dante, like many writers, seems deliberately to have kept details of his personal life screened. The constructed narrative tells us all he wanted us to know, all we need to know to appreciate the poem and understand its greatness. Biographers over the years have come up with some far-fetched ideas: that he spent ten years in Paris; that he studied at Oxford; that he had mystical visions; that he may have smoked hashish. Far more interesting than these speculative and unsubstantiated notions, for which there is no evidence at all, are the tantalizing glimpses of firsthand detail in some of the early commentaries on the poem. The author of the *Ottimo commento*, a Florentine, reports that he himself heard the poet explain that he never let the need to find a rhyme dictate what he wanted to say. On the contrary, he made language say things it had not said before.

The *Commedia* can indeed be read as an autobiography of a poet, as Contini hinted in the quotation used as an epigraph to this chapter. As Dante writes the poem, he finds a way of making sense of his own personal history and the role he finds himself fulfilling. He is not a political leader in Florence, as he had wished and hoped, setting his city on the right path, but a poet whose achievement will outlast that of political rivals and companions in exile. His role becomes willy-nilly that of a prophet, like Virgil; his poem a way of changing the world. Both the lives of individuals and the fate of cities and nations may be influenced by his words, if those words are heeded, and if they are sufficiently memorable.

What do we really know of Dante? We can say with confidence that he was a layman, not a churchman. A poet, not a mystic. An intellectual, whose close engagement with the scientific, historical and literary debates of his time and his evolving ideas on some issues have left clear traces in his work, as we shall see when we examine his views on language. But he was also a man of action, with direct and painful personal experience of politics and war. As a young man he had fought in battle to protect his city's interests against the Ghibellines of Arezzo at the Battle of Campaldino, where Corso Donati and Vieri dei Cerchi led the Florentine troops. A decade later he had acted as ambassador for his city in neighbouring San Gimignano and at the papal court in Rome. When he died in Ravenna in 1321 in the night between September 13 and 14— he had caught malaria making his way back through marshy terrain—it was on his return from a diplomatic mission to Venice.

We can say with certainly that he had great insight into human character and motivation, and great understanding of the moral predicaments of other people. He had an astounding capacity to convey the intricacies and complexities of human behavior as he saw it reflected in real-life stories from his own lifetime, projecting them into an imagined world where the fate in the afterlife of the protagonists conveyed their true moral essence. We can say with certainty that he believed that human actions should be judged by moral criteria, and that these criteria were objective (and divinely sanctioned). We may disagree with him—we certainly will disagree with him on many issues—but he is not rigid in his application of these criteria. On the contrary, he continually surprises us and confounds our expectations and forces us to think. Cato, an ancient Roman suicide, is the guardian of purgatory, and is destined for paradise. Ripheus, a Trojan, is already in paradise. Cunizza, a noblewoman renowned for her vigorous love life (she had four husbands and many lovers, among them the poet Sordello—a kind of upmarket Wife of Bath), is also in paradise. Francesca da Rimini is in hell.

Dante is certainly not, as one sometimes hears said, vindictive, spiteful, sadistic. He is not merely engaged in score settling with old adversaries by assigning them to hell. The punishments in hell are horribly cruel, but the world in which he lived was horribly cruel. He had been sentenced to death both by burning and by decapitation. Such sentences were almost routine. We think of the modern world as more civilised than his, but who could seriously argue that this is so, bearing in mind events on the world stage in the twentieth century?

Dante had insight into his own character and failings, predicting that he would spend time on the terrace of pride but very little on the terrace of envy. He was well aware of his exceptional gifts as a poet, both the linguistic virtuosity and the shaping imagination. He showed courage and fortitude on matters of principle in difficult circumstances, when he lost everything he held most dear, including his ambition to be effective as an agent for moral and political change in his beloved but benighted city. It was to be five hundred years (1865) before Florence erected a statue to its troublesome poetic genius, where it still stands in front of the church of Santa Croce where he may have studied as a young man.

The reaction of orthodox clerics to Dante's work—burning and banning—shows that he was perceived in certain religious quarters as a dangerous radical. Just eight years after his death the *Monarchia*—the treatise in which he argued that the emperor was not answerable to the pope, but received his authority directly from God—was publicly burnt in Bologna.

It was destroyed on the orders of Cardinal Bertrand du Poujet, a nephew of Pope John XXII, who was then engaged in a power struggle against the ambitious contender for the imperial crown, Ludwig of Bavaria. All copies of the book that could be found were burned. Dante was declared a heretic. There was a suggestion that his bones should be disinterred from their burial place in the church of San Francesco in Ravenna and brought to Bologna to be added to the pyre. It became dangerous to own a copy of the *Monarchia*. Almost half the surviving copies of the treatise have no title or author's name, indicating that this had become a clandestine text that circulated in secret. It was still considered dangerous more than two centuries later when the first Index of Prohibited Books was drawn up by the Vatican, in the context of the Reformation. It remained on the Index, astonishingly, until the twentieth century.

Official distrust and fear spread like an oil slick from the political treatise to the poetic masterpiece. In 1335, just fourteen years after Dante's death, the Dominican order in Tuscany was strictly prohibited from owning or reading *poeticos libros sive libellos per illum qui Dante nominatur in vulgari compositos*, "the books or booklets of poetry composed in the vernacular by the man who is called Dante." The *Commedia*, like the *Monarchia*, had become a banned book, a troubling and subversive work best kept away from impressionable readers.

But set against this official disquiet and censorship, the *Commedia* rapidly became a best-seller to rival that other medieval best-seller, the *Roman de la Rose*. There are around eight hundred surviving copies of the poem, compared, for example, with the eighty-odd copies that survive of Chaucer's *Canterbury Tales*. The richness of the manuscript tradition is equivalent in modern terms, it has been calculated, to a print run of many millions of copies. The poem was read by *non litterati*, people who did not know Latin. It spoke directly to a mass audience, inviting readers to engage directly with issues both on the public stage and in the privacy of individual conscience. An engagé writer of unique linguistic sensitivity and inventive energy and wider shaping and fashioning skills spoke directly to the broadest possible audience. That audience responded, as readers still do today, to a dangerous, passionate, unorthodox, questioning voice which compels attention through poetry, the most arresting of all written forms.

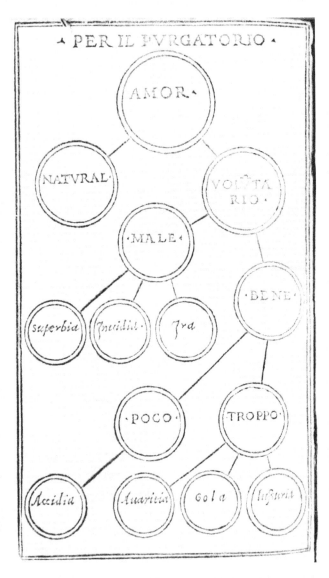

Diagram of love gone wrong.

4.

Love

amor sementa in voi d'ogne vertute
e d'ogne operazion che merta pene.
(*Purg.* xvii 104–5)
(love the seed in you of all virtue, and of
every action that deserves punishment.)

What will survive of us is love.
—PHILIP LARKIN, "AN ARUNDEL TOMB"

Desire haunts my dreams.
—PUSHKIN, EVGENY ONEGIN

HAT IS LOVE? WHAT CAUSES IT? WHAT ARE ITS EFFECTS? CAN anything be done about those effects, or is a person who is in love power-less in the grip of strong emotion? Italian vernacular lyric poetry began two generations before Dante, at the court of Frederick II in Palermo in the 1230s and 1240s; from its beginning, poets tried to define and analyse the nature of love. First Sicilian and then Tuscan poets explored this phil-osophical strand (what exactly *is* love?) alongside the more familiar psy-chological themes inherited from the Provençal troubadours: the poet's joy and suffering in love, the exalting effect on him of his lady's beauty, the pain caused by her indifference or her absence.

This exploring of a speculative strand alongside the psychological was a distinctively Italian development. Two of the most accomplished poems by Dante's predecessors deal with this theme. Both of them influenced him profoundly. One was Guido Cavalcanti's "Donna me prega," a text to be refuted and exorcised. The other was Guido Guinizzelli's "Al cor gentil," a formative influence on the young Dante, but now in his maturity to be reevaluated. Cavalcanti, as we have seen, figures in the *Commedia* only as an absence (an ever-present absence, perhaps). Guinizzelli, a poet of the previous generation from Bologna, was not known to Dante in person but was revered by him as a father figure to the younger generation, and was always spoken of with respect bordering on veneration. Dante will meet him at the top of the mountain of purgatory in a moving scene where the relationship between love and poetry—in effect, between life and literature, between lived experience and the written word—will emerge as a crowning concern at the end of the journey.

Cavalcanti's poem "Donna me prega" is a tour de force which analyses love as a negative and destructive passion in human life, beyond the control of the rational faculties and therefore an inescapable source of confusion and pain to those who experience it. (Ezra Pound made a brave attempt to translate this almost impossibly difficult work.) Guinizzelli's "Al cor gentil," by contrast, expresses a positive, if elitest, view of love and loving. The ethos known as courtly love, with its central conviction that love ennobles the lover, is presented by Guinizzelli in a version of extreme refinement and sensibility. Only the noble-hearted can truly love. Love's natural dwelling place is in the noble heart, just as birds naturally seek out the shade among the green leaves, and just as the heat of fire naturally rises. Love and ignoble hearts are as incompatible as fire and cold water. A series of analogies from the natural world makes a poetic yet quasi-scientific case for the link between nobility of heart on the one hand and susceptibility to love's influence on the other. To love, you must be noble. If you are noble, you will love.

Nobility no longer has the conventional meaning of bloodline or inherited wealth. Rather, it signifies innate intellectual and emotional qualities of character: intelligence, sensitivity, honour.

Dante echoed the opening line of Guinizzelli's poem (*Al cor gentil rempaira sempre amore*: "Love always makes the noble heart its dwelling place") in a sonnet he included in the *Vita nova*. Here the natural affinity between love and the noble heart asserted by Guinizzelli has become an outright identity: *Amor e il cor gentil sono una cosa* ("Love and the noble heart are one and the same thing"). Dante as a young poet has not just endorsed Guinizzelli's view; he has given it a more radical reformulation. In the *Commedia*, long before we meet Guinizzelli himself on the mountain of purgatory, this notion of a link between nobility of heart and the capacity to love is invoked in a celebrated encounter in the poem, that with Paolo and Francesca in the circle of the lustful in hell.

DANTE AND VIRGIL HAVE descended to the second circle, where they discover Minos, the fearsome judge who assigns new arrivals to the appropriate circle of damnation. Here they see sinners whirled about on a strong wind like a huge flock of starlings, buffeted in all directions, *di qua, di là, di giù, di sù* ("here, there, down, up"). Dante immediately understands that these are the carnal or lustful sinners, their punishment an emblematic mirroring of the turbulent force of the physical desire which in life they had been unable or unwilling to resist.

One group stands out from the rest because of the distinctive shape they make as they are borne on the wind, stretched out in a long line like cranes. Dante asks who they are. Virgil identifies famous lovers from history and legend: Cleopatra, Dido, Helen, Achilles, Paris, Tristram and many others. All of them died for love. Dante's attention is caught by a couple who are carried on the wind together, and he says he would like to speak to them. Virgil tells him to call out to them in the name of their love, and they will come to him. As indeed they do, like a pair of doves flying to their nest.

What follows is one of the most famous episodes in the *Commedia*. The pair are Paolo and Francesca, lovers murdered because of their love—killed by her husband when their passionate but adulterous relationship was discovered. This was a contemporary scandal, a real-life tragedy, far removed from the aura of legend and romance conjured up by the names of the heroes and heroines of old. Francesca da Rimini was married to Gianciotto Malatesta, but she fell in love with his brother Paolo, with whom she had an affair. This had happened in the mid-1280s, just a few years after Paolo had served as *Capitano del Popolo* (chief of military forces) in Florence in 1282, where the adolescent Dante may have known him. But these are not facts we learn from the text. If we follow the dialogue as it unfolds, the story emerges with very little by way of concrete circumstance or detail.

The woman (whose name we still do not know) addresses Dante with exquisite courtesy. If the king of the universe (God) were their friend, she says, she would pray for peace for Dante. She will tell him anything he wishes to know, and speak for as long as the hellish wind and noise allow her to, *poi c'hai pietà*, "since you have compassion" for our wretched state. She has sensed his sympathetic interest. She will tell him her story.

She was, she tells him, a native of Ravenna (now some miles inland from the sea but in the Middle Ages close to the coast):

> Siede la terra dove nata fui
> su la marina dove 'l Po discende
> per aver pace co' seguaci sui.   (*Inf.* v 97–99)

> (The city where I was born sits on the shore where the Po flows
> down to find peace with its tributaries.)

But she is not the protagonist of her story. She is the object, not the subject, of the action. The protagonist is Love.

> Amor, ch'al cor gentil ratto s'apprende,
> prese costui de la bella persona
> che mi fu tolta; e 'l modo ancor m'offende.
> Amor, ch'a nullo amato amar perdona,
> mi prese del costui piacer sì forte,
> che, come vedi, ancor non m'abbandona.

Amor condusse noi ad una morte.
  Caina attende chi a vita ci spense.   (*Inf.* v 100–7)

(Love, which quickly takes hold of the noble heart, made him
  fall in love with the beautiful body which was taken from me;
  and the manner of it still offends me. Love, which spares no
  one who is loved from loving in return, made me fall in love
  with his pleasing form so strongly that, as you see, it still does
  not abandon me. Love led us to one death. Caina [a zone in
  the depths of hell reserved for traitors] awaits the man who
  took our lives.)

The couple drawn together by their passion are hapless victims.

Dante is so moved by her words that he is silent, lost in thought, until
Virgil asks him what he is thinking. His answer (*quanti dolci pensier,
quanto disio / menò costoro al doloroso passo*: "how many sweet thoughts,
how much desire led them to the grievous step") shows how powerfully
he has been affected by her account, how completely he has engaged
imaginatively with her telling of the tale. Addressing her by name—he
has recognized who she is—he now asks how and when the two lovers
became aware of their feelings for each other.

Francesca's second great speech tells the story, and now there is more
detail:

Noi leggiavamo un giorno per diletto
  di Lancialotto come amor lo strinse;
  soli eravamo e sanza alcun sospetto.
Per più fiate li occhi ci sospinse
  quella lettura, e scolorocci il viso;
  ma solo un punto fu quel che ci vinse.
Quando leggemmo il disïato riso
  esser basciato da cotanto amante,
  quei, che mai da me non fia diviso,

la bocca mi basciò tutto tremante.
 Galeotto fu 'l libro e chi lo scrisse;
 quel giorno più non vi leggemmo avante.   (*Inf.* v 127–38)

(We were reading one day for pleasure about Lancelot, how love
 bound him; we were alone and had no suspicion. On several
 occasions that reading caused our eyes to meet, and took the
 colour from our faces; but it was just one point that over-
 came us. When we read that the longed-for smile was kissed
 by such a great lover, this man, who will never be separated
 from me, kissed my mouth all trembling. The book was a
 go-between, and so was the man who wrote it; that day we
 read no further.)

Responsibility for what happened has shifted to the book they were reading and its author. As Francesca speaks, her companion weeps. Dante
faints from emotion, and the canto ends.

The episode has often been seen as expressing the quintessence of
romantic love and sexual desire, a passion which survives beyond the
grave and conquers hell. The doomed lovers are still together even after
their violent death, indivisible in the afterlife. The feeling and eloquence
with which Francesca speaks are powerfully appealing, and have proved
inspirational to many later writers, composers and painters. (Various
plays, a symphonic fantasy, at least one ballet and an opera all bear her
name. Wikipedia tells us that no fewer than nineteen composers have
been moved to write operas about her; one of them, by Riccardo Zan-
donai, is still in the repertoire.) Nineteenth-century critics often spoke
of her as a heroine, as remarkable for her charm, delicacy and reticence
as for her passion and untimely end. Even the most jaundiced modern
reader will admit that her words make a profound impact.

No documentary evidence remains of the story, but it was clearly
alive in popular memory decades after the event. Early commentaries
on the poem savour the scandalous details and often add exonerating
circumstances. (The husband was deformed. Francesca was tricked into

marriage with him, believing she was marrying Paolo, with whom she was already in love.) But Dante's version gives no exculpating detail, just the compelling words of the protagonist, who tells her own story, presenting the lovers as blameless figures through whom ineluctable natural laws are operating.

It emerges only at the beginning of the next canto that the lovers are brother- and sister-in-law. The man Francesca refers to obliquely as "the one who killed us" is not only her husband but also her lover's brother. To medieval eyes the relationship was thus doubly illicit, incestuous as well as adulterous, since a married couple become one flesh. Francesca's account is reticent to the point of misrepresentation.

Her account is also bookish and literary, and not just because it was their reading of the story of Lancelot and Guinevere that led to their undoing. Gianfranco Contini noted rather unkindly that Francesca is *un'intellettuale di provincia*, "a provincial intellectual." Her conversation with Dante shows that she is well read, and well able to draw on her reading. She is also a keen student of rhetoric. The artful structuring of her first speech, with its three tercets beginning with the word *Love*, appears to give it the unanswerable logical force of a syllogism: two premises (the laws of love) and a conclusion (the outcome of their operation). Those laws of love—the particular susceptibility of the noble-hearted to the emotion of love, and its corollary, the impossibility of not loving in return if you are loved—were familiar to Francesca from her reading of vernacular love poetry. One of the poets whose words her words echo is Dante himself. He is implicated in her fate. Small wonder that he faints dead away as she finishes her story.

If readers react with shock and sympathy to Francesca's account of how she comes to be in hell, it is hardly surprising; Dante himself reacts in the same way. That is, Dante the character in the poem (the pilgrim, as he is sometimes called), as distinct from Dante the author of it (the poet, though one must not lose sight of the fact that the pilgrim is also a poet). The distinction between the two Dantes helps to explain the apparent contradiction between the sympathy of her portrayal and the stark fact of her damnation. It provides a useful key for thinking about all those episodes in hell where the damned sinner we encounter seems, in human terms, to have an undeniable moral stature. (Farinata is another case in point.) Where nineteenth-century readings of this episode assumed that Dante faints simply with compassion, modern readings emphasise, surely rightly, that his emotions are more complex. This is a first and harrowing instance of the journey in knowledge and understanding the pilgrim-protagonist undergoes in the poem. Reassessing his own past, including his own past as a poet, is a part of the journey.

For many nineteenth-century readers, Dante has created in Francesca a figure so compelling in human terms that it undermines his own theological system. If we sympathise with Francesca, we are calling into question the justice of her punishment. Dante the man, with his innate human sympathies, the argument goes, has unwittingly undermined Dante the moralist. In a more sophisticated version of this view, Dante the poet, unknowingly or even in spite of himself, has undermined the moralist by creating a figure so touchingly human, so single-minded in her passion, that the reader can only respond to her positively. According to this view, it is Dante's creative energies which are at war with his moral system. The creative imagination subverts theology.

These two ways of reading the episode see Francesca either as the innocent victim of a harshly punitive moral code or as a dangerously seductive spokeswoman for sin. The two opposing camps are sometimes described as "doves" and "hawks." But of course she is neither entirely innocent nor entirely demonic. The strength of Dante's art lies in this complexity, the impossibility of categorising her as purely good or purely bad. The tragedy is precisely that someone so attractive and potentially noble in human terms, so rich in admirable human attributes, should nonetheless have been damned. She is damned because of her fatal misreading—a fatally naïve misreading—of a literary tradition.

Distancing himself from his own earlier love poetry while nonetheless insisting on its value is one of the difficult things Dante does in the *Commedia*. After the death of Beatrice in 1290, he tells us in the *Convivio*, he found consolation in philosophical study. This new passion for philosophy manifested itself in his eager frequenting of *le scuole de li religiosi* and *le disputazioni de li filosofanti* ("the schools of the religious" and "the debates of the philosophers," *Convivio* II xii 7). The "schools" of which he speaks are the two great monastic institutions of Florence. Santa Croce (the Franciscans) and Santa Maria Novella (the Dominicans) were both flourishing religious communities with rich libraries and lectures open to laymen. (Unlike Bologna, Florence had no university at this time.) These formative intellectual experiences of the 1290s, like involvement in politics later in that same decade, lie behind the new direction his poetry took towards the turn of the century. But in 1300—the date of the journey to the afterlife—his reputation as a writer still rested primarily on his love poems.

It is as a love poet that Dante is recognised and celebrated by the poet Bonagiunta da Lucca on the terrace of the gluttons in purgatory. Bonagiunta was a Tuscan poet of the previous generation, whose poems were definitively outclassed by those of the new generation. Bonagiunta is eager to acknowledge Dante's role as a poetic innovator. He wants to understand exactly what it is that accounts for the novelty of the *nove rime*, the poems in the new manner. He uses the phrase *dolce stil novo*, the "sweet new style," to characterise that new manner, and to ask what sets Dante apart from his predecessors. Dante answers his question in terms of his relation to love:

> E io a lui: "I' mi son un che, quando
>   Amor mi spira, noto, e a quel modo
>   ch'ei ditta dentro, vo significando."   (*Purg.* xxiv 52–54)

> (And I said to him: "I am one who, when Love breathes within
>   me, takes note, and just as he dictates within me, I set forth
>   my meaning.")

Fidelity to love's inspiration, indeed to love's dictation, defines his way of writing poetry.

Perhaps more critical ink has been devoted to understanding these words than to any other single passage in the poem. The pivotal text in the *Vita nova* which introduces the "sweet new style" is the poem that begins *Donne ch'avete intelletto d'amore* ("Ladies who have understanding of love"). This poem marks the point at which Dante comes to understand that his task is to praise Beatrice, not to win her favour. The phrase *dolce stil novo* refers to the poems written after this, but it clearly implies not simply their content but—more importantly—their style.

The idea of writing under dictation is one often used of the authors of the Bible. Dante himself says as much in the *Monarchia*: "although there are many who record the divine word, it is God alone who dictates." His words here in purgatory, where he talks of taking dictation from love, have clear echoes of the Scriptures and the writings of the church fathers. And later in the *Commedia* he will describe himself explicitly as a scribe, talking of *quella matera ond'io son fatto scriba* ("that subject matter of which I have become the scribe," *Par.* x 27). In the *Commedia* a broader philosophical understanding of love includes yet transcends the more circumscribed emotional and psychological conception derived from Guinizzelli.

For Dante in the *Commedia* love is the mainspring of all human action, whether good or bad, praiseworthy or damnable. But Dante the pilgrim comes to understand this only halfway through his journey, when he asks Virgil to explain love to him: *Però ti prego, dolce padre caro, / che mi dimostri amor* ("Therefore I ask you, dear sweet father, to explain love to me"). In Virgil's explanation, love is no longer just romantic emotion or sexual passion linking two individuals. Desire is seen as a fundamental category of human experience, the driving force behind all human interaction with the world. It is the engine of moral agency.

Virgil's account of love as the source of all human action is at the very centre of the poem, conceptually and geographically. From it follows a notion which is somewhat paradoxical to modern eyes. The seven capital vices (in common parlance, the seven deadly sins) are to be understood in terms of love. Love gone wrong, to be sure: love misdirected, love too weak or love too strong. There are three ways in which love can be misdirected, one way in which it can be too weak, and three ways in which it can be too strong. The geography of purgatory with its seven terraces, as we shall see, embodies this analysis. Closely linked to this notion is the question of whether human beings can be held accountable for their actions. This in its turn raises the fundamental philosophical problem of free will and determinism.

The nature versus nurture debate is at the cutting edge of modern thinking in science and sociology. Do our genes or our upbringing determine the way we behave? The answer to this question has profound implications for our thinking about human behaviour. If our actions are determined by forces beyond our control, whether genetic or environmental, should we be held accountable for them?

The problem of human freedom and accountability has exercised thinking people since the early Greek philosophers, and continues to inspire writers today. (Ian McEwan's *Saturday* is a recent memorable exploration of the theme.) Are human beings free agents? Can they make choices? Or are their choices—to pursue one course of action rather than another, to be one kind of person rather than another—illusory because they are constrained, predetermined by their biology or their parenting? Dante's meditation on this question—medieval in the detail of the argument and at the same time surprisingly modern—lies at the heart of his poem. It is the philosophical and theological underpinning of the whole enterprise. There could be no justice in punishing and rewarding people in the afterlife for actions committed during their earthly existence if they had no possibility of acting otherwise than as they did. Dante places this central concept at the centre of his poem: he is exactly halfway up the mountain—on the fourth of the seven terraces—when the issue is addressed in *Purgatorio* xvii.

To understand how it is that human beings have free will one must understand the nature of love and how it works in the human world. This is what Dante asks Virgil to explain to him when they pause to take a rest on the central terrace of the mountain.

By way of preamble Virgil explains:

"Né creator né creatura mai,"
    cominciò el, "figliuol, fu sanza amore,
    o naturale o d'animo; . . ."   (*Purg.* xvii 91–93)

("No creator or creature," he began, "my son, was ever without
love, either natural or elective; . . .")

Natural love is the love any creature necessarily feels for its creator.
There is no choice involved. Elective love is love for any other aspect of
creation. It always involves choice.

The initial impulse to love, Virgil explains—to be attracted and
drawn to something outside ourselves and to seek to possess it—exists
in all of us. It is a given of human experience. The capacity for loving
becomes the actual experience of loving when something outside the
individual is perceived as attractive and the person feels drawn towards
it. There is no blame attached to the initial perception or to the feeling of
attraction. But before acting on the attraction, before actively pursuing
the object and attempting to possess it, there is a vitally important step,
a step which distinguishes human beings from animals. Animals act
instinctually and do not have the power of reason. Human beings have
reason, and they must use it if they are to lead fully human lives. Reason
or judgment is the link, the crucial intermediary stage, between desire
and action. To act instinctively on desire is to be an animal.

Reason must control desire. The lustful (che la ragion sommettono al
talento, "who submit reason to desire") do precisely the opposite. But
so do other sinners. Uncontrolled sexual appetite is no different from
uncontrolled appetite for other things—for food, for money and material
possessions. These things in themselves are good, not evil. Too great a
love for these things is punished on the top three terraces on the mountain: avarice, gluttony and lust. Too little love for the primal good (God)
expresses itself as sloth or spiritual laziness, accidia, punished on the central terrace of the seven.

Slightly trickier to reconcile with a modern sense of human behaviour
and psychology is the notion of love misdirected, the love of a malo obbietto, a "bad object or thing," which generates the sinful dispositions to
pride, envy and anger. Unlike hell, purgatory punishes sinful dispositions, not actual sins; thus its structure and organizing principle is very
different. Essentially, these first three sinful dispositions consist of lov-

ing and desiring something bad for or disadvantageous to fellow human beings. Wanting them to be inferior to ourselves (pride). Wanting them not to have the good fortune, talents or possessions they have (envy). Wanting them to be punished for some perceived wrong they have done us (anger). So the *malo obbietto* longed for is *malo* (bad, wrong, evil) because it is injurious and harmful to others, invidiously placing self above the community of which one is a part.

Dante is particularly alert to the poisonous effect of envy on personal relationships and the social fabric. The punishment of the envious in purgatory is peculiarly satisfying. The word *envy*—defined in the *OED* as "grudging contemplation of more fortunate persons"—is *invidia* in Italian, from Latin *invideo*, "to look askance at, to look maliciously or spitefully at." The punishment of the envious is to have their eyelids sewn shut with iron wire so that they can no longer see the good fortune of others they were so unable to contemplate with equanimity during their lifetime. They also wear hair shirts, whose itching expresses in concrete terms the prickling ill feeling which drove them in life. Envy is, for Dante, the opposite of love, of *caritas*.

As modern observers and analysts of human behaviour, we surely recognize these character traits or dispositions in ourselves and in others. And try as we may to be nonjudgmental, it is surely true that we recognize certain kinds of behaviour as reprehensible—as destructive and self-destructive, driven by impulses the individual seems unable or unwilling to acknowledge or control. Modern psychologists and commentators might give different names to these various dispositions. Pride might nowadays be called self-aggrandisement, arrogance, ambition, self-regard, grandiosity, narcissism (all words routinely used by journalists to describe the behaviour of certain politicians and the qualities displayed in their memoirs). Envy would be lack of empathy and inadequate socialisation. Anger is lack of impulse control. But where modern psychologists would locate the source of much aggressive and destructive behaviour in self-loathing, for Dante hating oneself is an impossibility. All things naturally desire their own existence and their own well-being.

Although this last point might suggest an unbridgeable gulf between

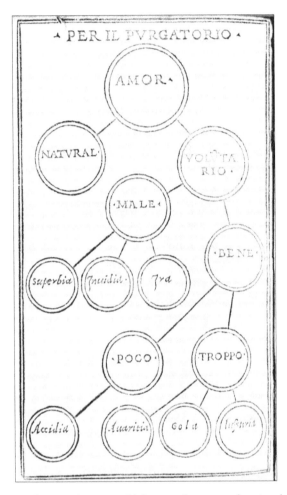

Fig. 25 This neat diagram, which comes from an early printed edition of the *Commedia* published by Aldo Manuzio in Venice in 1515, shows how all the seven deadly sins derive from love gone wrong. Love can be natural (of God), or elective (*voluntario*: of earthly goods). Elective love can be of something which is bad (*male*), giving rise to the sins of pride (*superbia*), envy (*invidia*) and wrath (*ira*); or it can be of something which is in itself good (*bene*), but loved too weakly (hence sloth: *accidia*), or too strongly (hence avarice: *avaritia*, gluttony: *gola*, and lust: *lussuria*).

Dante's view of human behaviour and a modern view, the distance is less great than it might seem. What Dante is saying here chimes strikingly with recent thinking about certain kinds of depraved behaviour and how we should think about it. The discipline of forensic psychotherapy has been developed in the last twenty-five years to treat perpetrators of the most appalling crimes (including incest, paedophilia and domestic violence and abuse). It tries to teach offenders guilty of perversion and deviance—offenders trapped in patterns of compulsive, damaging behaviour—to interpose thought between the impulse and the action. This is precisely what in Dante's view is the essence of being a human being and not an animal. Freedom from the tyranny of compulsion, of having no choice, is what forensic psychotherapy offers its damaged and destructive patients (whom the law treats as criminals and punishes). It sees the perpetrators as victims of dysfunctional relationships across the generations—nurture rather than nature being at the heart of their condition.

The hope that forensic psychotherapy offers perpetrators is that by learning to interpose thought between impulse and action they can achieve freedom. Virgil, at the beginning of purgatory, tells the guardian of the mountain that freedom is what Dante is seeking on his journey to the afterlife: *libertà va cercando* ("he is searching for freedom"). At the end of the journey up the mountain, in what proves to be his last speech in the poem, Virgil declares that Dante has achieved this goal: *libero, dritto e sano è tuo arbitrio* ("your will is free, straight and whole"). This is just what a forensic psychotherapist would hope to be able to say to a patient at the end of a successful course of dynamic psychotherapy.

We all spend a great deal of our time observing, talking about, analysing and judging other people's behaviour. This is a constant of the experience of being human. Dante gives us a structured, systematic account, and shows the negativity (the true nature, he would say) of bad behaviour in starkly graphic terms. His punishments are either an externalization of the aberrant impulse or a corrective to it. The avaricious in purgatory lie facedown on the ground, physically attached to the material world to which they were too attracted in life. The proud walk bent double under the weight of huge stones they carry on their backs, their posture a physical enacting of humility. We may find the *esprit de système* that informs Dante's thinking rigid, but the arresting visual impact of the punishments, and their capacity to stimulate thinking about our own and other people's personalities and behaviour, is undeniable.

Although it may seem a reductive approach to the rich variety of life and human behaviour to slot people into categories under a limited number of moral headings, this is counterbalanced in Dante's case by his acute awareness of the individuality of every human being. He says explicitly at one point in one of his minor works that people are so different from one another that it is as if each person constitutes a species of his or her own. This sensitivity to the uniqueness of every individual is reflected in the portrayal of the characters in the poem. A delicate balance is constantly maintained in the *Commedia* between the analytic impulse that establishes a system and the appreciation of every nuance of differentiation between people.

On the question of our accountability for our dispositions and actions, Dante's views on the nature-nurture debate are not very different from the latest conclusions of modern research. Nature and nurture both contribute to the formation of a human being, in a ratio that is impossible to quantify precisely. What we get from nature is a given. We cannot control it, whether it is (in modern terms) our DNA or (in medieval terms) the chemical makeup of our bodies which determines our "humour" or character, and the dispositions and aptitudes we are born with that are determined by astrological influences at the moment of our birth.

In accordance with the conceits of medieval astrological learning, Dante, born under Gemini, has a talent for study and writing. His "humours" make him passionate and proud. He tells us that he expects to put in serious time on the first terrace of the mountain purging pride when he returns after his death. But he expects to spend very little time on the terrace of envy. Working with the aptitudes and personalities we are born with, we can all, with education and training, learn to control and direct our natural inclinations. We can all learn to be good and fulfilled human beings. The task is to use what we have been given as best we can in order to lead fully human lives. No serious educationist today, religious or secular, would disagree.

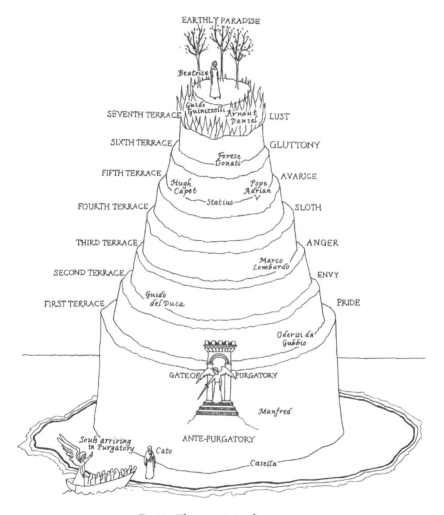

EARTHLY PARADISE

Beatrice

SEVENTH TERRACE — *Guido Guinizzelli* *Arnaut Daniel* — LUST

SIXTH TERRACE — GLUTTONY

Forese Donati

FIFTH TERRACE — AVARICE

Hugh Capet *Pope Adrian V*

— *Statius* —

FOURTH TERRACE — SLOTH

THIRD TERRACE — ANGER

Marco Lombardo

SECOND TERRACE — ENVY

Guido del Duca

FIRST TERRACE — PRIDE

Oderisi da Gubbio

GATE OF — PURGATORY

Manfred

ANTE-PURGATORY

Souls arriving in Purgatory — *Cato*

Casella

Fig. 26   The mountain of purgatory.

To understand the nature of love as it is expounded in the central cantos of *Purgatorio* is to attain a perspective that enables us to look back and reassess earlier episodes. From this perspective, Francesca's impassioned speech on love in the *Inferno*—in operatic terms, the encounter with Francesca is the first of the great highlights of the poem—can be seen for what it truly is. For all its charm and eloquence, it is a self-serving exercise. It is an exercise in justifying her actions and exonerating herself, in denying her personal responsibility. Love is to blame. The book is to blame. Anything is to blame except Francesca herself. And her self-justification echoes literary texts of Dante's own fashioning.

The connection with literature seems inescapable. If the lustful in hell are represented by Francesca, a reader of poetry, the lustful in purgatory are represented by writers of it. In purgatory we find the lustful in two categories: homosexuals and heterosexuals. In hell the homosexuals had a subcircle to themselves, for there homosexuality was classified as a sin against nature, not a sin of incontinence or weakness of will like lust. While modern readers may find this abhorrent, we can note the extraordinary lack of prurience in Dante's depiction of the homosexuals—to the point, as we have seen, that some scholars have argued that Brunetto Latini's sin against nature is not sodomy at all. The three noble Florentine leaders of an earlier generation who share Brunetto's circle (and whose homosexuality is not in doubt) so arouse Dante's admiration and gratitude for their contribution to civic life that he tells us he would have leapt down to embrace them had Virgil allowed it. Readers can make of this avowal what they will.

The view of love we find in the *Commedia* is very different from the views of Cavalcanti, Guinizzelli and the younger Dante. The whole poem might be seen as an attempt to express the truth of the matter with sufficient subtlety and comprehensiveness to do it justice. In the *Commedia*, love is the key not just to the workings of the individual human psyche but to the very functioning of the universe. Love literally makes the world go round. The created universe moves and functions out of yearning for its creator, as the pilgrim states in his profession of faith to Saint Peter in the *Paradiso*:

> Io credo in uno Dio
> solo ed etterno, che tutto 'l ciel move,
> non moto, con amore e con disio.   (*Par.* xxiv 130—32)

(I believe in one God sole and eternal, who moves the whole of
the heavens, unmoved, with love and with desire.)

The opening words are those of the Credo, which every believer recited
in the course of a church service. Believers today still do so.

Love is the starting point and the end of the narrative of Dante's
journey to the afterlife. It is love which moves Beatrice to intervene
and ask Virgil to come to his rescue when he is lost in the dark wood at
the beginning of the poem (*amor mi mosse*, she tells him, *Inf.* ii 72: "love
moved me"). Dante appeals to Virgil in the name of *'l lungo studio e 'l
grande amore* ("the long study and the great love") he has devoted to Virgil's work. Near the end of the poem, as Dante draws closer to his goal,
a famous image describes the whole of creation as the scattered pages
and gatherings of a book. Dante finally sees those pages *legato con amor
in un volume* ("bound with love in one volume"). The multifariousness
and fragmentariness of the created world and human experience makes
sense as a single artifact, intelligible and meaningful. It is love that binds
the book, love that holds everything together. In the final lines of the
poem, when he is absorbed in the beatific vision, Dante's desire and will
are attuned to and move in harmony with those of his maker:

> ma già volgeva il mio disio e 'l *velle*,
> > sì come rota ch'igualmente è mossa,
> l'amor che move il sole e l'altre stelle.   (*Par.* xxxiii 143–45)

> (but already, like a wheel revolving with an even motion, my
> > desire and will were turned by the love that moves the sun
> > and the other stars.)[1]

---

1 Literally, "the love which moves the sun and the other stars was turning my will
and my desire"; I have turned the active verb into a passive one—following many
translators of these famous lines, most recently Robert Durling and Robert and Jean
Hollander—in order to retain the impact of the last line of the poem. Italian word
order allows the subject to follow the verb and object, which English does not.

As well as erotic love and cosmic love, many other kinds of love are expressed in the *Commedia*. Love of one's birthplace (*la carità del natio loco*), and the natural affection one should feel for others born in the same place, is reflected in the spontaneous embrace of Sordello and Virgil on discovering that they both come from Mantua—in striking counterpoint to the wary mistrust and then open hostility of Dante and Farinata, fellow Florentines. Love of the natural world and its beauty is poignantly evoked in the words of sinners who are now deprived of it forever: *Li ruscelletti che d'i verdi colli / del Casentin discendon giuso in Arno* . . . ("The little streams that from the green hills of the Casentino flow down into the Arno . . ."). Every nuance of human affection, companionship and intimacy is caught at some point—nowhere more delicately than in the evolving relationship between Virgil and Dante. In *Inferno* i Virgil is Dante's *maestro, duca, segnore* ("master," "leader," "lord"); by the time he leaves he has become *dolcissimo patre* ("sweetest father"), and even *più che padre* ("more than father").

Above all else, there is love of knowledge. Aristotle's dictum that all men naturally desire to possess knowledge lies at the heart of Dante's understanding of what it is to be human. He cites it in the opening sentence of the *Convivio* almost as an epigraph to that work of encyclopedic aspiration. The philosophical studies he had immersed himself in to find consolation for his grief at Beatrice's death became a lifelong passion, a formative influence on his view of the world.

Dante cites two works explicitly as texts that set him on this course of philosophical enquiry. One is *The Consolation of Philosophy* by Boethius. The sixth-century Roman statesman and philosopher had sought consolation for the grief and injustice of wrongful imprisonment by Theodoric, king of the Ostrogoths. He wrote his masterpiece in prison in Pavia, where he was later tortured to death. The other is the *De amicitia* by the Roman writer and orator Cicero, a philosophical study of the nature of friendship. Dante says he found the texts difficult when he started to read them but immensely rewarding when he persisted. This intellectual passion, the passion to know and understand the world he lived in, remained with him for life. It continued undiminished after the spiritual crisis of which the *Commedia* is in some sense the record. Dante, it has been well said, is a repentant Christian but an unrepentant intellectual.

Celebration of the philosophers and thinkers who have contributed to our understanding of the world is a major theme in the *Paradiso*. It is hard to pinpoint with certainty which texts Dante had direct access to and which he knew only at second hand. We can't even be sure which works of Aristotle he had read (he refers specifically to a dozen of them), though certainly the *Ethics* was among them. By 1265, the year of his birth, around fifty-five of Aristotle's works had been translated into Latin. The 1260s and 1270s were a period of great intellectual ferment at the university of Paris, as the Aristotelian works and their implications were debated in their relationship to Christian thinking. Dante's indebtedness to scholastic philosophy and the intellectual and scientific heritage of Aristotle is strikingly apparent.

Foremost among those celebrated in the heaven of the wise in *Paradiso* x are figures from the thirteenth century. Thomas Aquinas, the scholastic theologian and philosopher (†1274). Albert the Great, Aquinas's teacher (†1280). Bonaventure, head of the Franciscan order (†1274). Sigier of Brabant, the cutting-edge Paris intellectual who was a professor at the Sorbonne (†c. 1283). Peter of Spain, author of an important treatise on logic who briefly became pope (until the ceiling of the papal palace in Viterbo fell in and killed him in 1277). To us these figures seem remote in time, and perhaps we do not easily distinguish them from figures from much earlier epochs. Their companions in the heaven of the wise are the sixth-century Boethius and eighth-century Bede, the great Anglo-Saxon churchman, along with the biblical King Solomon. The modern equivalents of these thirteenth-century figures would, for us, be intellectual giants of the mid-twentieth century like Wittgenstein, Freud, Einstein, Russell and Keynes. Dante is celebrating outstandingly original thinkers of the previous century, many of them still alive when he was young. Just a generation or two after Dante's death scholasticism was in crisis. Today it seems arcanely remote from modern science and philosophy in its methods and its reasoning. That should not blind us to the quality of Dante's engagement with the great thinkers of his age and his desire to honour them.

The love of knowledge—desire to know and understand the world—

is for Dante an overriding passion, of which the *Commedia* is a supreme expression. For human beings, he believes, there is a direct relationship between knowledge and happiness. As he puts it in the opening lines of the *Convivio: la scienza è ultima perfezione de la nostra anima, ne la quale sta la nostra ultima felicitade* ("knowledge is the highest perfection of our soul, in which our supreme happiness is to be found"). Yet we encounter Ulysses, the Greek hero renowned not just for his guile but also for his thirst to explore the world, in the depths of hell. The passion to know, his presence in hell forces us to conclude, is not without danger.

Ulysses is in the circle which punishes those who counselled fraud or deception. The stratagem of the Trojan horse that breached the walls of Troy was one of his wiles. There was also the trick that ultimately led Achilles to his death, and the theft of the statue of Pallas Athena from the citadel (the city's safety depended on it). Yet these episodes are referred to only briefly. Dante's interest lies elsewhere. Readers of the *Odyssey* know that the Homeric Ulysses returned to Ithaca and to his wife, Penelope, after many years of wandering. But Dante did not know Homer, and does not know the outcome of Ulysses' adventures. What became of him? How did he die? These are the questions he wants answered when he comes upon the Greek hero in the depths of hell. What we learn there of Ulysses' end may be Dante's own invention. There is no known source for the story he tells. Or it may reflect a source that has not survived. Either way, it is an unforgettable tale.

The encounter is prefaced by a statement of unprecedented explicitness, which alerts us to the importance of the scene that is to follow:

> Allor mi dolsi, e ora mi ridoglio
>   quando drizzo la mente a ciò ch'io vidi,
>   e più lo 'ngegno affreno ch'i' non soglio,
> perché non corra che virtù nol guidi;
>   sì che, se stella bona o miglior cosa
>   m'ha dato 'l ben, ch'io stessi nol m'invidi.   (*Inf.* xxvi 19–24)

> (I grieved then, and now I grieve again when I turn my mind to
>   what I saw, and I rein in my intellect more than is my habit,

lest it run without being guided by virtue; so that, if a favour-
able star or some better thing has given me this good, I may
not deprive myself of it.)

Dante's own intellect, his mind and the use he makes of it, are in play
here. There is a danger it would seem, in giving free rein to his mental
powers. Ulysses is the most obvious and most powerfully evoked of all
the stand-ins for Dante himself, representing an aspect of the poet's psychology which is at its very core.

The scene is set with one of those flashes of naturalistic description
that evoke the Tuscan landscape at a certain time of year and day. Here it
is late summer at dusk, with its *lucciole giù lungo la vallea* ("fireflies down
along the valley"). Dante looks down from a stone bridge into the deep
circular trench that contains the sinners in this circle, and he sees not people but moving tongues of flame. There is a heavy weighting of biblical
and classical allusion in the description of the scene. The flames are like
the flame in which the prophet Elijah was enveloped when he was caught
up to heaven, making him invisible to onlookers. Just so every flame here
enwraps and hides a sinner. Dante is so eager to gaze, so drawn to the
spectacle, that he has to cling to the rock in order not to fall down among
them. The physical danger mirrors the psychological danger, the allure of
the passion for knowledge of which we are about to hear.

Dante's attention is struck, not for the first time, by a pair of sinners who
suffer a linked destiny. One flame has two "horns," two flickering tongues
of fire arising from the same base. The twin flame, he tells us, is like the
funeral pyre of Polynices and Eteocles, the sons of Oedipus. They killed
each other, but their enmity lasted beyond the grave, so that even on their
joint funeral pyre the flame split in two. Virgil tells him that the twin-horned
flame hides the shades of Ulysses and his partner in guile, Diomedes.

In words of unmatched urgency Dante begs Virgil to be allowed
to speak to them. Virgil insists (and this too is unprecedented) that he
should be the one to speak—being Greeks, he explains, they might take
it amiss if an unknown person addressed them in the vernacular. There
is simultaneously a heightening and distancing in the narrative. We are

taken back to the world of Greek legendary heroes, far removed from the squalid misconduct of Dante's Florentine contemporaries so graphically enacted in the previous circle of the thieves. When Ulysses speaks, it will be in language of great force, one of the dramatic highlights of the poem.

In Ulysses' story, the passion for knowledge is represented as a geographical quest, a desire to visit unmapped regions of the world, places where nobody has ever been. The story of his death is the story of his last journey. Virgil, intuiting the focus of Dante's interest, puts the question to him. Where did he go to die? What became of him at the end? Ulysses' answer unfolds to fill the whole second half of the canto. The great characters in Dante's world are always allowed the space to reveal themselves through their own words. There is a speech within a speech, when, exactly at midpoint, Ulysses recounts how he encouraged his last remaining companions to sail on with him and not turn back. He urged them to set out on this final adventure in the name of their humanity and its highest aspirations.

Dante did not know the *Odyssey*. He took the story of Ulysses from the Roman poet Ovid, who recounts it in his *Metamorphoses*, written many centuries after Homer. (Like Dante, Ovid suffered the fate of exile and expulsion from the city he loved and died without returning to it.) Ovid's account of the story of Ulysses does not tell us what became of him. Dante picks up the narrative at the exact point at which Ovid's account breaks off, when Ulysses' companion Macareus concludes his recounting of their adventures by telling how he remained behind when the others departed from Circe, in just one ship. Dante's Ulysses in effect picks up the tale, telling how nothing could hold him back after he left Circe behind on the coast of southern Italy after his involuntary year-long sojourn with her:

> Quando
> mi diparti' da Circe, che sottrasse
> me più d'un anno là presso a Gaeta,
> prima che sì Enëa la nomasse,
> né dolcezza di figlio, né la pieta

del vecchio padre, ne 'l debito amore
lo qual dovea Penelopè far lieta,
vincer potero dentro a me l'ardore
ch'i' ebbi a divenir del mondo esperto
e de li vizi umani e del valore;   (*Inf.* xxvi 89–99)

(when I left Circe, who beguiled me for more than a year there
near Gaeta, before Aeneas gave it that name, neither the
sweetness of a son, nor the sense of duty to an elderly father,
nor the love I owed Penelope, which should have made her
happy, could conquer within me the passion I had to experience the world and human vices and worth;)

He set out on the sea journey with his small band of comrades:

ma misi me per l'alto mare aperto
sol con un legno e con quella compagna
picciola da la qual non fui diserto.   (*Inf.* xxvi 100–102)

(but I set out on the deep open sea with just one boat and with
the small group of companions who had not deserted me.)

They pass the familiar landmarks of the Mediterranean: the coasts on
either side as far as Spain and Morocco, Sardinia and the other islands. At
the Strait of Gibraltar they reach the Pillars of Hercules, set at the nar-
rowest point where Europe almost touches Africa. In classical mythology the Pillars of Hercules marked the limits of the known world, the
point beyond which men were forbidden by the gods to venture. On the
right hand, they passed Seville; on the left, they had already passed Ceuta
on the North African coast. Without preamble, Ulysses reports the "little
speech" he now made to his men:

"O frati," dissi, "che per cento milia
perigli siete giunti a l'occidente,
a questa tanto picciola vigilia

d'i nostri sensi ch'è del rimanente
  non vogliate negar l'esperienza,
  di retro al sol, del mondo sanza gente.
Considerate la vostra semenza:
  fatti non foste a viver come bruti,
  ma per seguir virtute e canoscenza."   (*Inf.* xxvi 112–120)

("O brothers," I said, "who through a hundred thousand dangers
  have reached the west, to this so brief vigil of our senses that
  is left us, do not choose to deny experience, following the
  sun, of the world without people. Consider your origin: you
  were not made to live like beasts, but to follow virtue and
  knowledge.")

Ulysses appeals to his companions in the name of their humanity,
the thing that makes them human beings and not animals, the desire to
know. To know the world, to pursue the twin goals of human living at
its best: *virtute e canoscenza*, "virtue and knowledge." It is not surprising
that in the face of this stirring rhetoric they agree to accompany him.
Indeed, he says, they were so eager after hearing it that he could hardly
have held them back.

So they leave the Mediterranean behind, setting out on a journey into
the unknown, following the path of the sun as it sinks in the west, holding to a southwesterly course across the ocean:

e volta nostra poppa nel mattino,
  de' remi facemmo ali al folle volo,
  sempre acquistando dal lato mancino.   (*Inf.* xxvi 124–26)

(and having turned our stern to the east, we made wings of our
  oars for the mad flight, always bearing to the left).

As they journey on, the stars in the night sky are no longer the familiar ones of the northern hemisphere, now barely visible above the hori-

zon. After five months of strenuous effort, they see a mountain higher than any they have ever seen, dark in the distance. They rejoice at the sight, but quickly their joy turns to tears. A whirlwind arises from this newly discovered land; it strikes the boat and spins it around three times, then upends it so that it sinks. In the last line of Ulysses' speech, which is the last line of the canto, the sea closes with a terrible finality over the shipwrecked vessel and its occupants:

Noi ci allegrammo, e tosto tornò in pianto;
    ché de la nova terra un turbo nacque
    e percosse del legno il primo canto.
Tre volte il fé girar con tutte l'acque;
    a la quarta levar la poppa in suso
    e la prora ire in giù, com'altrui piacque,
infin che 'l mar fu sovra noi richiuso.   (*Inf.* xxvi 136–142)

(We rejoiced, and quickly it turned to weeping; for from the new
    land a whirlwind arose and struck the front part of the boat.
    Three times it spun the boat around with all the waters; at
    the fourth it raised the stern up and made the prow go down,
    as it pleased another [i.e., as God willed it], until the sea closed
    over us.)

First-time readers of the *Commedia* encounter in Ulysses' story the tale of a heroic undertaking. It is an enthralling account of a journey into the unknown, against the odds, defying the elements, told with compelling power by a master storyteller. At the very heart of the story, right in the middle, is his stirring speech to his companions, urging them to accompany him. That speech is the hinge, the turning point between the known world and the unknown. Beyond that point, instead of the familiar landmarks of the Mediterranean, we have an immensely mysterious geography, then a whirlwind of devastating force, and the shipwreck which brings the adventure to an end.

Why do we find Ulysses so enthralling? And why is he in hell? The answer to the first question is easy, the answer to the second a little less so. Our first response is to the fascination of the story itself, and the human qualities it embodies: courage, tenacity, endurance, a will to continue in the face of the unknown. These are the qualities captured in the final lines of Tennyson's poem "Ulysses," partly inspired by Dante, where the emphasis is firmly on the heroic dimension of the enterprise: *One equal temper of heroic hearts, / Made weak by time and fate, but strong in will / To strive, to seek, to find and not to yield.* These lines are engraved on the memorial to the explorer Scott in the Antarctic, in a fitting tribute to a modern hero whose journey might be thought to parallel in audacity that of the Greek hero. Seen in this perspective, Ulysses is a figure to be admired and imitated. Indomitable, an inspiring leader of men. So why is he in hell?

To understand the significance for Dante of Ulysses' journey, one must understand his stirring words in the context of other journeys against which to measure his, and the geography of the otherworld in Dante's poem. In this broader context, Ulysses may come to seem not courageous, tenacious, indomitable so much as foolhardy, selfish, defiant. His journey may come to seem, as he himself indeed momentarily describes it, a *folle volo*, a "mad flight."

Ulysses' journey implicitly contrasts with the exemplary story of Aeneas's journey from Troy: and as though to underline the point, Ulysses mentions Aeneas by name at the very beginning of his account. The *Aeneid*, we remember, was often read in the Middle Ages as a model for the journey of human life. Both Homeric heroes set out from Troy at the same time; both sail the familiar waters of the Mediterranean. One completes his destined journey and lands on Italian soil, in spite of the temptations and distractions he faces on the way. His journey is a necessary preparation for the founding of Rome, city of destiny and seat of empire.

Ulysses sets out on his final adventure and sails on, regardless of social and family obligations. As Dante's son Pietro acutely noted in his commentary on these lines, the bonds which Ulysses ignores even as he acknowledges their force—the bonds of affection, respect and duty which link him to his son Telemachus, his father Laertes, his wife Penelope—are exactly those Aeneas calls to mind, in the same order—son, father, wife—as he sets out from Troy (*Aeneid* ii 666: *Ascanium patremque meum iuxtaque Creusam*: "Ascanius, and my father, and Creusa at their side"). Aeneas's voyage is the virtuous version of Ulysses' voyage, the version which acknowledges the force both of social bonds and of divine decrees.

The divine decree is the injunction not to venture beyond the Pillars of Hercules. With his typical willingness to draw on and use elements from the pre-Christian world and incorporate them into his own world-view, Dante accepts as binding in the Christian world prohibitions pronounced by the deities in the classical world. In just the same way he on occasion uses the name Jove (*Giove*) for the Christian God—nowhere more strikingly than when he addresses him as *o sommo Giove / che fosti in terra per noi crucifisso*: "O highest Jove, you who were crucified on earth for us." In the Pillars of Hercules mythology and geography coalesce in Dante's Christian otherworld. In retrospect it will become clear to the reader that Ulysses has tried to take a shortcut to purgatory, for the "mountain dark in the distance" that the sailors see just before the shipwreck is, precisely, the mountain of purgatory.

Ulysses has almost reached purgatory by relying on unaided human efforts: his own courage, his eloquence, his companions' loyalty and trust in his leadership, his unquenchable thirst for knowledge. He has done so bypassing divine grace, and his mission is therefore doomed to failure. In a medieval Christian world, this is the crux of the issue. But for us as readers, it is only as we look back from purgatory that these things will fall into place, when we encounter our first group of saved souls who disembark on the shore at the foot of the mountain after a sea voyage which exactly follows in its course the path taken by Ulysses on his final journey. The connection is underlined by the deliberate repetition of the final rhyme sequence of the canto. The *nacque—acque—piacque* of the last lines of *Inferno* xxvi becomes the *acque—piacque—rinacque* of the last lines of *Purgatorio* i: a fine example of the functional use of rhyme.

Journeys, what they are for and where they take us, and above all how they end, are a theme of perennial interest to human beings. The journey is a powerful metaphor for any experience with a beginning, a middle and an end and a trajectory that links them in a narrative arc.

Even though we travel with relative ease in the modern world compared to the difficulties of travelling in the Middle Ages, the idea has lost none of its resonance. Indeed, as the physical equivalent of a mental and psychological experience, it has become a commonplace of psychobabble.

The journey image is a fundamental one in medieval literature for the course of a human life. The poem starts *nel mezzo del cammin*, "in the middle of the journey." Even more specifically, the course of a human life is often likened to a pilgrimage, one of the commonest reasons for setting out on a journey in the Middle Ages. When Dante asks Sapia on the terrace of the envious if there is any soul there who is Italian, she gently corrects him: *tu vuo' dire / che vivesse in Italia peregrina* ("you mean, who lived in Italy as a pilgrim," meaning "while he was alive"). (The Catholic church today still talks of human life in these terms.) The theme of the *Commedia* is a journey, the journey to the afterlife, which will end well with Dante's vision of the divinity. It too can be thought of as a pilgrimage, to paradise, to the holy city, to *quella Roma onde Cristo è romano* ("that Rome of which Christ is a citizen").

No less significantly, the arduous sea voyage over uncharted waters is a metaphor for the writing of a long literary work on a demanding theme. The sea-voyage image is used by Dante at the beginning of both the *Purgatorio* and the *Paradiso*. The *Purgatorio* begins:

> Per correr miglior acque alza le vele
>   omai la navicella del mio ingegno,
>   che lascia dietro a se mar sì crudele;
> e canterò di quel secondo regno . . .   (*Purg.* i 1–4)

> (To cross better waters the little ship of my genius now hoists its
>   sails, leaving behind it a sea so cruel; and I will sing of that
>   second realm . . .)

The *Paradiso* addresses its readers with the same image, but now warning them to turn back if they are not up to facing the difficulties of the journey across uncharted waters that is to follow:

O voi che siete in piccioletta barca
  desiderosi d'ascoltar, seguiti
  dietro al mio legno che cantando varca,
tornate a riveder li vostri liti:
  non vi mettete in pelago, ché forse
  perdendo me, rimarreste smarriti.
L'acqua ch'io prendo già mai non si corse . . .   (*Par.* ii 1–7)

(O you who are in a little boat, eager to listen, having followed
  my ship which goes on its way singing, turn back to gaze on
  your own shores; do not set out on the open sea, for perhaps,
  losing me, you would be quite lost. The water I am setting
  out over has never been crossed . . .)

This last line could have been spoken by Ulysses, whose journey thus
stands in counterpoint both to Aeneas's journey and to Dante's writing
of his poem. Those experiences, unlike his, have a positive, indeed joyous, outcome.

How did Dante intend us to see Ulysses? as magnificent but flawed,
a figure of heroic stature but fatally misguided? or as an embodiment
of arrogance and pride? Ulysses' words are thrilling. We respond to the
quality of the language and the artistry of the execution. He is appealing to the best there is in human nature, to our highest instincts, the
pursuit of virtue and knowledge. When Primo Levi was a prisoner of
the Nazis in the concentration camp at Auschwitz, he kept himself sane,
he tells us in his autobiography, by attempting to reconstruct Ulysses'
great speech in the *Commedia* from memory. The two values Ulysses
invokes as defining what it is to live as a human being rather than as an
animal—intellectual activity (*canoscenza*) and the practice of the moral
virtues (*virtute*)—are the two things Aristotle had held to be the source
of human happiness. In the ghastly context of Auschwitz, the modern
version of Dante's hell, Ulysses' words and the values they appealed to
must have been a touchstone of humanity and civilisation, just as in that
context of pure evil and destructiveness it must have been comforting

to cling to a memory of human artistry and creativity. I think we can
be sure that Levi did not agonise over whether the Greek hero's stirring
lines to his companions were to be taken at face value or were evidence
of his deviousness and guile:

> Considerate la vostra semenza:
>> fatti non foste a viver come bruti,
>> ma per seguir virtute e canoscenza.

> (Consider your origin: you were not made to live like beasts, but
>> to pursue virtue and knowledge.)

Can we fail to respond to these words even when we are aware of the
medieval context which makes them sinful and leads to hell? Some people might argue that there are dangers in the pursuit of knowledge with
no limitations, no restraints, even in modern life. A modern equivalent
might be uneasiness about some aspects of genetic research and where it
might lead. A proper sense of the limitations of human reason and understanding, the need for curbs and checks, is not necessarily a medieval or
even a religious imperative.

The *Commedia* is not a sermon, in spite of its author's desire to change
the world for the better. More often than not the teaching is implicit.
Dante the protagonist learns, and we the readers share his experiences
and learn with him. Sometimes he is instructed by his mentors on points
of special scientific or doctrinal difficulty, as he is by Virgil on love. More
often, and more engagingly, he learns directly from his encounters with
the shades of the dead, by observing them or talking to them. The process is dynamic and interactive. It is because Dante doesn't spell out the
moral point that the encounters with some of the shades of the damned
are so compelling. We must work out for ourselves why figures as sympathetic as Francesca or as courageous as Ulysses are in hell, and we must
do this in spite of the charm and eloquence with which they tell their
own stories. That readers have always been divided in their response to
such episodes is testimony to the undogmatic quality—the tact, the indi-

rectness, the obliqueness—of Dante's narrative strategy. The poem may embody moral certainties in its design, but the telling of the tale confronts us with the ambiguities, the reticences, and the self-deceptions of real human behaviour in a real human world.

In Dante's view love is the key to understanding the way the universe functions. It causes the circling motion of the heavenly bodies. It drives all human behaviour. In its central section, the *Commedia* enunciates this principle with magisterial clarity, and demonstrates how its operation is consistent with the notion of free will and personal moral responsibility. It is right and just that people be called to account for their actions.

The *Commedia* shows how the simplicity of the basic underlying principle is reflected in the world in the infinite variety of individual human actions and choices, enmeshed as they always are in the intricacies of human personality and historical circumstance. Over its length, the poem shows the myriad ways in which the underlying principle works itself out. The love for another human being that drove Francesca, the love of knowledge that drove Ulysses—both are experienced subjectively as supremely important and valuable aspects of human life. But Dante gives us a more philosophical and thought-through take on the problem, and leaves readers to decide for themselves on the ultimate value of their experience.

Although the values of our modern world are so different from those of a medieval Catholic, one central concern of human beings remains the same: human behaviour and how we judge it. Dante sees the key to understanding human behaviour in the idea of love. The idea is as fascinating now as it was in Dante's time, as it has always been. For lovers of poetry, there is the added delight of the medium in which the message is delivered.

5.

Time

Time . . . worships language and forgives
Everyone by whom it lives . . .
—W. H. AUDEN, "IN MEMORY OF W. B. YEATS"

It is unthinkable to read the cantos of Dante without
aiming them in the direction
of the present day. . . .
They are missiles for capturing the future.
—OSIP MANDELSTAM

The past is never dead. It's not even past.
—WILLIAM FAULKNER, REQUIEM FOR A NUN

AS DANTE STARTED TO THINK ABOUT WRITING HIS IMMENSELY
ambitious long poem, one early decision must have made many things
fall into place: the decision to set his imagined journey to the afterlife
in 1300. By 1300 he had lived long enough to know many people who
had died. He would be able to encounter them in the afterlife as personal acquaintances. Yet when he started writing the poem 1300 was far
behind him. He began around 1307–1308 and finished not long before
his death in 1321. There was an ample period (some twenty years by the
end) which was in the past at the time of writing but in the future from

the perspective of the narrative. He is thus able to "prophesy the past"—
to prophesy future events in the certain knowledge that they will take
place. This opens up possibilities of dramatic and poetic effect, hauntingly exploited in the troubling theme of his own destined exile from
Florence.

The timing of the journey is as important as its date, but for very different reasons. The journey takes place in spring, a time of year that signifies rebirth, a new beginning. More specifically, it takes place at Easter,
which for Christians signifies mankind's salvation through the crucifixion and resurrection. Some details of Dante's journey seem deliberately
to echo the timetable of the Easter narrative. He goes down into hell at
dusk on Good Friday and emerges onto the shore of purgatory at dawn
on Easter Sunday, calling to mind the time between Christ's death and
resurrection. So we have a chronology accurately pinpointed in historical time combined with a time frame which has universal resonance.
These two strands—one firmly anchored in history, the other outside or
beyond history—run in counterpoint throughout the poem. The inter-
play between them is an essential part of its meaning.

The passing of time is the simplest measure of a human existence. We
conceptualise space (the other determining condition of life in this world)
in terms of three dimensions. Time in modern thinking is the fourth
dimension. But to medieval thinkers its most striking aspect was its tripartite structure: past, present, future. Whereas human beings move
easily within the three spatial dimensions they inhabit, time moves in
one direction only, its inexorable forward movement allowing no devia-
tion, no illusion of freedom or control to those who live out a sequence
it is not in their power to change. Human beings, caught in the here and
now of the passing moment, experience the past through memory and
contemplate the future through anticipation. The ability to summon the
past and think forward to the future was considered then, and is still
considered now, distinctive of human beings. We live forward, but we
understand backwards.

The linear forward movement through time in everyday living is
similar to the experience of reading a text from beginning to end. But

set against the simplicity of that onward movement as we live and read, there are complexities in the handling of time within Dante's imagined world. Past, present and future are all powerfully present in the *Commedia*. The way time plays out in the narrative of the journey to the afterlife is one of its most compelling features.

The experience the poem records is almost always recounted in the simple past tense of narrative: *mi ritrovai per una selva oscura* ("I found myself in a dark wood"). Yet just as strong as the sense of a story set in the past is the sense of the artist struggling with his medium, struggling to find words that will do justice to his story. This aspiration and ongoing effort is described in the present tense. The here and now of writing the poem is evoked whenever the poet addresses the reader directly (as he does on sixteen separate occasions), when he comments on the challenges his theme presents, or calls on the muses for help: *or m'aiutate* ("help me now"). The present tense is also used when he breaks the narrative flow and erupts into denunciation of the sorry state of the world. And it is used in comparisons which draw on universal human experiences: *E come fantolin che 'nver' la mamma / tende le braccia . . .* ("And like a small child who holds its arms out towards its mother . . .") or observations of the natural world: *E come a l'orlo de l'acqua d'un fosso / stanno i ranocchi pur col muso fuori . . .* ("And just as frogs sit at the edge of the water in a ditch, with only their snouts poking out . . ."). Such comparisons are not linked to a particular moment in time, but evoke common experience shared across the generations and the ages.

Beyond the immediate narrative past of the journey to the other-world the text points further backwards to the more distant past of the poet's earlier life. Beyond that it points still further back to the turbulent political fortunes of Tuscany in the thirteenth century, and ultimately beyond that to the whole of human history. Equally, it looks forward, not just to the proximate future of Dante's own political misfortunes and his ignominious exile but also to the broader future of the human race and its possibilities for happiness. That imagined future even encompasses us, the readers of his poem now, who look back to the time it was written as the far-distant past. We are those *che questo tempo chiameranno antico* ("who will call this time long ago"). Dante's fame as a poet will be known to us, to far-off future generations, if he speaks out as a bold friend of truth.

As we move downwards through upper hell, our first impression is of the moral squalor of Florence now in 1300. A shocking portrait emerges of the city. In *Inferno* vi Dante comes across the first of the many fellow Florentines he will meet in the afterlife, in the circle of the gluttons. The gluttons lie on the ground under a relentless barrage of icy rain, hail and snow. The ground they lie on stinks. Dante and Virgil tread on them as they walk, their feet passing through the insubstantial shadow bodies of the sinners. Although the bodies of the souls in the afterlife look exactly like real bodies, they have no solidity or weight. Their contrast with Dante in this respect was established at the beginning of the journey. Charon's boat was filled with souls being ferried across the river Acheron; only when Dante stepped into the boat did it sink lower in the water.

Now as he walks over the bodies of the gluttons, one of them sits up abruptly. He has recognised Dante, though Dante fails to recognise him. But as soon as he identifies himself as a Florentine, Dante has a question for him: *a che verranno / li cittadin de la città partita?* ("what will become of the citizens of the divided city?"). The shade tells him: *dopo lunga tencion / verranno al sangue* ("after long conflict they will come to bloodshed")—a first presaging of the events which will unfold in the opening years of the new century. The cause of the discord is pinpointed in moral failings: *superbia, invidia e avarizia sono / le tre faville c'hanno i cuori accesi* ("pride, envy and greed are the three sparks which have set hearts on fire"). Whenever Dante meets a Florentine in the afterlife, the painful subject of the city's state, and fate, is likely to arise. An escalating sense of its turbulent present, its political instability and its citizens' inability to govern it well, is orchestrated throughout the *Inferno*.

But the state of Florence is part of a wider malaise. Other Italian cities are equally war-torn, equally ungovernable. Vast regions are degenerate. In a sustained passage of invective in *Purgatorio* xiv the whole of Tuscany and adjacent Romagna are described as places where what seems to be an irreversible moral decline has set in. Here on the terrace of envy, the penitents sit slouched against the dark bruise-coloured inner rock wall of the mountain, like beggars huddled together outside a church. The cloaks they wear are the same colour as the stone, so that at first it is hard to pick out the sinners against the rocky backdrop. Dante overhears two voices discussing him as he passes. "Who is that person . . . ?" one of them says to the other. "I don't know . . . You ask him . . . ," the other replies.

When they have established that Dante is a Tuscan, one of the speakers, Guido del Duca, a penitent soul from Romagna, launches into an attack on the valley through which the Arno flows. It is, in a dismissive and explosive line, *la maledetta e sventurata fossa* ("the cursed and unlucky ditch"). With contempt and sorrow in equal measure, he traces the course of the river from its origins in the Casentino area in the foothills of the Apennines to the sea at Pisa. The cities which lie along it form a symbolic bestiary of degradation, their inhabitants transformed in Guido's angry rhetoric into animals. The Casentinesi are swine, the Aretines ineffectual yapping dogs, the Florentines deeply sinister wolves, the Pisans cunning foxes.

Guido changes tack when he talks about Romagna, focusing not so much on the present as on the past. The *ubi sunt* theme ("where are they now?") is a traditional literary motif. Here Dante revitalises it in Guido's outpouring of grief for what is gone and seems unrecoverable. Where are the great men of the past, the noble families and individuals whose behaviour and traditions brought honour to the region? The litany of names of the great families who have no worthy descendants shows Dante's ability to make moving poetry out of not much more than a list of names. (Compare the lists of great pagan thinkers in *Inf.* iv and of some forty noble Florentine families of an earlier generation in *Par.* xvi.)

> Ov'è 'l buon Lizio e Arrigo Mainardi?
> > Pier Traversaro e Guido di Carpigna?
> > Oh Romagnuoli tornati in bastardi!
> Quando in Bologna un Fabbro si ralligna?
> > quando in Faenza un Bernardin di Fosco,
> > verga gentil di picciola gramigna?

Non ti maravigliar s'io piango, Tosco,
   quando rimembro, con Guido da Prata,
   Ugolin d'Azzo che vivette nosco,
Federigo Tignoso e sua brigata,
   la casa Traversara e li Anastagi
   (e l'una gente e l'altra è diretata),
le donne e ' cavalier, li affanni e li agi
   che ne 'nvogliava amore e cortesia
   là dove i cuor son fatti sì malvagi.   (*Purg.* xiv 97–111)

(Where is worthy Lizio and Arrigo Mainardi? Pier Traversaro
and Guido di Carpigna? Oh men of Romagna become bas-
tards again! When will there be another Fabbro in Bologna?
When will there be another Bernardin di Fosco in Faenza,
noble offspring from modest stock? Do not be amazed if I
weep, Tuscan, when I remember, with Guido da Prata, Ugolin
d'Azzo who lived in our parts, Federigo Tignoso and his companions, the Traversari family and the Anastagi (both families
without an heir), the ladies and the knights, the hardships and
the leisure which love and courtesy made us desire, where
now hearts have become so wicked.)

The roll call of honour of the noble men of an earlier generation whose
families have died out or whose heirs are unworthy continues with the
same intensity for another dozen lines.

   The past is evoked with this same fierce sense of loss in the encounter
at the midpoint of *Paradiso* when Dante meets his great-great-grandfather
Cacciaguida, in the heaven of Mars, where we find the spirits of warriors
who fought for the faith. Cacciaguida, who was born around 1091, had died
in about 1147 in the Second Crusade, fighting against the infidel. The three
central cantos of *Paradiso* (xv–xvii) form a triptych, evenly balanced between
past and future. Themes touched on earlier—the moral decline of Florence,
Dante's future expulsion from the city—here move to centre stage.

   In canto xv Cacciaguida's words carry us back to an age when things

were as they ought to be—the not-so-distant past, just four generations
back, less than two hundred years earlier, when Florentines lived simply
and in peace. This idealised past is evoked with poetic force in lines most
Florentines know by heart:

> Fiorenza dentro da la cerchia antica,
>> ond'ella toglie ancora e terza e nona,
>> si stava in pace, sobria e pudica.   (*Par.* xv 97–99)

> (Florence within the ancient circle [of the city walls], from which
>> she still takes tierce and nones, was at peace, sober and modest.)

These are the original walls of the city, dating from Roman times.
The Roman walls enclosed the small central nucleus of early medieval
buildings at the city's heart: the baptistery, the cathedral church of Santa
Reparata, as it then was, the ancient Benedictine abbey (Badia) with its
church. The old walls were rebuilt in Cacciaguida's time to enclose a
larger area. They were extended, as we have seen, in 1258 and then again
in Dante's lifetime, beginning in 1284, to enclose a vastly larger area (see
the map on p. 12). Set right up against the original wall was the church of
the Badia whose bells rang out the canonical hours: tierce and nones are
roughly speaking 9:00 A.M. and 3:00 P.M. In an age before the invention
of clocks, the ringing of the church bells told people the time of day and
helped organise daily life. An early commentator tells us that guild workers regulated their working day around the striking of the Badia bells.
The sound of the bells marking the hours seems to be the only thing that
survives from the Florence of Cacciaguida's time.

In this vanished age of sobriety and modesty, Cacciaguida tells us,
there was no flaunting of wealth, no ostentation. Citizens dressed simply and decorously. Fathers were not afraid of having daughters, since
daughters were not promised in marriage too young and with excessive
dowries, forcing their fathers into sharp business practices to meet their
financial obligations. The buildings, palaces and towers of Florence did
not outdo those of Rome, as they now do. Wives were not abandoned by

husbands going to France to pursue their business interests. They were content with their domestic role, working at home with spindle and distaff, caring for infants, handing down stories of the city's origins. None of this is true in the Florence of Dante's time.

This celebration of an idealised past might make it seem almost mythically remote, a lost golden age. That way of life becomes instantly real when Cacciaguida mentions by name an illustrious citizen whose high-minded plain living he evokes with just one concrete detail:

> Bellincion Berti vid'io andar cinto
>> di cuoio e d'osso, e venir da lo specchio
>> la donna sua sanza 'l viso dipinto.   (*Par.* xv 112–14)

> (I saw Bellincion Berti wearing a belt made of leather and bone,
>> and his wife come away from the mirror without makeup on
>> her face.)

The leather belt with its simple bone fastening gives the stamp of authenticity to the description of a sober, healthy, orderly society—a way of life now seemingly lost forever.

As well as looking back, the Cacciaguida episode points forward, pulling together all the hints and veiled references encountered along the way and making explicit what has puzzled and troubled the pilgrim as shades in the afterlife allude to a painful destiny of which he himself still knows nothing. In canto xvii, the very centre of the *Paradiso*, that destiny is finally spelled out. His fate, Cacciaguida tells him, is already being plotted *là dove Cristo tutto dì si merca* ("where Christ is bought and sold every day")—that is, in Rome, at the papal court, by those responsible for the betrayal of the White party in Florence and its expulsion from the city. Dante will leave his beloved home:

> Tu lascerai ogne cosa diletta
>> più caramente; e questo è quello strale
>> che l'arco de lo essilio pria saetta.

Tu proverai sì come sa di sale
  lo pane altrui, e come è duro calle
  lo scendere e 'l salir per l'altrui scale.   (*Par.* xvii 55–60)

(You will leave behind every thing you love most dearly; and this
is the first arrow the bow of exile shoots forth. You will experience how salty is the taste of another man's bread, and how
hard a road it is to go up and down another man's stairs.)

After a few years of fruitless attempts to return to the city, his companions in exile will turn against him. Their shameful behaviour will leave
him isolated and alone: *sì ch'a te fia bello / averti fatta parte per te stesso* ("so
that it will be to your honour that you have formed a party on your own").
The phrase has become proverbial for anyone taking an independent
stand above factional interests and intrigues. He will become a solitary
figure, associated with no political grouping. (In fact, this disillusionment
with his companions in exile, his fellow White Guelfs, was the seedbed
for the development of his mature political views.) He will find refuge in
the early years of exile at the court in Verona with a generous host whose
hospitality he must cherish. He must write a full account of his journey to
the afterlife: *tutta tua visïon fa manifesta* ("tell everything you have seen").

In this encounter with his great-great-grandfather, the meaning of
Dante's life is made clear to him. He is to be a poet with a prophetic
mission. His poetry is to enlighten and to change the world. Like Aeneas
visting the underworld to see his father Anchises, who explains to him
the significance of his journey to Italy, which will lead to the founding of
Rome and the establishing of Roman rule over the world, Dante finally
understands the true significance of the journey to the afterlife.

One of the glories of the *Commedia* is the effortless sense it gives of
its author's panoramic view of human history as a single, purposeful
sequence of events. That history is an intelligible narrative, the acting
out of a providential divine plan for the human race. This is not a view
a modern reader is likely to share, but that should not blind us to its
grandeur. This view sees King David, the author of the psalms, and Vir-

gil's hero Aeneas as contemporaries. Each contributed to the unfolding pattern of history which ultimately led to the founding of the Roman Empire and the birth of Christ in the twelve-year period of peace under the rule of Augustus. In *Paradiso* vi the emperor Justinian's account of the founding of the Roman Empire majestically conveys that sense of the purposefulness of history. In Dante's eyes Rome has a special destiny as the seat of both empire and church. The *Aeneid* celebrates the backstory of the city's founding with its account of the wanderings of Aeneas after the Trojan War and his eventual landing in Italy. It is a poetic text of unique importance—the "Bible of the Empire," as it has been called.

Dante's mature political conviction is that proper government of the human race requires two leaders, an emperor and a pope, responsible respectively for the secular and spiritual lives of human beings. Neither is subordinate to the other. Each receives his authority directly from God. This is the lesson of history that Dante the pilgrim learns on his journey. His political education is enacted over the length of the poem. He ceases to be the White Guelf so swiftly embroiled in an acrimonious exchange with Farinata early in the *Inferno*. His experience in the after-life profoundly alters his understanding of politics, of the way the world should be ordered and governed. He becomes a different man.

A key encounter near the centre of purgatory spells out the political message and links it indissolubly to the question of free will and human accountability. (Prompted by what he learns here, Dante will quiz Virgil in the following canto on this central philosophical problem.) Dante meets a courtier called Marco Lombardo, a contemporary character of whom we know very little. Dante clearly admired him, since he has given him this important speech:

> Soleva Roma, che 'l buon mondo feo,
> > due soli aver, che l'una e l'altra strada
> > facean veder, e del mondo e di Deo.
> L'un l'altro ha spento; ed è giunta la spada
> > col pasturale, e l'un con l'altro insieme
> > per viva forza mal convien che vada; . . .   (*Purg.* xvi 106–111)

(Rome, which made the good world [i.e., provided a model for
good government], used to have two suns [sc., papal and
imperial authority], which illuminated the two paths, the
world's path and God's path. The one sun has extinguished
the other; and the sword has been joined with the crook, and
linked together by force they inevitably proceed badly; . . .)

The message of the poem is that if human beings choose wilfully to
ignore or pervert divine intentions, the providential plan for humanity
cannot be fulfilled. In the current state of the world something has gone
terribly wrong. It must be put right. What Dante learns from Cacciaguida confirms and reinforces what Beatrice had told him in the earthly
paradise, that he must write *in pro del mondo che mal vive* ("for the benefit
of the world which lives badly"). Dante the poet and politician manqué is
changing before our eyes into Dante the poet and prophet.

There are two kinds of prophecy in the *Commedia*, both embedded
in the past of the narrative, both teaching the pilgrim things he does
not know at the outset of the journey. There are prophecies made by
the souls he meets bearing on his own future. These are a puzzle to be
solved, finally clarified by Cacciaguida. Then there are prophecies made
by his guides in the afterlife concerning the broader political future of the
human race. The wording of these latter prophecies is perforce more elusive and gnomic. It is impossible to pin down with certainty the identity
of the *veltro* (greyhound) whose coming is announced by Virgil in *Inferno*
i, and the *dux* (leader) foretold by Beatrice in *Purgatorio* xxxiii in the mysterious language of numerology. But the general sense of the prophecies
is clear. A saviour figure will come. He will set the human family back
on the right path. This saviour is almost certainly an emperor to act as
head of human beings in their secular life alongside the pope, who leads
them in their spiritual lives.

Frederick II, the last effective Holy Roman Emperor, had died in 1250,
fifteen years before Dante's birth. The courtier Marco Lombardo explicitly blames Frederick's struggle against the popes in the decades before his
death for the splitting of Italian cities into Guelfs and Ghibellines, and the

ensuing long history of conflict and turmoil in northern and central Italy. But he also makes it clear that the fault for the disaster ultimately lies with the church, not with the emperor. The church usurps an authority that does not belong to it: *la Chiesa di Roma, / per confondere in sé due reggimenti, / cade nel fango, e sé brutta e la soma* ("the Church of Rome, by joining in itself two forms of government, falls in the mud, and dirties itself and its burden"). That is, ecclesiastical authority, by taking on the burden of secular power, defiles both itself and the secular power it usurps.

After the failed attempts of Frederick's heirs, including Manfred, to win victory for the imperial cause in the second half of the century, finally in 1310, to Dante's great joy, Henry VII of Luxembourg came to Italy in an attempt to reestablish imperial overlordship in the peninsula. He had been appointed by the electors in 1308. He was crowned in Aachen in 1309, then came down into Italy to be crowned again, first in Milan (1311) and then in Rome (1312). His coming was fiercely opposed by Florence ("the viper that turns against the vitals of her mother," as Dante puts it in one of his Latin letters). But Henry died in 1313, before his mission was accomplished. Some said he had been killed by poison administered by a monk in the consecrated wafer, though probably a malarial fever was the true culprit. There was no other credible candidate in the picture. The urgency and despair of Dante's message was his response to this bleak political reality.

The prophecies in the *Commedia* powerfully link the poet's sense of what the future holds (for him, for the human race) to the larger past of history and to the present of the poet's struggle with his medium, with language and its limitations, and to the value of the poem he is writing. The interweaving of past, present and future becomes a part of the poem's fabric and fashioning, handled with great virtuosity as Dante moves between these different planes, orchestrating his various themes. This is all the more striking an achievement because time does not exist in hell and paradise, which are eternal and unchanging.

One of the great incidental pleasures of the *Commedia* is Dante's ability to evoke times of day and times of year, quintessential aspects of human living in this world. There are two dazzling examples as he is about to set out on his journey. The haunting opening to *Inferno* ii describes dusk with a sense of weariness and melancholy as all living creatures end their day's labours and Dante alone prepares for his arduous journey:

> Lo giorno se n'andava, e l'aere bruno
>   togliea li animai che sono in terra
>   da le fatiche loro; e io sol uno
> m'apparecchiava a sostener la guerra
>   sì del cammino e sì de la pietate . . .   (*Inf.* ii 1–5)

(The day was departing, and the dark air took the living creatures that are on earth from their toil; and I alone was preparing to undergo the battle, both of the journey and of pity . . .)

Equally magical is the close of the canto, after Virgil's words of encouragement have stilled Dante's doubts. His spirits rise, as though responding to the revitalizing effect of the early-morning sun's rays:

> Quali fioretti dal notturno gelo
>   chinati e chiusi, poi che 'l sol li 'mbianca,
>   si drizzan tutti aperti in loro stelo,
> tal mi fec' io . . .   (*Inf.* ii 127–30)

(Just as little flowers bent and closed by the night frost, when the
   sun shines on them, stand upright all open on their stalks, so
   I became . . .)

At the beginning of canto iii Dante and Virgil pass through the gate of hell and enter a region where time does not exist, as the gate declares in its inscription. The natural phenomena that mark the passing of time in our world—the rising and setting of the sun and moon, the positions of the stars and planets, the changing seasons—have no place in this gloomy underground realm. The final line of *Inferno* is a pivotal moment in the narrative because we have been deprived of light for so long: *quindi uscimmo a riveder le stelle* ('then we emerged to see the stars again'). The line restores Dante and Virgil, and us with them, to our proper ter-

rain, the surface of the terrestrial globe. Dante's first reaction when he
emerges on to the shore of purgatory is a joyous sense of wonder at the
intense deep blue of the pre-dawn sky.

Dolce color d'oriental zaffiro,
   che s'accoglieva nel sereno aspetto
   del mezzo, puro infino al primo giro,
a li occhi miei ricominciò diletto . . .   (*Purg.* i 13–16)

(Sweet colour of oriental sapphire, which grew deeper in the
   cloudless aspect of the air, pure as far as the horizon, renewed
   delight to my eyes . . .)

Where exactly is purgatory? Dante's answer to this question is one of
his most satisfying inventions. Medieval theologians, if they addressed
the problem at all, tended vaguely to locate purgatory as a kind of annex
to hell. (Modern theologians are no less vague.) Dante's solution to the
problem, by contrast, is very precise. The geography of the known world
in his time centred on the Mediterranean, around which are arranged
the three continents of Europe, Asia and Africa. This threefold landmass
constitutes the habitable part of the globe, located in the northern hemisphere. Educated people believed that the southern hemisphere con-
sisted entirely of water. Hence the courage, or foolhardiness, of Ulysses
in setting out over the uncharted ocean beyond the Straits of Gibraltar.
The Hereford map, which dates from c. 1300, gives a good sense of this
worldview, with Jerusalem emblematically at the centre of the inhabited
landmass and the world spreading out from that centre.

    Dante's mapping of the otherworld onto this accepted medieval
model of the known world is strikingly original. Purgatory is at the
antipodes of Jerusalem (the very centre of the inhabited world), a huge
mountain which rises from the ocean in the southern hemisphere. At the
top of this mountain is the earthly paradise, the original home of Adam
and Eve. Thus—the point is worth repeating because the geography so
satisfyingly reflects the theology—the place of man's fall (the Garden of

Eden) and the place of his salvation (Jerusalem, site of the crucifixion) are on the same axis, which passes right through the centre of the earthly globe. (See Fig. 2 on p. 7.)

But none of this geographical detail is spelled out for us. We get our bearings in purgatory as Dante gets his. He uses the heavenly bodies, now newly visible, some familiar and others never seen before, to work out where he is: at the antipodes of the northern hemisphere with its familiar night sky. He sees the planet Venus, which he recognises, but he sees other stars he has never seen before, which have never been seen by anyone except Adam and Eve.

> Lo bel pianeta che d'amar conforta
>> faceva tutto rider l'orïente,
>> velando i Pesci ch'erano in sua scorta.
> I' mi volsi a man destra, e puosi mente
>> a l'altro polo, e vidi quattro stelle
>> non viste mai fuor ch'a la prima gente.
> Goder pareva 'l ciel di lor fiammelle . . .   (*Purg.* i 19–24)

(The beautiful planet which moves us to love [sc., Venus] made the whole of the eastern sky smile, outdazzling the Fishes which accompanied her [i.e., the planet Venus lit up the eastern sky so brightly that the constellation of Pisces, with which she was in conjunction, was hard to make out]. I turned to the right, and gazed at the other pole, and I saw four stars which had never been seen except by the first people. The sky seemed to rejoice with their lights . . .)

The verbs *ridere* ("smile") and *godere* ("enjoy") suggest a natural world delighting in its own radiance and beauty. The limpidity and clarity of the language convey vitality and serenity. We are as far as it is possible to be from the gloom, the disarray, the turbulence of hell. Dante's mood—and the focus in this opening sequence is all on Dante's reactions, not on Virgil—is one of joyous hopefulness.

The stern figure of an old man appears and questions the newly arrived travellers about their unorthodox point of entry. Souls do not normally reach purgatory by climbing up through a hole in the ground. He then instructs them on the steps they must take before proceeding to climb the mountain. They must enact a ritual of cleansing and purification down by the shore. Dante's face must be washed clean of the grime of hell, and a rush plucked from the water's edge must be tied around his waist. The old man proves to be the Roman Cato. This is one of the boldest and most mysterious choices made by the poet when assembling his cast list.

Cato was renowned in antiquity for his moral stature and integrity. He took his own life at Utica after the defeat of Pompey in the battle with Julius Caesar. He would seem to be trebly disqualified to be the guardian of the penitential realm in the Christian afterlife. He is a pagan, a suicide, and on the wrong side politically (he had fought against Caesar, who in Dante's eyes was the founder of the imperial line).

Cato's presence in this crucial role is a mystery never explained or commented on. Dante's view of Cato's suicide must be the key issue, but it is difficult to untangle the various possible meanings it may have had for him, and which set it apart from the suicides punished in hell. The idea of dying nobly for one's country, of suicide as a quest for liberty, and (possibly) a perceived parallel between Cato's suicide and the voluntary sacrifice of Christ for the good of mankind may all be factors.

Dawn arrives, with light victoriously advancing and putting the darkness to flight:

> L'alba vinceva l'ora mattutina
> che fuggia innanzi, sì che di lontano
> conobbi il tremolar de la marina.   (*Purg.* i 115–17)

> (Dawn was defeating the last hour of night which fled before it,
> so that in the distance I made out the shimmering of the sea.)

The victory of light over darkness in the daily cycle underscores the profoundly hopeful atmosphere.

In these early cantos of *Purgatorio*, the easy familiarity with which movements of the heavenly bodies are noted and interpreted gives a new sense of cosmic scale to the story, reminding us that our globe is a small part of a vastly larger system of planets and stars. This newly expanded horizon puts human existence into perspective. We are only a tiny part of the cosmos. The change in perspective that starts here will be completed when in *Paradiso* Dante looks back down to earth from the constellation of the heavenly twins, his birth sign. He looks past all the seven circling spheres of the planets to see the earth at the centre, so small that he laughs at the insignificance of *l'aiuola che ci fa tanto feroci* ("the little patch of ground that makes us so fierce").

Purgatory differs from hell precisely in respect of time. It is a realm of transition, of change, of making progress, of going from one place to another: of time passing and time pressing. Like Dante, its occupants are engaged in a journey, albeit a journey that will take many hundreds of years to complete. But it is a journey whose outcome is assured, however long it takes and however painful it may be. The penitents' assured goal is paradise. Just as human life on earth can be thought of as a journey or pilgrimage towards a heavenly home, so too the progress up the mountain of purgatory is a kind of pilgrimage.

One of the delights of the second cantica is the pleasure Dante takes, and we take with him, in registering the passing of time from hour to hour, from dawn to dusk, from one day to the next. Back in a world where light marks the passage of time, we reconnect with the diurnal rhythm of human experience. Dante's three days and nights on the mountain produce some of the most lyrical and arresting canto openings in the poem. Here is dusk on the first evening:

> Era già l'ora che volge il disio
> ai navicanti e 'ntenerisce il core
> lo dì c'han detto ai dolci amici addio;
> e che lo novo peregrin d'amore
> punge, se ode squilla di lontano
> che paia il giorno pianger che si more . . .   (*Purg.* viii 1–6)

(It was already the time of day which makes travellers at sea
    think back with longing and makes their hearts grow tender,
    the day they have said good-bye to their dear friends; and
    which makes the pilgrim newly set out feel a pang of love, if
    he hears a bell ringing in the distance, which seems to mourn
    the dying day . . .)

Byron translated these lines in *Don Juan* (canto iii, stanza 108), adding
a concluding couplet to round off his stanza:

Soft hour, which wakes the wish and melts the heart
Of those who sail the seas on the first day
When they from their sweet friends are torn apart,
Or fills with love the pilgrim on his way
As the far bell of vesper makes him start,
Seeming to weep the dying day's decay.
Is this a fancy which our reason scorns?
Ah, surely nothing dies but something mourns.

Not a bad stab at it. But Byron's lines seem overripe compared with
Dante's. Byron adds words (*"soft* hour," "day's *decay"*). He uses more
emphatic verbs to describe the emotions (*"are torn apart," "makes him
start"*). His alliterations verge on the heavy-handed (*"sail the seas," "which
wakes the wish," "dying day's decay"*). The delicate musicality of Dante's
lines, with their distillation of feeling reaching a high point in the last line
of each tercet, is diluted and at the same time coarsened. Dante's simplicity
and intensity have been overlaid with a more self-consciously "romantic"
melancholy, filtered through an early-nineteenth-century sensibility. The
expressions "overegging the pudding," or "laying it on a bit thick," come
to mind. Dante is purer, more quintessential, closer to universal emotions.
    A few hours later, just one canto on, Dante plots the time in purga-
tory against the time in Italy on a global clock. The concubine of ancient
Tithonus is Aurora, or dawn. Tithonus is ancient because Aurora asked
the gods to give her lover eternal life but forgot to ask for eternal youth.

The constellation of Scorpio is visible in the pale eastern sky. There is an unmistakable surge of linguistic power and energy as Dante hits his stride:

> La concubina di Titone antico
>   già s'imbiancava al balco d'orïente,
>   fuor de le braccia del suo dolce amico;
> di gemme la sua fronte era lucente,
>   poste in figura del freddo animale
>   che con la coda percuote la gente . . .   (*Purg.* ix, 1–6)

(The concubine of ancient Tithonus was already growing pale
   at the balcony of the east, rising from the arms of her sweet
   lover; her brow shone with gems, set in the shape of the cold
   animal that strikes people with its tail . . .)

We recognise what Seamus Heaney, talking about true poetry, calls "forcibleness . . . the attribute that makes you feel the lines have been decreed, that there has been no fussy picking and choosing of words but instead a surge of utterance." The lines pose an interpretative puzzle, about which commentators disagree. This hardly seems to matter.

Time is sequence, movement, progression, succession, change. In human life we pass from generation to corruption, from birth to death, as a continuous sequence measured in hours, days, seasons, years. Time is linear (a forward movement), but its patterns are also cyclical: "grief returns with the revolving year," in Shelley's beautiful phrase. This same combination of linearity and circularity shapes the narrative movement of Dante's journey. There is forward momentum through time, as Dante journeys and as we read. And there is a spiralling movement through space, as he circles down through hell and up the mountain of purgatory on a continuous helical trajectory. There is also what we might call a spatial organisation of the narrative and its component parts which is reminiscent of painting or architecture. This too has a temporal dimension.

Medieval narrative artists (fresco painters) could arrange their sequence of events spatially in two dimensions, and sometimes even in three, in order to create meaning. The frescoes in the basilica at Assisi representing scenes from the life of Saint Francis, painted around 1300 and traditionally believed to be by Dante's contemporary Giotto, illustrate the point especially well. They are arranged not just horizontally along the walls of the nave in groups of three and vertically in a double tier at each point, but across the nave as well. Patterns of meaning are established by reading along, or up and down, or across the central space.

Something similar is done by what is often called the "architecture" of the *Commedia*, the overall structural framework that carries the narrative. It is no accident that the word *architecture* implies a spatial, three-dimensional quality. Significant symmetries across the *cantiche* reinforce and enrich meaning. One casts one's eye back to appreciate parallels, contrasts or reinforcements in related themes. Reading about Sordello and his spontaneous embrace of Virgil as a fellow citizen of Mantua (while still unaware of his identity as a famous poet), we think back to Farinata and the initially guarded and soon hostile encounter between the two Florentines. Reading Cacciaguida's account of the domestic contentment and modesty of Florentine women of old, we think back to Forese's *sfacciate donne fiorentine* ("shameless Florentine women"), whose extravagant fashions cause them to go *mostrando con le poppe il petto* ("showing their chests with their breasts").

Echoes and contrasts of this kind are everywhere in the *Commedia*. For example, each section of the poem ends with the word *stelle* ("stars"). Each occurrence of the word marks the completion of a stage in the protagonist's journey: *e quindi uscimmo a riveder le stelle* ("then we emerged to see the stars again"), as he leaves hell behind and emerges into the predawn light on the shore of mount purgatory. When he has completed the arduous journey up the mountain and is ready to rise up through the heavens, he is *puro e disposto a salire alle stelle* ("pure and ready to rise to the stars"). At the very end of the poem, his will and desire are attuned to those of his maker: *l'amor che move il sole e l'altre stelle* ("the love which moves the sun and the other stars").

Each canto vi is political in theme but increasingly broad in its geographical scope and its wider political implications. *Inferno* vi deals with the troubled state of Florence, torn apart by factional discord within the ascendant Guelf party. *Purgatorio* vi deals with the decadence of Italy, where city-state fights city-state and there is no effective secular leader to control warring Guelfs and Ghibellines. *Paradiso* vi deals with the condition of Europe and beyond, when the emperor Justinian recounts the history of the Roman Empire and shows how it provided a model for good government, if only perverse modern rulers would choose to understand. The geographical focus has broadened to include the whole inhabited world.

Members of the same family are found in different realms of the afterlife, their fates all the more telling for their family connection. The three Donati siblings—Forese, Piccarda and Corso—end up in purgatory, paradise and hell respectively. There is a striking intergenerational example—father and son—in the Montefeltro family. Guido da Montefeltro is in hell, while his son Bonconte is in purgatory, their destiny in the afterlife reversing commonsense expectations of where they should have ended up. Guido, the great Ghibelline warlord from Romagna, had turned to the religious life in old age and become a friar, seeming to distance himself from the political guile of his earlier years. Bonconte had died unshriven on the field of battle.

The contrast in their destinies makes a polemical point about repentance (genuine repentance must be heartfelt, with no calculating of risk or self-interest). It makes an even more polemical point about the limitations on the power of the pope (Boniface again). Boniface had guaranteed absolution to Guido in advance for committing a sin. But it was not in his power to grant absolution, since absolution can only follow repentance, and it is a logical impossibility that repentance can precede an act one is about to perform. Guido had counselled guile to Boniface, telling him how he could defeat his opponents in the papal curia and overthrow their impregnable stronghold Palestrina. He told the pope to revoke their excommunication and make a pact with them for peace; then, when it was too late for them to take evasive action, to betray them. Palestrina was razed. Boniface was triumphant.

But this counseling of duplicity costs Guido his place in paradise. The wily old fox is shame-faced that he has been outfoxed by Boniface. He is willing to tell his story only because he believes Dante cannot return to the world of the living and destroy his reputation for having made a good end. But once again his calculated risk does not pay off. The lines T. S. Eliot used as the epigraph to "The Love Song of J. Alfred Prufrock" show him in the very act of making the miscalculation. We witness the same mental process that was his undoing on earth. Like Ulysses, another counsellor of fraud, Guido is enveloped in a flame. The movement of the tip of the flame is the way he articulates speech:

> S'i' credesse che mia risposta fosse
>> a persona che mai tornasse al mondo,
>> questa fiamma staria sanza più scosse;
> ma però che già mai di questo fondo
>> non tornò vivo alcun, s'i' odo il vero,
>> sanza tema d'infamia ti rispondo.   (*Inf.* xxvii 61–66)

> (If I thought my reply was to someone who might ever return
>> to the world, this flame would remain without further flick-
>> ering; but since, if what I hear is true, no man ever returned
>> alive from this depth, I answer you without fear of infamy.)

But Dante will return to the world of the living, and he will tell the tale in his poem. In the *Convivio* Dante had expressed a high opinion of Guido, at a time when it was widely known that he had become a friar in old age. Guido had seemed to offer an exemplary role model of how a human life should be conducted. But between the writing of the treatise and of the poem, news of his final counselling of Boniface on the matter of Palestrina must have leaked out. In spite of his wiliness, the fox is out-foxed once again.

A sense of time and its significance operates in the poem at a very human level as well. Dante has a strong sense of the ages of a human life and the conduct appropriate to those ages. Part of the folly of Ulysses' behaviour in setting sail for the unknown world beyond the Pillars of Her-cules is his age: *io e ' compagni eravam vecchi e tardi* ("I and my companions were old and slow"). Guido da Montefeltro as an old man had lowered his metaphorical sails and come into harbour by ceasing to be a warlord and becoming a friar (though he had not foreseen the pope's skullduggery, which would be his undoing). This is an essential point. While still within time, human beings can choose or change their eternal destiny.

Fig. 27 Botticelli: Dante and Virgil look down
on the counsellors of fraud.

Time is a vital component in the drama of Ugolino, perhaps the most moving of all the stories told in hell. It is the story of a father forced to see his children die of hunger, unable to help them or offer comfort in their hour of need. Ugolino's long speech explaining the horrifying circumstances of their deaths is another one of the poem's great operatic arias.

Dante comes upon Ugolino at the bottom of hell, where traitors are punished in the ninth and last circle. The floor of hell is a frozen lake of solid ice. The traitors are trapped in the ice, with just their heads poking out. Some have their heads tilted forwards, so their tears can drain away. Others hold their heads upright. Yet others have their faces upturned, so their tears form an icy mask over their eyes. Treachery is for Dante the worst sin of all. It involves the misuse of human reason not just against a fellow human being but against someone who has a special reason to trust the perpetrator—some special bond of trust which the act of treachery violates. There are four categories of traitors: against family, against country or political party, against guests (a particularly shocking form of treachery in medieval eyes, where the bond of hospitality was considered sacred) and against benefactors.

In this circle Dante's attitude to those he meets has lost any trace of compassion. In one particularly shocking encounter, as he picks his way between the heads protruding from the ice, he inadvertently kicks the face of one sinner. (Or was it deliberate? he wonders. Or was it destined to happen?) He asks the sinner who he is, and, when the sinner refuses to reveal his name, Dante grabs him by his hair and pulls out several chunks. The sinner howls, and a neighbour complains: What the devil has got into you, Bocca? Thus he reveals the name its owner was trying to hide. This is Bocca degli Abati, the Florentine traitor at Montaperti. He had ensured the Sienese victory against the Florentine Guelfs by cutting off the hand of the Florentine standard-bearer at the height of the battle, so that the troops no longer knew where to go and scattered in disarray. His desire for the world to forget him has been thwarted. Dante has revealed his miserable destiny in the afterlife to posterity.

Ugolino too is in the section of the circle of treachery reserved for political traitors. He was from a Ghibelline family in Pisa but had gone over to the Guelfs. He had later been betrayed in his turn by the Ghibelline archbishop Ruggieri, a man he had trusted. Dante finds the two sinners—a churchman and a layman, on opposite sides politically— sharing their eternal destiny. They are frozen in the ice in a single hole, with just their heads emerging. Ugolino is behind Ruggieri, gnawing at the base of his old enemy's skull, in a gesture of animal-like ferocity and cannibalism. He breaks off to speak to Dante in one of the most arresting canto openings of the whole poem:

La bocca sollevò dal fiero pasto
    quel peccator, forbendola a' capelli
    del capo ch'elli avea di retro guasto.
Poi cominciò: "Tu vuo' ch'io rinovelli
    disperato dolor che 'l cor mi preme
    già pur pensando, pria ch'io ne favelli."   (*Inf.* xxxiii 1–6)

(That sinner raised his mouth from the fierce meal, wiping it
    on the hair of the head whose back he had ravaged. Then he
    began: "You want me to renew a desperate sorrow which
    presses on my heart even just thinking about it, before I speak
    of it.")

You know that I died as the result of Ruggieri's scheming, he tells
Dante, but you don't know *how* I died. And he proceeds to tell the story.
He had been seized by the archbishop and locked up in a tower along
with his four children. A disturbing predawn dream left them with a
premonition of impending disaster.

Quando fui desto innanzi la dimane,
    pianger senti' fra 'l sonno i miei figliuoli
    ch'eran con meco, e dimandar del pane.
Ben se' crudel, se tu già non ti duoli
    pensando ciò che 'l mio cor s'annunziava;
    e se non piangi, di che pianger suoli?   (*Inf.* xxxiii 37–42)

(When I awoke before the daybreak, I heard my sons who were
    with me weeping in their sleep, and asking for bread. You are
    very cruel, if you are not already grieving at the thought of
    what my heart was telling itself; and if you do not weep, what
    could make you weep?)

The prisoners hear the door to the tower being nailed shut below them.
They realise they are to be left to starve to death.
    The remorseless measuring out of the eight days it takes Ugolino to

die of hunger in the tower is set against the fact—unstated but inescapably clear—that time is running out in a different sense: the chance for repentance and making his peace with God. For all the horror of his circumstances, Ugolino is in the theologically privileged position of knowing he is to die soon. He could have died a good death, but chose not to, implacably obdurate in his consuming hatred of his old enemy. This state of mind is immortalized in hell in his animal-like gnawing at the base of Ruggieri's skull.

The behaviour of his children is very different. They reach out to their father. They offer their own flesh to him to assuage his hunger, in a sacrificial gesture. Their words echo those of Christ. Ugolino is unable to respond, does not talk to them, offers them no comfort, is unreachable in the pain and despair of his final days. *Poscia, più che 'l dolor, poté 'l digiumo.* "Then hunger did what sorrow could not do," in Longfellow's rhythmically pleasing translation. But this translation loses the chilling ambiguity present in the Italian. Literally, the line reads "Then hunger was more powerful than sorrow." Did Ugolino die of hunger rather than of grief? Or was his hunger more powerful than his grief? Did he, in his despair, bite into the flesh of his own children? The line which ends his story leaves this possibility hanging in the air. A contemporary chronicle reports that there were signs of cannibalism when the bodies were recovered.

Ugolino's mental state is precisely that denial and rejection of God which is the essence of damnation. (The story is retold by Chaucer less than a century later in "The Monk's Tale," where the emphasis is all on the pathos of the children's fate rather than on the mental state of their father: 'And with hym been his litel children thre; / The eldest scarsly fyf yeer was of age.") Here in a single human being we have an example of supreme hatred, expressed in the animal gesture of devouring its object, and the supreme suffering of a father unable to help or comfort his children as they starve to death. The hatred and the suffering are intimately linked. The hatred is both the cause of the suffering and its effect.

It is illuminating to compare Ugolino with the three figures who talk to Dante in *Purgatorio* vi, the canto which celebrates those who died violent deaths and turned to God only in extremis. They were all *peccatori infino a l'ultima ora* ("sinners until the last hour"), but at that moment they turned to their maker: *pentendo e perdonando, fora / di vita uscimmo a Dio pacificati* ("repenting and forgiving, we departed from life having made our peace with God"). Having repented only at the very moment of death (all of them were young), they cannot begin their progress up the mountain until they have passed an equivalent length of time in ante-purgatory.

Jacopo del Cassero had been betrayed by those he trusted and had died fleeing from his enemies through the marshy ground between Venice and Padua. He tells how he watched his life blood flow out from his deep wounds to form a pool on the ground where he lay. Bonconte da Montefeltro had died on the battlefield at Campaldino, where he had led the Ghibelline forces of Arezzo against the Florentine Guelfs. His body had never been found. Dante, who had fought at Campaldino, is eager to learn of his fate. Bonconte describes how, wounded in the throat, *fuggendo a piede e sanguinando il piano* ("fleeing on foot and bloodying the plain"), he reached the river Archiano, a tributary of the Arno. He died there with the name of Mary on his lips, his arms forming a cross over his chest. A violent thunderstorm carried his body into the swollen main river, and then far downstream, where it disappeared under the debris of the storm, never to be found.

Bodies, wounds, blood. These are graphic descriptions of very physical deaths. By contrast, Pia de' Tolomei's death is almost disembodied. After an exquisitely courteous preamble, in which she asks Dante to remember her when he has recovered from the hardships of his long journey, just three allusive lines tell the tale. *Siena mi fé, disfecemi Maremma* ("Siena made me, Maremma unmade me"—that is, "I was born in Siena, I died in Maremma"). The man who first betrothed her and then married her with his ring knows the story. With extraordinary reticence, she says no more than this, merely implying that her husband had her killed when it became politically expedient to form a marriage alliance with another family. Although we do not know the circumstances of her death, several early commentators tell us that she was hurled from a window of her husband's castle to her death on the rocks below. Her whole earthly existence from birth to death is condensed into a single line. Compare this with the story of Ugolino, with its agonizing sense of the slow and inexorable passing of the eight days it took him to starve to death. These are just two examples of the kinds of poetic effect created by Dante's handling of time.

It is only in the *Paradiso* that we will be given an account of the nature of time. That account is both philosophical and poetic. Dante is about to emerge from the created world, in which alone the concept of time has meaning. Time came into being with the creation of the cosmos. Temporality is a dimension of the created world within which human experience unfolds. (Modern physicists and psychoanalysts would have no difficulty with this observation.) An arresting visual image describes time as a tree with its roots in the *primum mobile*.

The *primum mobile* is the outermost of the moving spheres of the heavens, the one that moves most swiftly and imparts motion to all the other spheres contained within it. It is, in other words, the outermost enclosing shell of our universe. Beyond it is God and paradise. The experience recounted in the poem—Dante's journey—is a movement from time to eternity, from a realm that is time-bound and flawed, enclosed within the *primum mobile*, to a realm beyond the *primum mobile* where justice and sanity reign. On emerging into this new realm the poet says: *a l'etterno dal tempo ero venuto* ("I had come from time to eternity"); and he cannot refrain from adding, *e da Fiorenza in popol giusto e sano* ("and from Florence to a just and sane people").

Human beings, caught in the here and now of the present as they live from moment to moment, recover time past through memory. Memory and language defeat time. Dante's first encounter with a saved soul in purgatory shows the depth and richness of meaning within time made possible by memory and language, even while the narrative line remains straightforwardly in the present of the journey.

As Dante and Virgil stand on the shore at the beginning of *Purgatorio* ii, a light approaches rapidly across the sea. The description is cinematic

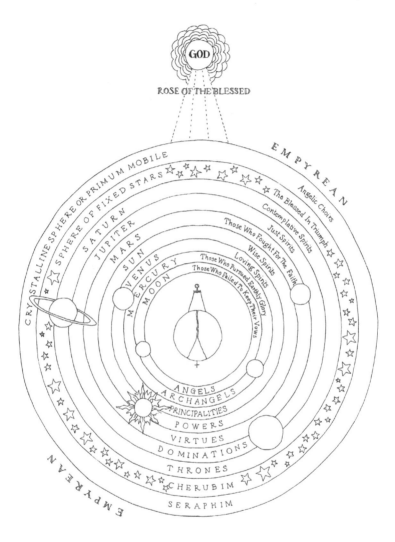

Fig. 28 Nine spheres circle the earth: the seven planetary spheres, the eighth sphere of the "fixed" stars (including the constellations of the zodiac), and the outermost ninth sphere, or *primum mobile*, which imparts motion to the other spheres nested inside it. The nine orders of angels correspond to the nine spheres.

in its suggestion of movement, speed and power. The light proves to be the radiance from the wings of an angel helmsman who is ferrying a group of saved souls across the water towards the shore, having collected them (we will learn) from an assembly point at the mouth of the river Tiber—the orthodox route to purgatory. The souls are singing in unison the exodus psalm *In exitu Isräel de Aegypto* ("When Israel went out of Egypt"). They disembark, and the boat speeds off. By now it is full daylight, described in a marvellously vital image:

> Da tutte parti saettava il giorno
>   lo sol, ch'avea con le saette conte
>   di mezzo 'l ciel cacciato Capricorno, . . .   (*Purg.* ii 55–57)

(The sun, which with its expert arrows had chased Capricorn from
   the zenith, was now shooting out daylight on all sides . . .)

The newcomers ask for directions. Virgil explains that he and Dante are also newcomers who do not know the way (the word he uses is *peregrin*, "pilgrims"). The disembarked souls have become aware from Dante's breathing that he is still alive, and they press forward in astonishment.

> Io vidi una di lor trarresi avante
>   per abbracciarmi, con sì grande affetto,
>   che mosse me a far lo somigliante.
> Ohi ombre vane, fuor che ne l'aspetto!
>   tre volte dietro a lei le mani avvinsi,
>   e tante mi tornai con esse al petto.   (*Purg.* ii 76–81)

(I saw one of them move forward to embrace me, with such
   great affection that he moved me to do the same thing.
   Alas, empty shadows, except in appearance! Three times I
   grasped my hands behind the shade, and three times my arms
   returned to my own breast.)

Dante's astonishment at his inability to embrace the shade causes it to smile—the first smile we have seen since Virgil in Limbo smiled at the welcome given to Dante by the ancient poets. He draws back, and Dante follows. The shade invites him to halt. Dante recognises the voice of an old friend—a musician called Casella, who set love poems to music—and asks him to stop a little so that they can talk.

After a discussion of how one gets to purgatory when one dies, the conversation changes direction. Dante asks his friend to sing a song, just as he used to do back in the world of the living:

> E io: "Se nuova legge non ti toglie
> > memoria o uso a l'amoroso canto
> > che mi solea quetar tutte mie voglie,
> di ciò ti piaccia consolare alquanto
> > l'anima mia, che, con la sua persona,
> > venendo qui, è affannata tanto!"   (*Purg.* ii 106–11)

> (And I said: "If a new law does not take from you the memory or
> > practice of the love songs that used to quiet all my longings,
> > please sing one now to refresh my soul, which, coming here,
> > burdened with its body, is so wearied!")

Casella immediately obliges with a song:

> "*Amor che ne la mente mi ragiona*"
> > cominciò elli allor sì dolcemente,
> > che la dolcezza ancor dentro mi suona.   (*Purg.* ii 112–14)

> ("*Love which speaks to me in my mind,*" he then began so sweetly
> > that the sweetness still resounds within me.)

The tact with which Casella chooses one of Dante's own songs to cheer up his old friend suggests the closeness and affection of their friendship. We know nothing of Casella at all from surviving documentary evidence. This delightful episode is our only source of information.

The group of souls is spellbound listening to the performance. The spell is broken when Cato reappears from nowhere and rebukes them for their slackness. They should be hastening to the mountain to cleanse themselves, to begin the process of purification. The group abandons the song and scatters towards the slope like startled doves. Dante and Virgil depart with equal speed.

Perhaps the first thing to notice about this episode is how beautifully it conveys the new sense of urgency about time that will mark purgatory. An innocent pastime, listening to a soothing song to raise one's spirits, is inappropriate behaviour in this new realm, sternly rebuked by its guardian. Only a strenuous pursuit of spiritual perfection will do here. But this is not something the new arrivals understand immediately. Two old friends slip into their old ways; the musician sings to please his friend the poet. The two are linked by a creative bond, since the words the musician sings are the poet's own. But this apparently harmless interlude is now to be understood as time-wasting.

The contrast between the two songs sung in the canto unobtrusively underscores the point. The first is the psalm that recalls the exodus of the Israelites in the time of Moses and the entry into the Promised Land. Figurally, it signifies the salvation of Christian souls from sin through Christ. On a more practical note, it was the psalm that in medieval funeral services accompanied the procession carrying the coffin to the church and then to the graveyard. It is strikingly appropriate that the souls should be singing it in unison as they arrive on the shores of purgatory in the afterlife. Their choral celebration of the promise of liberation from sin and the reaching of the promised land suggests a proper sense of spiritual focus in the singers.

The second song, the one sung by Casella, in which the shades take such pleasure, is a secular love song. Not a licentious or erotic song, indeed a rather chaste and intellectual exploration of the theme of love. The lady it celebrates, Dante tells us in the *Convivio*, is Lady Philosophy, not a flesh-and-blood human being. But nonetheless, it is inescapably a song of this earthly world. The love that speaks to the poet in his mind in this song is not the love of God, nor of Beatrice.

Dante's self-citation here, in the mouth of Casella, is a way of recovering his own past, of taking us back in time to an earlier stage in his own life. This is not the only time a shade quotes from one of Dante's lyric poems. It will happen again with Bonagiunta da Lucca on the circle of the gluttonous in *Purgatorio* xxiv, and again with Charles Martel in *Paradiso* viii. We saw that Francesca's account of her fatal involvement with Paolo incorporated a tissue of words and phrases from Dante's early love poems. All these self-citations, direct and indirect, are a way of presenting Dante's own past in a new light, where its significance may be subtly but irrevocably altered.

Intertextuality is the word now used to refer to the many different ways in which one text inescapably calls to mind other texts. Direct quotation is a simple form of it. Another is what used to be called "sources and analogues." A later work can allude to an earlier one not just by verbal reminiscences but by echoing incidents or plot points or structural features.

The Casella episode has an echo of this second kind: the failed embrace. Dante's inability to embrace Casella, with his arms passing right through the shadow body of his old friend—the gesture repeated three times to underline how astonished and incredulous he is— inescapably calls to mind the similar episode in the *Aeneid* where Aeneas attempts to embrace the shade of his father Anchises, and fails just as Dante does. Virgil's use of the motif is in its turn an even more remote echo of Homer, though Dante probably did not know that. Echoes and recurring narrative patterns of this kind establish meaningful connections across the vast field that is earlier literature and civilisation.

Where there are allusions to and echoes of earlier texts, time is always involved. Such echoes are an enacting of cultural memory. Dante's text is a palimpsest, with earlier texts visible through or behind or underneath its surface. As we read of Dante's failure to embrace Casella, we perceive through it or behind it Aeneas's failed embrace of Anchises, just as behind Manfred's display of the wound on his chest we see Christ and doubting Thomas. Evoking an earlier figure or episode or phrase from history or poetry or Scripture creates a sense of depth in time.

The encounter with Statius near the top of purgatory is another example. At the centre of the episode is an emotional encounter between two great poets of antiquity. Virgil, author of the *Aeneid*, had died in 19 B.C. Statius, the author of the *Thebaid*, was born some sixty years later, c. 40 A.D. Dante has them meet here in purgatory so that Statius can express his gratitude to a great poet whom he never met in life. His gratitude is not just for poetic inspiration, as we might expect, but, much more surprisingly, for moral and spiritual enlightenment as well.

Statius himself is unequivocally a *figura Christi*, "a figure of Christ." The opening lines of *Purgatorio* xxi, where he first appears on the scene, make this quite clear. As Dante and Virgil walk along the terrace of the avaricious and the prodigal they become aware of a third figure who has joined them from behind:

> Ed ecco, sì come ne scrive Luca
> che Cristo apparve a' due ch'erano in via,
> già surto fuor de la sepulcral buca,
> ci apparve un'ombra, e dietro a noi venìa . . .   (*Purg.* xxi 7–10)

> (And lo! as Luke writes that Christ, already risen from his
> burial place, appeared to the two who were on their way [to
> Emmaus], a shade appeared to us, and it was coming along
> behind us . . .)

The parallel between Christ's appearance to the disciples on the road to Emmaus and Statius's appearance to Dante and Virgil is exact in every detail. Two travellers are joined by a third figure, who is suddenly, unaccountably present, walking along behind them.

Statius will be the only example Dante encounters in purgatory of a soul who has completed the process of purgation, so the connection with Christ is fundamental. Every saved soul reenacts the resurrection.

Just as the choice of Cato, the pagan suicide, as guardian of the Christian realm of purgatory is startling, so too is the choice of Statius, a pagan poet not known to have been a Christian, as the first and only purified soul we meet on the mountain. Dante presents Statius as a secret convert to Christianity who did not publicly profess his faith. Like Casella, he is used by Dante to give crucial information about the realm of purgatory. First he will explain about weather conditions on the mountain. Later he will give an important speech about the development of the embryo in the womb, and the moment in time when the foetus becomes a person.

But the poetic energy source is the central encounter between the two ancient poets. There is a delicious irony as Statius explains his indebtedness to the *Aeneid* without realising that it is Virgil he is talking to. He makes the highly unorthodox claim that he would willingly put in an extra year of penance on the mountain for the chance to have met Virgil while he was alive. His whole achievement as a poet is due to Virgil:

> Al mio ardor fuor seme le faville,
> > che mi scaldar, de la divina fiamma
> > onde sono allumati più di mille;
> de l'Eneïda dico, la qual mamma
> > fummi, e fummi nutrice, poetando:
> > sanz'essa non fermai peso di dramma.   (*Purg.* xxi 94–99)

> (My poetic ardour was set alight by the sparks, which warmed
> > me, of the divine flame which enlightens thousands; I mean
> > the *Aeneid*, which was a mother to me in writing poetry, and
> > a nursemaid: without it I would have achieved nothing of any
> > weight.)

There is a clear allusion here to the end of Statius's own poem the *Thebaid*, where he takes leave of his poem and urges it to follow in the footsteps of the "divine *Aeneid*." This is the only time in the *Commedia* that the word *divine* is used of anything except God. And of course Dante did not call his poem the *Divine Comedy*. Its title is simply the *Comedy*. The word *divine* was added by editors of early printed editions of the poem to reflect its theme and acknowledge its greatness.

But Statius's indebtedness goes beyond the poetic. Virgil asks what caused him to convert to Christianity, of which there is no trace in his work. Statius tells him:

> Tu prima m'invïasti
> verso Parnaso a ber ne le sue grotte,
> e prima appresso Dio m'alluminasti.
> Facesti come quei che va di notte,
> che porta il lume dietro e sé non giova,
> ma dopo sé fa le persone dotte,
> quando dicesti: "Secol si rinova;
> torna giustizia e primo tempo umano,
> e progenïe scende da ciel nova."
> Per te poeta fui, per te cristiano . . .   (*Purg.* xxii 64–73)

(You first sent me towards Parnassus to drink in its grottoes,
    and you first enlightened me concerning God. You did what
    a man does who travels by night, carrying a lantern over his
    shoulder which does not benefit himself, but casts light for
    people who follow him, when you said: "The age is renewed;
    justice returns and first human time, and a new offspring
    descends from heaven." Because of you I was a poet, because
    of you a Christian . . .)

From earliest Christian times the lines of Virgil's Fourth Eclogue which Statius here quotes had been interpreted as an unwitting prophecy on Virgil's part of the coming of Christ. In reality, the lines celebrated in somewhat extravagant terms the birth of a child to a Roman consul. Statius reads these lines with their seemingly prescient understanding and is persuaded that a new age has dawned. A miraculous child has come from heaven. What Dante shows here is not just that Virgil's lines have prophetic insight into the future, as many in the Middle Ages believed, but that they could actually effect a conversion.

Statius goes on to describe how he began to frequent the early Christians in Rome, was moved by their goodness and piety, grieved when they were persecuted by the emperor Domitian, helped them while he was alive, and was himself secretly baptised before he finished writing the *Thebaid*. But out of fear he remained a secret convert. For this spiritual slackness he spent more than four hundred years on the terrace of sloth. (Another five hundred years were spent here on the terrace of avarice, where, as he explains to a puzzled Virgil, he was not purging the sin of avarice, but its opposite, prodigality. For those pedants among you who are doing the maths and are wondering, this leaves some two hundred years unaccounted for. We assume these were spent on the lower terraces of the mountain in some unspecified proportion.)

These lines throw light on Dante's deepest convictions about the power of poetry. Poetry can be prophetic; poets have access to truths denied to other men; poetry can change human lives. Statius's lines take us back in time to just before the birth of Christ (the lines from Virgil's Fourth Eclogue were written in 40 B.C.); and to early Christian settlements in Rome and to the persecutions of the early Christians in the first century A.D. The two ancient poets now at ease in each other's company talk about literary friends they have in common: *dimmi dov'è Terrenzio nostro antico* ("tell me, where's our old friend Terence"). Dante follows in their footsteps, listening to their conversation and learning from it, offering us a tantalising glimpse of literary shoptalk. Botticelli alone of all illustrators of the poem captures this delicious detail:

> Elli givan dinanzi, e io soletto
>   di retro, e ascoltava i lor sermoni,
>   ch'a poetar mi davano intelletto.   (*Purg.* xxii 127–29)

> (They went on ahead, and I followed behind them on my own, and I listened to their talk, which gave me insight into writing poetry.)

Fig. 29   Botticelli: Dante follows in the footsteps of Virgil and Statius.

Statius will remain with Dante and Virgil until the top of purgatory, the trio of poets facing the final section of the journey up the mountain together. When on the final terrace Dante meets the vernacular master he so greatly admired, Guido Guinizzelli, it will be in the company of the two classical poets whose example enabled him to outdo his contemporaries and produce a poem that could stand alongside the great epics of antiquity.

In both the Casella and the Statius episodes, there is simplicity and complexity simultaneously in the organisation of the narrative. With Casella, we have a simple sequence of events, a delightful vignette of friendship and creative companionship. But that vignette is enriched by the depth in time which single elements in the composition effortlessly summon up: the exodus psalm, the self-citation, the literary antecedents. With Statius we have something more complex. One great poet of the ancient world acknowledges his poetic and spiritual indebtedness to another (and through him, so does Dante). His words convey a message about the power of poetic language to affect human lives.

These methods of creating meaning through echoes, patterning, parallels—intertextuality and figuralism, to give them their unwieldy technical names—enable Dante to encompass the whole of human history, culture and poetry. The present does not simply follow the past. It contains the past and relates to it in meaningful ways. The Virgilian and biblical originals that lie behind Dante's surface are perceptible through it, just as light shines through an alabaster window, enabling us to appreciate the detailed veining of the stone as well as its polished surface. For a lover of poetry the process of identifying the countless echoes and allusions in the *Commedia* is endlessly pleasurable.

From our twenty-first-century vantage point, such echoes and allusions work through time forwards as well as backwards. When we read Milton's *Thick as autumnal leaves that strew the brooks / In Vallombrosa . . .* , or Shelley's *Far from the shore my spirit's bark is driven . . .* , or Eliot's *Stand on the highest pavement of the stair . . .* , or Pound's *Pull down thy vanity, I say pull down*, we think back to Dante and the originals of those beautiful lines. When Heaney reworks his translation of lines 127–32 from *Inferno* ii and incorporates those lines into a new poem of his own, where they take on a subtly different meaning, the effect matches the original in its beauty and delicacy:

> As little flowers that were all bowed and shut
> By the night chills rise on their stems and open
> As soon as they have felt the touch of sunlight,
> So I revived in my own wilting powers
> And my heart flushed, like somebody set free.

This is comparable with Dante's own translations and appropriations of Virgil. At the climactic moment when he finally sees Beatrice in the earthly paradise after an interval of ten years since her death, he tells us: *lo spirito mio . . . / . . . d'antico amor sentì la gran potenza* ("my spirit . . . felt the great power of its old love"). He then turns to Virgil to share the moment. What he says is: *conosco i segni de l'antica fiamma* ("I know the signs of the ancient flame"), echoing Dido's words to Aeneas in *Aeneid* ii (*adgnosco veteris vestigia flammae*). This poetic homage acknowledges but subtly transforms a formative influence, illustrating the fertilising power of one great poet on another. These are in fact Dante's last words to Virgil in the poem. This is the very moment that he discovers Virgil is no longer with him.

We may conclude with a paradox. The *Commedia* is extremely specifically tied to the historical circumstances of Dante's own time, to the year 1300, and the events of the immediately preceding decades. But it spreads out to encompass all time, the whole of human history, including us, its twenty-first-century readers. As the poem progresses, the time frame extends outwards in both directions, and space opens up as well, from the dark wood to the circling cosmos. One of the things that makes the *Paradiso* so powerful is that just as the poem becomes more esoteric, more spiritual, it takes in more of lived human experience on this planet. We are taken further and further back in time. By Cacciaguida to the beginning of Dante's own family history. By Justinian to the beginning of the Roman Empire. By Saint Peter to the beginning of the church. By Adam to the beginning of the human race.

The *Commedia* is firmly anchored in time, yet it transcends time. To those of a religious disposition, this is because it connects with what is beyond time and space, the limiting conditions of mortal existence on earth. To nonbelievers, it must be because aesthetic value transcends or defeats time. Dante speaks to us as powerfully as he did to his own age, perhaps more so, because the circumstantial and the incidental have dropped away. We return to the paradox that a poem so firmly anchored in a precise historical moment, whose key figures are so specifically linked to a certain period and place, nonetheless transcends those temporal limitations and has universal resonance. Francesca, the adulteress; Ugolino, the traitor; Bonconte da Montefeltro, who died on the battle-field at Campaldino and whose body was never found; Brunetto Latini, the revered role model; Forese, the friend of Dante's youth with whom he exchanged rude sonnets; Guido da Montefeltro, the warlord

turned friar; Casella, the musician friend; and Boniface, the evil pope—
all lived out their earthly destinies in the last two decades of the thirteenth century. Yet seven hundred years later, countless lines from the
Commedia are incised in the Italian national memory. Words that lodge in
the mind, unforgettable because of their expressive and rhythmic force,
survive the passage of time. Poetic form defeats time: *ars longa, vita bre-
vis.* The nature of that poetic form is what we will consider in the next
two chapters.

Quando mi fui umilmente disdecto

dauerlo uisto mai el disse oruedi

a mostromi una piaga a somol pecto.

Poi sorridendo disse io son Manfredi

nepote di Costancia Impidrice

ondio ti prego che quando tu riedi.

Uadi amia bella figlia genitrice

del honor di Cicilia e da Ragona

e dinne alei il uer s altro si dice.

Poscia chi ebbi rocta La persona

didue puncte mortali io mirendi

piangendo aquei che uolontier perdona.

Orribil furo li peccati miei

ma la bonta infinita a si gran braccia

che prende cio che si riuolge alei.

6.

Numbers

As yet a child, nor yet a fool to fame,
I lisped in numbers, for the numbers came.
—ALEXANDER POPE, AN EPISTLE TO DR. ARBUTHNOT

. . . per costui ogni bellezza di volgar parlare
sotto debiti numeri è regolata . . .
(. . . he brought every beauty of vernacular speech
under the rule of due numbers.)
—BOCCACCIO, LIFE OF DANTE

Nature uses only the longest threads to weave her patterns,
so each small piece of her fabric reveals
the organization of the entire tapestry.
—RICHARD FEYNMAN, THE CHARACTER OF PHYSICAL LAW

FREUD'S WOLF MAN SUFFERED FROM AN OBSESSIVE-COMPULSIVE disorder with a religious twist. He saw signs of the Trinity (Father, Son and Holy Spirit) all around him, even in dollops of horse dung lying in the road. Readers of the *Commedia* may sometimes feel they are suffering from a similar affliction. The number three is so much the informing principle of the poem—so omnipresent in its shaping and structuring—

that it becomes tempting to see a trinitarian allusion even in apparently trivial details. The artist Tom Phillips, in his lithographs illustrating the *Inferno*, captures this obsessional quality brilliantly in the sheet devoted to "Infernal Trinities," covered as it is with densely packed notes on instances of the number three in hell.

While it is wise to be wary of the literal-mindedness that detects a trinitarian allusion in every instance of the number three in the *Commedia*, it remains true that the resonance of the number enriches the poem by connecting it meaningfully with the view of the world it celebrates. Even in modern church ritual allusions to the Trinity can take surprisingly concrete and unsubtle forms. When the Swiss Guards whose job it is to protect the pope are sworn in, for example, they raise an arm with three fingers extended and open to signify the Trinity. Before we consider how the principle of threeness operates in Dante's poem, we must understand how that principle connects with the world as the poet understood it—and not just the world of organised religion.

The notion of the Trinity—the three-personed deity of Christian belief—is a central tenet of Christianity which distinguishes it from the other two great monotheistic faiths, Judaism and Islam. All three monotheistic religions reject the *dei falsi e bugiardi*, the "false and lying gods," of the pagan world of Greece and Rome. Christianity is set apart from the other two by the notion of its three-personed God: one substance, the Godhead, in three equal persons, Father, Son and Holy Spirit. Dante warns us explicitly that this is a mystery of the faith which is beyond human comprehension:

> Matto è chi spera che nostra ragione
> > possa trascorrer la infinita via
> > che tiene una sustanza in tre persone.
> State contenti, umana gente, al *quia*.   (*Purg.* iii 34–37)

> (Mad is he who hopes that our reason can go down the infinite
> > path taken by one substance in three persons. Be content,
> > human kind, with the *quia*.)

Be content, that is, with the *that*—the fact that it is so. This resound-ing admonition, with its clinching technical term in Latin, has become proverbial for Italians when they are forced to accept that something is the case even though its unfathomability defeats human understand-ing. The line is characteristically cited in connection with the country's more arcane bureaucratic procedures. Some things just are beyond comprehension.

When Dante makes his confession of faith to Saint Peter in the *Par-adiso*, he offers a grammatical gloss on the mathematical conundrum of three-yet-one:

> e credo in tre persone etterne, e queste
> credo una essenza, sì una e sì trina,
> che soffera congiunto "sono" ed "este."   (*Par.* xxiv 139–41)

> (and I believe in three eternal persons, and I believe them to be
> one essence, an essence so one and so threefold that it takes
> "are" and "is" simultaneously.)

That is to say, the verb *to be* is used of it correctly in the plural (*are*) and in the singular (*is*) at the same time. (This last line confirms to my mind that Dante has the temperament of an intellectual and not of a mystic.) For Dante, as for his Christian contemporaries, Judaism was the neces-sary precursor of Christianity. The New Testament is the fulfilment of the Old. Islam, by contrast, was seen as a heresy of Christianity, a devia-tion from true belief which deprived the church of a significant portion of its adherents.

The Trinity is nowhere mentioned directly in the Bible. The Ortho-dox church sees a premonition of it in the three angels in the Old Tes-tament who visit Abraham. Passages in the New Testament refer to the Holy Spirit, and New Testament scholars see the doctrine of the Trinity adumbrated in Paul's words at the beginning of Ephesians. The doctrine was elaborated in the early years of the Christian church (the three or four centuries immediately following the crucifixion). It was formulated definitively by Saint Augustine in the fourth century in his *De Trinitate*. Augustine tells a story that conveys the disproportion between what human beings are capable of understanding and the mystery of a three-personed God. He dreamed he was walking on the seashore, pondering the mystery of the Trinity, when he came across a child playing with a seashell. He asked the boy if he thought he would ever succeed in emptying the ocean with the shell. The child, wise beyond its years, replied, "Certainly, before you've understood the essence of God."

Human beings cannot by their own efforts understand the Trinity: only revelation (God's grace) gives us knowledge of it. Had such knowledge been accessible to unaided human reason, the great philosophers of the ancient world, who had intuited the oneness of the divinity, would have understood it. As it is, they are forever excluded from the beatific vision because revelation was unavailable to them.

The double nature of Christ, human and divine (*una persona in due nature*), is the other central numerical mystery of Christian belief. While all Christians accept this last doctrine as fundamental to their faith, not all of them accept the doctrine of the Trinity. (Isaac Newton was famously the fellow of Trinity at Cambridge who did not believe in the Trinity. The Unitarian church rejects the doctrine in its very name.) But for most Christians, and certainly for Dante and his contemporaries, belief in the Trinity is one of the tenets that defines the essence of their faith.

The Old Testament tells us that God created man "in His image and after His likeness." Dante draws a distinction between the two terms: "in His image" can only properly be said of human beings, whereas "after His likeness" can be said of the whole of the created world. That created world bears the mark of its maker: *totum universum nihil aliud [est] quam vestigium quoddam divine bonitatis*. "The whole universe simply *is* an imprint of divine goodness" (*Mon.* I viii 2). *Vestigium* is literally a "footprint." Twenty-first-century physicists at CERN in Switzerland using the Large Hadron Collider have used this same image of the footprint to describe what they were looking for and indeed have now found—evidence from which they infer the existence of the Higgs boson, which is believed to give mass to all the other subatomic particles.

Dante uses another image, with a venerable tradition going back to Plato, when he talks of God's creative act in fashioning the universe in terms of wax and seal. Just as wax bears and reveals the image of a seal that has been imprinted on it, and the imprinted image remains visible even when the seal itself cannot be seen, so the cosmos displays in itself evidence of its divine origin: *occulto exisente sigillo, cera impressa de illo quamvis occulto tradit notitiam manifestam.* "Although the seal is hidden, the wax stamped by the seal (hidden though it is) yields clear knowledge of it" (*Mon.* II ii 8).

Specifically, it is the order apparent in creation that mirrors the divinity:

> Le cose tutte quante
> hanno ordine tra loro, e questo è forma
> che l'universo a Dio fa simigliante.   (*Par.* i 103–5)

> (All things have an order which relates them one to another, and this is the form which makes the universe resemble God.)

We have it on biblical authority that this order in creation can best be understood by means of mathematics or numbers: *omnia mensura et numero et pondere disposuisti.* "You have arranged all things by measure and number and weight" (Wisdom of Solomon 11, 21). The search for mathematical principles in how the universe is structured is endorsed by the Bible.

This is not quite the same thing as the "argument from design," which evolutionary biologists have dismantled with such relish. The argument from design holds that just as the intricacy and complexity of design which enables a watch to fulfil its purpose requires the existence of a watchmaker, so too the universe must have a maker. (The argument was put forward by the seventeenth-century theologian William Paley, whose ideas provided Richard Dawkins with the title of his book *The Blind Watchmaker.*) In Dante's thinking the emphasis is not on teleology, but on genesis. That is, it is not on the fulfilling of a purpose, but rather on the beauty and perfection of the blueprint or ground plan that lies behind the cosmos and reflects those qualities in its creator. Dante is not so much interested in trying to prove the existence of God through the ingenious workmanship displayed in the created world as he is in understanding how that world works.

The search for mathematical principles at work in the structure and functioning of the universe is not just a medieval preoccupation. That same search continues to drive the endeavours of modern physicists and astronomers. When Nobel Prize–winning theoretical physicist Richard Feynman (a Jewish nonbeliever) talked of his awe in the "mathematical beauty of nature," he was expressing an emotion that Dante and his contemporaries would have understood perfectly.

If both human beings and the whole of creation reflect the likeness of their creator, and that creator is a three-personed deity, then it would not be surprising to find the principle of threeness operating in the observable world. As it happens, the existence of such a triform principle in the natural world had the backing of a scientific tradition going back to Aristotle in the fourth century B.C. Aristotle's analysis of the evidence could not have been influenced or distorted in any way by Christian doctrine. It thus seemed to Dante and other medieval thinkers that science and theology came together independently to offer an account of reality that was in some respects very similar. This convergence between two antithetical traditions was powerfully persuasive.

To Dante and his contemporaries threeness seemed to offer a key to understanding the nature of reality in two fundamental areas of human experience. What is it to be and to function as a human being? What is the nature of the physical world we live in? The modern terms for these areas of enquiry are *physiology* and *psychology* on the one hand, and *astronomy* and *physics* on the other. It hardly needs saying that we are working with a conceptual model that predates Colombus, Copernicus, Darwin, Einstein, Freud, and all the thinkers who have shaped our modern understanding of the world and human behaviour. But it is a model that is subtle, sophisticated and deeply engaging nonetheless.

Aristotle's account of the great chain of being places human beings above plants and animals in the natural order. Yet human existence presupposes and includes the qualities and capacities of plants (plants are alive) and of animals (animals have sensation and the power of autonomous movement). It has in addition a third distinctive quality, consciousness or self-awareness. This is the capacity to reflect on one's self and on one's own experience, the capacity we call rationality or reason. As a human embryo forms in the womb, these are three successive stages of its development. The first two capacities are the product of nature or natural forces; the last came to be seen in Christian thinking as a direct gift from God. The end product of gestation is a human being: a single soul which is alive (like a plant) and experiences sensation (like an animal) and turns things over in its mind or reflects on itself (the uniquely human attribute):

> un'alma sola
> che vive e sente e sé in sé rigira.   (*Purg.* xxv 74–75)

(a single soul which lives and feels and reflects on itself.)

The tautness and energy of the single line that lays out this threefold way of being is typical of Dante when he is setting out complex ideas.

Human beings are three-in-one creatures. It is their rationality, their distinctively human quality, which makes it appropriate to say of them that they are made not just "in God's likeness" but "in His image" as well.

The mind or rational faculty has in its turn three powers, and thus three modes of operation or ways of functioning. As Dante enumerates them in the poem, they form another perfect line:

> memoria, intelligenza e volontade   (*Purg.* xxv 83)

(memory, understanding and will).

Augustine argued that the interconnected working of these three powers constitutes the soul's trinitarian nature. Before we dismiss this account of our mental functioning as a product of a medieval theologian's obsession with threes, we might reflect that the twentieth century's most influential account of human psychic life is equally threefold: Freud's id, ego and superego.

Scholastic theology adds to Aristotle a threefold explanation of how the cosmos was created. Dante touches on this idea near the end of the *Commedia*, in the ninety-sixth of the one hundred cantos, as we approach the vision of God. This is an exceptionally important moment of transition, when he is about to leave behind the created world and enter the Empyrean, beyond time and space. To describe the moment of creation Dante uses the arresting image of a three-stringed, three-arrowed bow:

> Forma e matera, congiunte e purette,
>> usciro ad esser che non avia fallo,
>> come d'arco tricorde tre saette.   (*Par.* xxix 22–24)

> (Form and matter, conjoined and in their pure state, came forth
>> into being with no imperfection, like three arrows from a
>> three-stringed bow.)

It requires an imaginative leap on our part to engage with the vital and mysterious image of the three shooting arrows which bring the world into existence. (Modern accounts of the big bang are, for nonspecialists, equally mysterious, though less poetic.) We can read most of the *Commedia* before we need to grapple with the problem of how the world came to be, the medieval equivalent of modern particle physics and astronomy.

What Dante means is something like this. At the moment of creation three orders of reality were brought into being, as though shot forth simultaneously like three arrows from a three-stringed bow. A three-stringed bow might seem a purely hypothetical idea, but one early commentator assures us that such things really existed. Those three orders of reality are: pure form, pure matter, and form conjoined with matter. Pure form is the Empyrean and the angels. Pure matter (or prime matter, as it is often called) is the matter from which the sublunary world is made—that is, our world of human experience, the earthly globe and its atmosphere right up to the level of the moon. Form conjoined with matter is the heavens, containing the circling heavenly bodies, the stars and planets, which mediate between the earthly and the divine. The whole of creation thus mirrors the three-personed deity who brought it into being. Our world is the central core or kernel of a system that is tripartite by its very nature.

There is no suggestion that the three persons of the Trinity are individually responsible for different aspects of creation. Nor was Augustine suggesting that different aspects of human mental activity can be matched to different persons of the Trinity. It is the pattern of three in one which is significant. The image of the shooting arrows compresses into an arresting poetic image a complex history of debate about the nature of creation that had developed over many centuries.

The material world, our world, is enclosed within and surrounded by the circling heavens; beyond the heavens is the Empyrean, where God, the angels and the souls of the blessed exist; the heavens mediate between the human and the divine. This view of humanity's place in the universe, bounded by time and materiality but permeable by higher influences, remained the conceptual model of the cosmos accepted by all educated people in Europe until well beyond the Renaissance. This is a Christianised version of the Ptolemaic model inherited from the ancient world, that of a system of nesting crystalline spheres (see Fig. 28 on p. 161).

The last part of Dante's journey, as it is recorded in the *Paradiso*, takes him from the material, sublunary world through the planetary spheres in order to leave behind the earthbound existence of humankind and reach the divinity, beyond the outermost visible revolving sphere of the fixed stars. (The stars are "fixed" in that their relationship to one another never changes, but the sphere which carries them revolves.)

For Dante it is not just the fabric of the cosmos that yields the pattern of three-in-one. Time and space, the defining conditions of human existence, embody a three-in-one principle: past, present and future; height, depth, width. Human activity within our world also lends itself surprisingly well to analysis in these terms. Three key kinds of human functioning—thinking, doing, making—all invite examination, albeit in somewhat different ways, in terms of three stages or three aspects or three constituent parts that make up a single whole.

Thinking in its most rigorous form involves logic, the discipline which enables one to argue from premises to valid conclusions. Aristotle analysed the forms valid arguments can take, and Aristotelian formal logic remained a part of the education of any serious thinker throughout the Middle Ages. Syllogistic argument, as it is called, was for Dante and his contemporaries the only legitimate "scientific" way to arrive at the truth—a discipline that provided a rigorous training in detecting fallacies in arguments, and that enabled one to frame conclusive proofs when arguing a case.

Syllogistic argument is structured around the number three. A syllogism has three terms, and these terms are arranged in three propositions (major premise, minor premise, conclusion). Thus, to give the simplest possible example of a syllogistic argument: all *a* is *b* (major premise); all *b* is *c* (minor premise); therefore all *a* is *c* (conclusion). The very possibility of valid deductive argument, of proving propositions to be true or false, involves a structure that is tripartite in nature. For Dante, logic (think-' ing) provides an unassailable model of a central human activity which embodies the trinitarian principle of three-in-one.

Indeed any kind of human action proves on examination to involve three stages. Action in effect constitutes a "practical" syllogism, a three-stage operation with a major premise, a minor premise and a conclusion. Dante spells out the parallel between the procedures involved in taking action and in arguing logically to a conclusion (*Mon.* I xiv 7). The procedures in each case consist of three steps, the third of which "concludes" the operation (with a deduction in the case of a syllogism, or, in the practical sphere, with the carrying out of an action). Here is a simple example of a practical syllogism. I'm thinking of planting a hedge. Major premise: privet and Leylandii plants make good hedges. Minor premise: my garden is small, so it would not be wise to plant Leylandii. Conclusion: I plant privet.

In a remarkable and little-commented-on phrase in one of his letters, Dante refers to Christ the syllogiser, as though the peace which marked the birth of Christ could somehow be understood as the completing of a syllogistic argument (Epistle v 9). Although it is difficult to be sure exactly what Dante had in mind, he seems clearly to be implying that a syllogistic pattern could be detected in the broad pattern of history as well as in individual human actions. Dante is not the only medieval thinker to write as if syllogisms can be perceived in places where we would not normally think of looking for them. The twelfth-century monk Honorious of Autun tells us that syllogisms lurk in the Bible: *syllogismi latent in sacra Scriptura, ut piscis in profunda aqua* ("syllogisms lie hidden in holy Scripture, like a fish in deep water"). The syllogism, with its three-in-one form, is a structuring principle perceptible to the medieval mind not just in formal logic but in sacred texts and in the broad pattern of history.

But even more than thinking, making is the human activity that it is most illuminating to consider in relation to the number three and the notion of three-in-one. Dante saw direct parallels between the act by which God created the universe, the workings of the natural world, and the productive activities of human beings who operate within that world. In other words, in our everyday lives we are all engaged in activities that are in some way analogous to the way God works. The relationship between these three things—in Dante's terminology, between God, nature and art—is described in *Inferno* xi.

Virgil and Dante are still in the circle of the heretics. In canto x Dante had talked to the two Florentines who thought there was no afterlife, Farinata degli Uberti, the Ghibelline leader, and Cavalante de' Cavalcanti, the father of his friend Guido. Now he and Virgil strike out towards the centre of the circle on a path that leads down to a valley. But the stench that rises from the valley stops them in their tracks. They huddle against a sarcophagus which, we are told in an almost throwaway aside, bears the name of Pope Anastasius—a pope guilty of heresy. Dante suggests they make good use of the time while they get used to the stench. Virgil starts by explaining the layout of hell and the way sins are ordered within it.

At the end of this lengthy explanation (to which we will return shortly), Dante has a final question which bears directly on the subject of human making. Why is usury sinful? To modern readers usury—the charging

of interest on loans—may seem relatively innocuous. It is, after all, the
basis of capitalism and modern Western society. But in medieval times it
was regarded as morally wrong, and still is in Muslim societies today. All
of us would probably agree that the actions of loan sharks who prey on
vulnerable people, or of hedge-fund speculators who make vast sums of
money by playing the money markets, are morally questionable. Virgil's
explanation of why usury is a sin leads him to explain the relationship
between God, nature and art, and their connected ways of working. His
explanation helps us to understand how Dante saw human making.

Virgil describes the relationship between God, nature and art as a
family one, citing Aristotle explicitly as his authority.

> "Filosofia," mi disse, "a chi la 'ntende,
>   nota, non pure in una sola parte,
>   come natura lo suo corso prende
> dal divino 'ntelletto e da sua arte;
>   e se tu ben la tua Fisica note,
>   tu troverai, non dopo molte carte,
> che l'arte vostra quella, quanto pote,
>   segue, come 'l maestro fa 'l discente;
>   sì che vostr' arte a Dio quasi è nepote."   (*Inf.* xi 97–105)

> ("Philosophy," he said, "to those who understand it, explains—
>   and not just at one point—how nature takes its course from
>   the divine intellect and its art; and if you read your *Physics*
>   attentively, you will find, quite near the beginning, that your
>   [human] art follows her [*sc.*, nature] as closely as it can, as a
>   pupil follows a teacher, so that your art is, as it were, God's
>   grandchild.")

Human art or making, being the child of nature, which in its turn is
the child of God, is (metaphorically) the grandchild of God. This idea is
not Dante's invention. It has a long history, and continues well into the
Renaissance. Two hundred years after Dante we find Leonardo da Vinci

saying exactly the same thing in his notebooks. It is worth looking at this family relationship a little more closely.

Human making, from the work of the humblest artisan or craftsman to artists in the full modern sense of the word ("creative" artists, as we now call them), is intelligible in terms of a threefold principle in two quite different ways. The first involves the relationship between the artist's mind, his material and his tools. The second considers human creativity against the wider background of the way the universe works. For Dante there was a strict parallel between these two things. Understanding the first will throw light on the second.

Any act of making involves three components. There is a mental component: the idea in the mind of the person making the object. There is an instrumental component: the tools necessary to make it, and skill in their use, often a result of training, though natural aptitude plays its part. And there is a material component: the raw material to be worked on, essentially a given, though choice may be involved. Thus, to use the classic example, a potter has a mental picture of a pot he wishes to make. He uses his instrument or tool (his potter's wheel) to fashion his material (potter's clay) into a pot of the size and shape he has in mind. No object can be fashioned without these three essential elements.

The interconnected working of these three elements in human making has a precise parallel in the operations of the natural world. Art mimics nature. But the meanings of the terms *art* and *nature* here are not quite the same as in modern usage. Art is the skill or expertise or craftsmanship required to make something, or indeed to bring to successful completion any human action. The art of navigation will enable the captain of a ship to bring it safely into port. Nature is specifically the workings of the heavenly bodies and their influences.

Dante spells out the analogy between art and nature explicitly: "just as art is found at three levels, in the mind of the craftsman, in his instrument, and in the material shaped by his craft, so too we can consider nature at three levels. For nature is in the mind of the first mover, who is God; then in the heavens, as in the instrument by means of which the image of eternal goodness is set forth in fluctuating matter" (*Mon.* II ii 2).

Let's try to translate Dante's thinking out of the rather abstruse language of medieval philosophy. God is the divine artificer. Nature, the revolving heavens, is God's instrument, the tool set with which he worked in fashioning the world. The mind of God, like the mind of the potter (or the poet), is where the creative act is initiated. The heavens (including the heavenly bodies such as planets and constellations) function like the potter's tools. Prime matter, like the potter's clay, is the material shaped and fashioned by the divine creative act. God's likeness is imprinted on prime matter through the mediating influence of the heavenly bodies, just as the potter's mental picture of the pot he wishes to make is "imprinted" on the clay he works with his wheel.

Dante's understanding of the idea of nature thus breaks down into yet another trinity, in that it can be considered under three aspects. It is God's art, in his mind (*Mon.* I iii 2). It is the instrument of that art, the heavens (*Mon.* II ii 3). And it is the end product of that art, the natural world we inhabit and the laws which govern it. God creates; nature generates; man makes. What God creates is eternal (*e io etterna duro*, we read over the gate of hell). What nature generates is subject to change and decay, birth and death. What man makes, being part of the natural world, is subject to that same law of corruption. Man-made things do not last, though they may outlast their maker.

Dante's is a world where the number three seems to be a key to understanding reality in many of its fundamental aspects. The numerical pattern three-in-one is built into the very structure of things, a medieval version of what modern thinkers call a "fractal." (Fractals are self-similar patterns: at whatever degree of magnification one uses, one sees the same pattern reappearing.) It is perhaps not surprising that Dante used the principle of three-in-one to structure his imagined world and the poem which celebrates it. What is astounding is how successfully he did so.

The *Commedia* as a product of human making—a man-made work of verbal art—was designed by Dante to embody the three-in-one principle. With satisfying symmetry, it does so both in its overall structure and in its individual component parts. The poem has three sections—*Inferno, Purgatorio, Paradiso*—which constitute one poem, the *Commedia*. The basic building block from which it is constructed is the *terzina* or tercet, a single metrical unit consisting of three lines. Dante invented this metrical scheme, and by so doing made three-in-oneness a part of the very fabric of his poem.

Purgatory, like the Trinity, is not mentioned in the Bible. There are isolated hints and phrases in the Scriptures that theologians from the early Middle Ages on developed into a fully fledged theory. By the thirteenth century the idea was a matter of lively debate within the church. But it was only at the Second Council of Lyons in 1274, when Dante was nine years old, that the notion of a transitional state of cleansing and purification was officially accepted as Catholic doctrine. (Twenty years earlier, a letter of Pope Innocent IV to the Greeks had offered the first definition of purgatory, a definition which remains authoritative today.) Historians explain this development as an attempt on the part of the church to extend its power. Control over the afterlife became a way of increasing control over this life, through the twin institutions of prayers for the dead and the sale of indulgences. The Second Council of Lyons stated that the prayers of the living help the dead in the afterlife (and we have seen how Dante exploits this idea in his encounter with his old friend Forese Donati). Indulgences bought remission of sin for those in purgatory by the payment of money to the church on earth.

For Dante the intervention could not have been more timely. With the birth of purgatory a binary system became tripartite. Previously there had been a series of polarised opposites (not just heaven and hell but also the corresponding notions of good and bad, light and dark, the realm of God and the realm of Satan). Purgatory introduced a third, intermediary state—a state that retains two of the fundamental characteristics of human existence, time and change. It became possible for Dante to create a poetic structure which is trinitarian. This satisfyingly echoes and alludes to many of the other kinds of three-in-oneness we encounter in the world of human experience and human history.

We can only speculate about how Dante came to invent the metre of the *Commedia*, the *terza rima* (for an account of how he may have come to invent it, see "The Invention of the *Terza Rima*" on pp. 265–66). *Terza rima* consists of a linked series of *terzine* or tercets. It is the linking mechanism—

the rhyme-scheme—that is the stroke of genius. The first and third lines of the tercet rhyme, but the middle line introduces a new rhyme, which will then become the paired rhyme of the following tercet. This intricate interlocking sequence of rhymes creates a chain of *terzine*—each tercet generates the next one, and is incomplete without it. Each tercet provides closure but also a new opening. There is a strong sense of action concluded but also suspense about the action still to come. Dante's metre propels us forward in a way that makes it ideal for a narrative poem.

In addition to the strong sense of forward propulsion, there is another advantage of the metre, less often noted. Although it is a tightly controlled metrical form, which both tests and displays the poet's virtuosity, a canto written in *terza rima* can be as long or as short as the poet chooses. Dante's cantos vary from 115 to 160 lines. The form offers significant flexibility in canto length without sacrificing exacting technical demands. Furthermore, each canto is symmetrical, in that it starts and ends with a double rather than a triple rhyme. All the rhymes occur three times except the opening and closing pairs. The scheme can be represented as a sequence of letters: aba bcb cdc . . . xyx yzy z.

A further practical advantage of the metrical scheme is that it makes Dante's poem virtually tamperproof. Medieval scribes often took liberties with the texts they copied. They cut bits they didn't like, added lines of their own, rather as a musician might treat a score as a basis for skilled improvisation. There is a whole scholarly industry devoted to scribal reworkings of the *Roman de la Rose*. Given the controversial nature of some of Dante's material, scribes might well have been tempted to censor the text by cutting awkward passages. But this is virtually impossible with the *terza rima*. Any cut will leave a text which is obviously botched. Any attempt to add material is likewise doomed to failure. The demanding form ensures that only a very good poet can handle it with confidence. In English, as has often been noted, the phonetic character of the language—the dense consonant clusters, which are so unlike the natural musicality of Italian, with its higher proportion of vowels—makes *terza rima* especially demanding. Only Shelley's unfinished "The Triumph of Life," the poem on which he was working at the time of his death, gives a sense of effortless mastery of the form which recalls Dante.

The use of *terza rima* means that the manuscript tradition of the *Commedia* is in one respect unproblematical. The six hundred or so complete surviving copies of the poem present no missing portions and no interpolated passages of any significance. Any desire to suppress material must be fulfilled in a very different way. One obvious passage for censorship is the episode where Dante has the corrupt popes stuffed head down in holes in the rock. In the beautiful illuminated British Library ms. Yates Thomson 36, this offending material in *Inferno* xix has been scraped away from the parchment, leaving only a blank page with its exquisitely executed gold initials ranged down the left-hand side as a ghostly reminder that something has gone missing. Gold leaf was clearly too valuable just to scrape off. The editor of the *Commedia* will face many problems connected with the textual substance and linguistic form of the poem, but doubt about its length and shape will not be one of them.

If we narrow our focus to the single lines of which the tercet is composed, it is important to take on board that Italian versification is syllabic, not accentual. What this means is that Dante's lines are measured out very precisely by the number of syllables in them. Every line of the *Commedia* has—must have—eleven syllables. The hendecasyllable form is fundamentally different in its governing principles and its rhythmic structure from the English iambic pentameter which it superficially resembles in length. For a full account and a comparison between the two, see "The Hendecasyllable" on pp. 263–65.

The mirroring of patterns in the poem from overall structure to individual metrical unit goes even further. Because each line of the poem has eleven syllables, each tercet has thirty-three syllables, matching the thirty-three cantos in *Purgatorio* and *Paradiso*. *Inferno* has an extra canto, which functions as a preface to the whole work, making a total for the poem of one hundred cantos, the perfect number. (The perfect number is ten squared, ten itself being a perfect number, or so medieval mathematicians thought, because it is the sum of $1 + 2 + 3 + 4$.) So the poem is not just a verbal artifact but a mathematical one as well.

These are not trivial considerations. The poem incorporates numerical patterns which echo the very ordering or structuring of reality itself. Dante, as the creator of that poem, is mirroring the creative activity of his maker. Human art (or creativity as we now call it) is the grandchild of God.

Anyone determined to see even more intricately complex number patterns incorporated into the shaping and structure of the poem will have no trouble finding them. It would have been difficult for medieval readers to detect such patterns, since lines were not numbered in medieval manuscripts. But that does not mean Dante was not using them to build his poem. He gives a strong sense of a shaping and ordering imperative dictating his procedures. Sometimes he articulates this explicitly, as when he describes drinking the waters of the river Eunoë at the end of *Purgatorio*:

> S'io avessi, lettor, più lungo spazio
> da scrivere, i' pur cantere' in parte
> lo dolce ber che mai non m'avria sazio;
> ma perché piene son tutte le carte
> ordite a questa cantica seconda,
> non mi lascia più ir lo fren de l'arte.   (*Purg.* xxxiii 136–41)

> (Reader, if I had more space to write, I would continue to sing in part the sweet drinking that never would have sated me; but because all the pages set out for this second cantica are full, the bridle of art does not allow me to go further.)

Modern printed editions, where the lines of the poem are numbered, make it easier for us to detect number patterns. But there are losses as well as gains with print technology. The layout of the poem in medieval manuscripts emphasises the structure of the tercet in a way that modern editions do not. A typical manuscript page puts a large capital letter, often decorated with a coloured line through it, hanging left at the beginning of each tercet (irrespective of the syntax), so that the three-in-one basis of the metrical scheme is subtly yet constantly reinforced by the layout of the text on the page. And although lines are not numbered in manuscripts, there

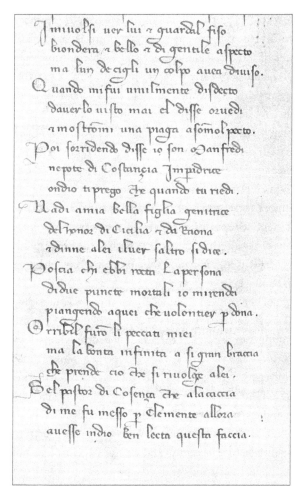

Fig. 30 The layout of the text on the page, with the large
initial letter at the beginning of the tercet hanging left, reinforces the three-in-one structure of the *terza rima*.

is clear evidence that early copyists sensed the importance of numerical
considerations.

There are of course practical reasons why scribes and those who prepared the parchment for copying needed to be alert to the number of

lines in the text. The preparation of the manuscript (the number of pages needed, the layout of those pages) required precise numerical calculations. Traces of those calculations are still visible in some manuscripts. Intriguingly, some very early manuscripts have almost exactly one hundred leaves, making one wonder if in an ideal version of the poem the tally should have been precisely one hundred. A more mundane practical consideration is reflected in one early manuscript in a number visible at the end of each canto. It represents a calculation of the number of tercets in the canto, plus one for the concluding line. This figure probably served to work out the payment owed to the scribe.

The number three, and more particularly the notion of three-in-one, is an important structuring principle in the way Dante imagines the three realms of the afterlife. This is true both in the geographical and the conceptual sense. Geography and theology (or ethics) characteristically go hand in hand.

In the pit of hell sins are classified under three major headings (incontinence, violence and fraud), and they are distributed across nine circles. Sins of incontinence are sins committed by people who lack willpower, like the gluttons. They harm only the perpetrator. Sins of violence commonly involve other people as victims, but violence can also be used against oneself (suicide, profligacy) or against the deity. The circle of violence thus divides into three subcircles. Violence against the deity in its turn has three further subcategories: violence against God (blasphemy), violence against nature (sodomy) and violence against *arte*, human productivity or honest toil (usury).

Sins of fraud—guile or deceit—are worse than sins of violence because they involve misusing reason, the distinctively human attribute, to harm another person. There are two major kinds of fraud. The first is fraud practised against any fellow human being. This heterogeneous and, to modern eyes, rather surprising collection of ten sins includes the simoniacs stuffed head downwards in their holes and the counsellors of duplicity wrapped in their tongues of flame; but it also includes pimps, flatterers, hypocrites, impersonators, counterfeiters and thieves. The second kind of fraud is treachery—that is to say, fraud perpetrated against those to whom one is linked by a special bond of trust. As we have seen, there are four such categories: family members, one's birthplace or political party, guests, and benefactors. With its many subdivisions, fraud occupies the eighth and ninth circles in hell, which between them take up almost half the physical terrain and narrative space of the *Inferno* (cantos xviii–xxxiv).

Treachery, the opposite of love, is punished in the icy wastes at the bottom of the pit. In Dante's value system ice rather than the traditional fire and brimstone punishes the worst sins in hell. This is anything but an orthodox view. Ice reflects the coldheartedness of the traitor, who acts with no trace of normal human warmth or empathy. The worst sin of all is to betray a benefactor towards whom one should feel grateful.

At the very centre of the pit—imprisoned at the centre of the earth, which is the centre of the universe, the point farthest from God—is Lucifer. His huge figure looms like a windmill on the horizon, embedded in the ice from the waist down. His three monstrous mouths in his three grotesque heads are a clear parody of the Trinity. They chew on Judas, Cassius and Brutus, the betrayer of Christ and the betrayers of Caesar (who in Dante's eyes was the founder of the Roman Empire). Lucifer is immobile, impotent, defeated. He weeps with rage, having become no more than an instrument of divine justice. But he makes no sound: no wailing, no lamentation, no cursing, no words at all. There is no possible risk that a reader might feel, as Blake felt about Milton's Satan, with his heroic posturing and stirring rhetoric, that the author was of the devil's party without knowing it.

Dante's scheme of hell is a blend of Aristotle's and Cicero's notions of wrongdoing and evil (the key texts are Aristotle's *Ethics* and Cicero's *De officiis*), with the addition from Christian thinking of heresy. If we add to the nine circles an initial area just inside the gate, where we find those who are excluded from hell because they did neither good nor evil, living their lives *sanza 'nfamia e sanza lodo* ("without disgrace and without praise"), then again we have the perfect number ten. This unorthodox entry zone embodies a notion unique to Dante, not known from theological sources or from Greek philosophy. It is here that he passes by in contemptuous silence the shade of the man *che fece per viltade il gran rifiuto* ("who out of cowardice made the great refusal"): Celestine V, whose abdication allowed Boniface to become pope. No one here is named. The souls run after a whirling banner moving at great speed, in pointed contrast to their failure to commit to any cause or take any moral stand during their lives. The vast number of souls guilty of this fatal moral indifference is captured in the line echoed by T. S. Eliot, expressing the same sense of astonishment at the sheer numbers of people, when he sees the crowds flowing over London Bridge: *i' non averei creduto / che morte tanta n'avesse disfatta*: "I had not thought death had undone so many."

Like hell, the mountain of purgatory divides into three major geographical sections: ante-purgatory at the foot of the mountain, the mountain itself with its seven terraces, and the Garden of Eden at its summit. Again the overall total is nine. The seven terraces subdivide into three groups arranged in the pattern 3 + 1 + 3. The richly imagined geographical detail of this conception is in striking contrast to other medieval representations of purgatory: as noted, the few that exist usually conceive of purgatory simply as an annex to hell. Dante by contrast melds the seven capital vices on to the geography of the imagined mountain. If we count ante-purgatory with its two distinct zones as two sections rather than one—the zone for those who died excommunicate, like Manfred, and the zone for those who repented only at the moment of death, like Bonconte—then purgatory, like hell, has ten sections rather than nine.

Like hell and purgatory, paradise has three major sections, and nine sections altogether, again with the number seven playing an important role. There are seven planetary spheres and thus seven heavens to be traversed before Dante reaches the heaven of the fixed stars and then the *primum mobile*, making a total of nine circling spheres or heavens, which constitute the created world. The hierarchy of heavenly spheres matches the hierarchy of the nine angelic orders, the guiding intelligences which cause the spheres to revolve. The angelic orders are arranged in three tiers, each with three subdivisions. Modern readers will have heard of the two bottom tiers: angels and archangels. They may also recognise the names of the two top tiers: seraphim and cherubim. They are unlikely to know the intermediate ranks of angels, in ascending order after archangels: thrones, dominations, virtues, principalities, and powers. (There was some disagreement among theologians about the correct order.) Dante's matching of the nine angelic orders to the nine revolving spheres is not part of official church doctrine and appears to be another mark of his originality.

In paradise the model is based on Dante's understanding of astronomy. Seven planets (the only ones known in the Middle Ages) circle the earth. The fixed stars lie beyond the planets and constitute the eighth sphere. The ninth sphere is the *primum mobile*—the largest sphere of all, enclosing the whole created world. It is transparent and invisible to observers on earth, but necessary to explain the motion of the other spheres. Nine becomes ten if we add the Empyrean—beyond time and space, the place where God is and where the souls of the blessed reside.

This is the barest schematic outline of the geography of the otherworld in the *Commedia*, showing the structural symmetries between the three realms. Dante varies the pattern in many different ways, and draws on a vast array of sources to flesh it out.

The number three is often an important element in the shaping and structuring of individual cantos and episodes in the *Commedia*. Just one example can serve to show the possibilities. The encounter with the proud in *Purgatorio* xi can be thought of as a triptych, a painting on three panels. Here on the first terrace of the mountain Dante meets and talks to three penitent souls. The central figure is Oderisi da Gubbio, an artist famous for the brilliant colours of his painted manuscript illuminations. His pride is pride in artistic talent. He is flanked on one side by a soul called Omberto Aldobrandeschi, who sinned through pride in social status and noble ancestry, and on the other by Provenzan Salvani, whose pride was in political position and power.

But canto xi is itself flanked by two parallel and balanced cantos, x and xii. So it is a triptych which itself becomes the central panel in a larger group of three cantos—a triptych within a triptych.

The purgatorial routine for those on every terrace of the mountain includes meditating on examples of the virtue opposed to the sin they are purging, and on examples of that sin itself punished. With his characteristic willingness to use pagan stories alongside Christian ones, Dante draws the examples from both the Bible and classical literature. The examples of the virtue always begin with an episode from the life of the Virgin Mary, followed by episodes from the Scriptures and/or Roman or Greek history or myth. These examples present themselves to the sinners in a different way on every terrace. On the terrace of pride they take the form of rock carvings which the sinners contemplate as they move around the terrace.

In canto x the virtue of humility (the opposite of pride, and therefore a proper subject for meditation by those who sinned through pride) is illustrated by three rock carvings. First we see the annunciation to the Virgin Mary, *umile e alta più che creatura* ("humble and exalted more than any other creature"), as she will later be described. She is the supreme example of the virtue of humility, paradoxically also more exalted than any other human being. Then we see David, the Old Testament prophet and author of the psalms, dancing naked in front of the ark as a sign of his humility before the Lord, while his wife Micol gazes down at him scornfully from the palace window. Finally we see the Roman emperor Trajan, who ruled from 98 to 117 A.D. and who was renowned for his integrity, on horseback surrounded by his troops, with eagle standards fluttering in the breeze. He stops to listen to the plea of a widow who begs him to avenge her son's death before he sets out for war. A divine hand has carved these stories with wondrous artistry into the vertical inner rock wall of the terrace. Although they are marble reliefs, the workmanship is so miraculously lifelike that gazing at them one seems to smell the incense and hear the words.

As Dante "reads" the stories carved into the marble surface, his gaze is drawn onwards, from left to right, and this sets him walking in the right direction around the mountainside. In purgatory he always turns to the right (*must* always turn to the right), just as in hell he had always turned to the left, the "sinister" side. Thus his journey through the afterlife follows a continuous helical trajectory, as he first spirals down into hell and then spirals upwards around the mountain of purgatory.

The examples of pride punished in canto xii are carved into the floor of the terrace, to be trodden underfoot by those who walk along it, like tomb carvings in a church floor. There are thirteen such examples, ranging from the fall of Lucifer to the fall of Troy (another instance of Christian and pagan examples coexisting in Dante's Christian afterlife).

The proud are bent double under huge stones they carry on their backs, an obvious corrective to the pride they displayed in life. Dante, listening to the first speaker, turns his face down the better to hear him, adopting the symbolic posture of humility with bowed head. A second shade recognizes him and calls out, gazing at him with difficulty from under the crushing weight of the stone. Dante in his turn recognises the shade:

> "Oh!" diss'io lui, "non se' tu Oderisi
>   l'onor d'Agobbio e l'onor di quell'arte
>   ch'alluminar chiamata è in Parisi?"   (*Purg.* xi 79–81)

> ("Oh!" I said to him, "aren't you Oderisi, the honour of Gubbio and the honour of that art which in Paris is called illumination?")

The shade's reply is exemplary for a penitent soul. He deflects the compliment and praises the work of another, better artist:

> "Frate," diss'elli, "più ridon le carte
>   che pennelleggia Franco Bolognese;
>   l'onore è tutto or suo, e mio in parte.
> Ben non sare' io stato sì cortese
>   mentre ch'io vissi, per lo gran disio
>   de l'eccellenza ove mio core intese."   (*Purg.* xi 82–87)

> ("Brother," he said, "the pages coloured by the brush of Franco from Bologna smile more brightly; the honour is now all his, and mine only in part. I would certainly not have been so courteous while I was alive, because of the great desire to excel on which my heart was set.")

Then Oderisi reflects on the vanity of human achievement. How short a time artistic reputations last, unless an age of decadence follows. He spells out the point with reference first to contemporary painters, and then to poets, in lines among the most famous in the *Commedia*.

> Credette Cimabue ne la pittura
>> tener lo campo, e ora ha Giotto il grido,
>> sì che la fama di colui è scura.
> Così ha tolto l'uno a l'altro Guido
>> la gloria de la lingua; e forse è nato
>> chi l'uno e l'altro caccerà del nido.   (*Purg.* xi 94–99)

> (Cimabue thought he held the field in painting, and now Giotto
>> is all the cry, so that Cimabue's fame is darkened. In the same
>> way one Guido has taken from the other the glory of lan-
>> guage; and perhaps someone is born who will drive both of
>> them from the nest.)

Cimabue, with his linear, stylised Byzantine forms, had been preeminent in painting. But his reputation has been eclipsed by Giotto, just one generation later (Cimabue was Giotto's teacher). Giotto's new capacity to represent solidity and depth on the flat surface of the painted panel or wall was revolutionary for Italian art. The Uffizi Gallery in Florence shows large panel paintings of the Madonna by the two artists in the same room, bringing Dante's point instantly to life. (Several early commentators tell us that Dante met Giotto in Padova when he was working there on the Arena Chapel frescoes: a pleasing idea.)

In poetry the same thing has happened. Guido Cavalcanti has eclipsed Guido Guinizzelli—and perhaps the man is born who will outdo both of them. This can only be a not-very-veiled allusion to Dante himself, destined to become a greater poet and more famous than either of the two Guidos. The fact that this claim should be made on the circle of pride, showing Dante the author committing the very sin the sinners here are purging, is one of the piquancies of the episode. Some readers think that

Dante for this very reason cannot possibly be referring to himself. The explicit allusion to Cavalcanti is a timely reminder of Dante's own poetic origins. This last generous reference to the friend of his youth is at the same time a confident assertion of his own role as a poet destined for greatness.

Dante's outdoing of his *primo amico* is asserted but immediately undercut by Oderisi's reflection on the vanity of all human fame or reputation.

> Non è il mondan romore altro ch'un fiato
> di vento, ch'or vien quinci e or vien quindi,
> e muta nome perché muta lato.
> Che voce avrai tu più, se vecchia scindi
> da te la carne, che se fossi morto
> anzi che tu lasciassi il "pappo" e 'l "dindi,"
> pria che passin mill'anni? ch'è più corto
> spazio a l'etterno, ch'un muover di ciglia
> al cerchio che più tardi in cielo è torto.   (*Purg.* xi 100–8)

> (Worldly fame is nothing but a breath of wind, which blows now
> from one side and now from another, and changes its name
> because it changes direction. What more fame will you have
> if you put off your flesh when it is old [i.e., if you die in old age]
> than if you had died before you stopped saying *"pappo"* and
> *"dindi"* [i.e., in infancy, before you stopped using baby talk],
> when a thousand years have passed? which is a shorter time
> compared with eternity than the blinking of an eyelid com-
> pared to one turn of the slowest circling sphere in heaven.)

The time frame suggested here, which puts artistic achievement and reputation in the context of eternity, is infinitesimally small.

Instances of the number three are everywhere in the *Commedia*. They are everywhere, of course, in other aspects of ancient and medieval and indeed modern life and thought. In the biblical account of the nativity there are three wise men, who are traditionally taken to represent both the three regions of the world (Europe, Asia, Africa) and the three ages of man (youth, maturity, old age). In medieval and Renaissance paintings of the nativity one of the Magi is usually black, to represent Africa, and one is old and another young. The three sons of Noah also represent the three parts of the world, and are connected with the idea of migration and linguistic diversification.

In myth there are three Graces, three Furies, three Fates. In children's stories we have three little pigs, three billygoats gruff, three bears whose porridge Goldilocks tries. In nursery rhymes there are three blind mice. Shakespeare gives us three witches in *Macbeth*, three caskets and three suitors in *The Merchant of Venice*. The number three seems to have an irresistible appeal for writers and storytellers at whatever level of sophistication.

Whether we see instances of the number three in the *Commedia* as always having a trinitarian resonance is a matter of individual temperament. But what is not in any doubt at all is that the notion of three-in-one was for Dante as he crafted the poem a vital dimension of his shaping and ordering imagination.

Writing "in numbers"—that is, in a strict metrical form based on numerical principles—is a way of imposing a pattern of meaning on (or drawing out a pattern of meaning from) the mass of experience and language of our everyday lives. All poets aim to create a verbal structure whose shape and form render more perceptible or forceful the reality that it embodies. Some go so far as to make the physical shape of the words on the page mirror the thing those words describe. George Herbert's poems "Easter Wings" and "The Altar" come to mind.

Other poets pattern language rhythmically to connect in less visual but still vital ways with the subject matter of their poems. The classical scholar Bernard Knox has suggested that the Homeric hexameter mirrors in its structure and rhythm the wanderings of Odysseus and his final safe return home, so that the poem's overarching theme is enacted rhythmically in every line of the text. A. S. Byatt points to a similar perfect match between the metre of the *Rubáiyát of Omar Kayyám* and its content: "Our hearts beat five times for each of our breaths, and the iambic pentameter FitzGerald used is the rhythm of our passing lives themselves."

What is unique in the *Commedia* is the perfect match between the belief system it embodies—philosophical and scientific as well as theological—

and the structural and metrical form the poet invented to express it. William Empson is reported to have planned to write a long poem in *terza rima* on troilism (a sexual entanglement with three partners), where subject and stanza form might have achieved a similar perfect match, but it seems the plan was never carried out. That Dante found a way of incorporating the mathematical pattern which was at the core of his religious belief so satisfyingly into the structure and fabric of his poem is one aspect of his genius. The satisfaction for the reader is aesthetic and intellectual as much as religious.

T. S. Eliot used the term *objective correlative* to describe the relationship between the verbal artefact, the poem, and the state of mind the poet is expressing in it. We might use the term in relation to Dante in a slightly different way. The *Commedia* is an objective correlative not so much of the poet's state of mind as of the whole of the medieval world as he understood it, incorporating numerical principles that embody and reflect his deepest beliefs about the nature of reality and of human life.

Galileo said that mathematics is the language in which God wrote the universe. A nonbeliever might prefer a formulation in the passive: mathematics is the language in which the universe is written. And if, in the words of Ian McEwan in *Saturday*, the genotype is "the modern variant of a soul," then modern readers have an additional source of pleasure, for the genotype exhibits a triform principle just as surely as Augustine's version of the soul did. Dante would surely have felt awe and delight had he lived to hear what molecular biologists discovered as recently as 1959—that a principle of three-in-one is the very basis of life itself at a molecular level. The unit of meaning in the genetic code is a triplet—a sequence of three base pairs which specifies a particular amino acid. As the sequence of words in a book creates meaning, the sequence of triplet codons gives rise to the sequence of amino acids in a protein—and from this sequence its form and therefore its function arises. And from the properties of proteins comes all of biology. So in the book of life itself, every word has three letters. Modern readers who love Dante's poem must surely find this knowledge curiously satisfying.

7.

Words

A poet is, before anything else, a person who
is passionately in love with language.
—W. H. AUDEN

Poetry cannot afford to lose its fundamentally self-delighting
inventiveness, its joy in being a process of language
as well as a representation of things in the world.
—SEAMUS HEANEY

IT MIGHT SEEM A DOOMED UNDERTAKING TO TRY EXPLAINING TO
English readers what is remarkable about the language of the *Commedia*.
But the rewards of a close encounter with Dante's language are so great
that it has to be worth a try: *I' mi sobbarco* ("I'll take it on"). That a pithy
Dante quotation immediately springs to mind seems an auspicious start.
We can begin with a few facts, then move on to Dante's own views on
language and the kind of language he thought best suited to poetry.
Those views changed dramatically in the course of his life. Understanding
how they changed will take us a long way towards engaging with the
language of the poem.

First, our facts. Eighty percent of the *Commedia* is immediately intelligible to a native speaker of Italian today. Conversely, the two thousand
core words of modern Italian vocabulary are all there in Dante's poem.

By contrast, today's native speakers of English find Chaucer's *Canterbury Tales*, written two generations after the *Commedia* in the late fourteenth century, largely unintelligible in the original Middle English ("A povre widwe, somdeel stape in age"). It is unthinkable that a reading of Chaucer in the original could draw the kind of audiences that Tuscan actor Roberto Benigni's readings of Dante in large public venues such as Piazza Santa Croce in Florence have regularly attracted in recent years in Italy.

It is sometimes said that by choosing to write his masterpiece in Italian rather than in Latin Dante invented the Italian language. Just what does this extravagant-sounding claim mean? Attempting to understand *why* he chose to write the poem in the vernacular takes us to the heart of this question—and to the heart of his achievement as a poet.

Dante nowhere explains his decision, although he had given a great deal of thought to the relationship between the two languages, and written about it twice at some length. There is a story that he began writing an early version of the *Commedia* in Latin but gave up after the opening lines and started again some time later in Italian. If the story is an invention, its medieval inventor went to the trouble of supplying the opening lines of the poem in Latin. Boccaccio, who reports the story in his life of Dante, quotes them.

Dante's view of the place of language in the great scheme of things is the medieval view, ultimately derived from Aristotle, but adapted to a Christian perspective by the inclusion of angels. He believed that human beings are midway on the scale of creation between animals and angels. Mind, or rationality, is humanity's distinctive feature. Language is its necessary instrument. Animals have no need of language, since they act on instinct alone, and have no thoughts to communicate. (Apparent examples of talking animals, he explains, prove to be mere mimicry.) Angels communicate directly by thought transference. Only human beings—that unique hybrid of materiality and spirit, of body and soul—need language.

The nature of language, with its two essential features (sound and meaning), reflects this hybrid character. Language must have meaning in order to convey thought from one mind to another. It must have sound because human beings are embodied creatures and meaning can only be conveyed from one embodied mind to another through the senses.

The views outlined in the last two paragraphs are those expounded in the opening chapters of Dante's unfinished treatise—written in Latin—on vernacular speech: *De vulgari eloquentia*. (The title translates as *Eloquence in the Vernacular*: I will refer to it henceforth as *De vulgari*.) These are views the author shares with his educated contemporaries. But this nucleus of conventional thinking is embedded in what is in other respects a work of startling originality.

Dante was already an established poet when he wrote the *De vulgari* in the early years of his exile, around 1304–1307. The lyric poems collected in the *Vita nova* and the longer philosophical poems which followed would ensure his reputation as a major poet even without the *Commedia*. The main thrust of the treatise is to analyse the kind of language a poet should adopt when aiming to write with distinction in Italian. Its method is to examine systematically the varieties of Italian spoken in different regions in Italy. Dante had by now been in exile for a number of years and had travelled widely in the peninsula. He is speaking from firsthand knowledge. His conclusion is that no spoken variety of Italian is a fitting medium for serious poetry. The aspiring poet must aim at a linguistic form that somehow transcends regional variation but is nonetheless intelligible to all.

This ideal form of the language is found, in effect, only in good poetry, though it is not without civic and political resonance. In the course of producing his theoretical defence of this ideal, Dante cites phrases to illustrate the shortcomings of all the regional forms of the language. There are some regional forms—Sicilian, for example, or Bolognese—for which a case might be made, at least in theory. But even they on examination fall short of the ideal. Others can be dismissed out of hand as uncouth.

Dante doesn't pull his punches. The language of Forlí is so soft that men speaking it sound like women. The language of Verona, Vicenza and Padua is so harsh that the women sound like men. The people of Puglia *turpiter barbarizant* ("use vile barbarisms"). The people of Aquileia and

Istria *crudeliter accentuando eructuant* ("belch forth with a harsh accent"). If the Genoese lost the letter z they would not be able to speak at all. Appalled revulsion at what is judged rough and coarse, to be shunned by any person of linguistic sensitivity, underlies the search for the elusive ideal form of the language which poets who hope to write well should use.

Dante has, almost by accident, produced a pioneering work in the study of dialects, albeit one with a strong ideological and literary under-pinning: the first-ever survey—with examples—of the dialects of Italy. To illustrate the ideal form of the language he is advocating, he quotes from earlier and contemporary vernacular poets (himself included) who have written with distinction. The treatise is thus also the first system-atic survey of vernacular poetry in Italy, an embryonic history of the nascent literature. That literature had begun less than a hundred years earlier at the court of Frederick II in Palermo, as a transplant from south-ern France and the troubadours; from there it had then spread to the Tuscan cities. No one before Dante had attempted to write about it.

The *De vulgari* is a monument to extreme linguistic fastidiousness. Within the *vulgare illustre* (the "illustrious vernacular"), as Dante calls the ideal form of the language he is describing, forms are rejected which are too local or regional, or too concrete and earthy. Even words with certain sounds or combinations of sounds are best avoided: the "double" consonants z and x, for example (both z and x consist of two distinct pho-nemes); or double l or r; or l or r following certain consonants.

Furthermore the whole book is informed by a strict principle of hierarchy. Traditional rhetorical training taught that there were high, middle and low subjects, and that one's style must be adapted accord-ingly. There is a form of language that is better than other forms, and there are metres and subjects for poetry that are superior to or "higher" than other metres and subjects. Dante is working within this traditional framework in seeking to define and pinpoint the "illustrious" form of the vernacular. The best poets will use the best, most demanding metri-cal form (the *canzone* or ode). They will write only on the three subjects best suited to this lofty form (prowess in arms, amorous passion, and moral rectitude—in effect war, love and virtue). And they will use the exalted form of the language he is so painstakingly seeking to describe. The three suitable subjects for serious poetic composition equate with the threefold nature of human beings—that is, with what medieval thinkers called the vegetative, sensitive and rational components of the human soul (*De v. E.* II ii 6–7).

The *De vulgari* articulates Dante's thinking at a precise, relatively early, point in his poetic career. But he clearly changed his mind at some point after writing it. The way he writes in the *Commedia* stands in stark contrast to the ideas expounded in the treatise. To use the treatise to illuminate Dante's practice in the *Commedia*, as Ezra Pound on one occasion sought to do, is fundamentally misguided.

Indeed, in the *Commedia* Dante is at pains to correct a misconception about the very nature of language enshrined in the earlier work. Thinking about language, its nature and its use as a medium for poetry, powered his activity as a writer throughout his career. His ideas changed radically, and to understand the originality and power of the language of the *Commedia* one must understand this evolution.

The misconception about language which Dante endorses in the *De vulgari* and then corrects in the *Commedia* is a crucial piece in the puzzle. In the treatise he describes language as God-given, created by God (*concreatam*) along with Adam, its first user. In this view language is a given, not a human creation. In the *Commedia*, with brilliant appositeness, it is Adam himself who enlightens the pilgrim on the nature of language. Adam, the first human being—the first speaker—is the last person Dante encounters in the poem before he emerges from the created world into the Empyrean, beyond time and space.

Dante and Beatrice have reached the sphere of the fixed stars, the outermost visible sphere, which encloses all the nested smaller spheres of the planets. Dante has just undergone a searching viva examination on faith, hope and charity conducted by the three apostles who were closest to Jesus: Peter, James and John. He has satisfied his examiners that he is fully up to speed on the three theological virtues. Now suddenly a new luminous presence is with them: Beatrice explains that it is Adam. Dante, addressing him as *padre antico / a cui ciascuna sposa è figlia e nuro*

Fig. 31   Botticelli: Dante meets Adam.

("ancient father, to whom every bride is both daughter and daughter-in-law"), begs him to speak.

Intuiting the pilgrim poet's eager interest, and formulating his questions for him, Adam reveals that God gave him not a language, but the capacity for language. He himself invented the language he used by exercising this innate capacity. He speaks of *l'idïoma ch'usai e che fei* ("the language that I used and that I made"). Language use from its very beginning was a creative activity. Adam is setting out a principle with radical implications for all poets.

Adam also clarifies a related point. In the *De vulgari* language was said to be in origin both God-given and immutable. Until humans in their folly attempted to reach heaven by building the Tower of Babel (*turris confusionis*, "the tower of confusion"), there had been no linguistic change. The splitting into different languages was a punishment inflicted on sinful humanity for hubris—the third great punishment of the human race after the expulsion from the Garden of Eden and Noah's flood. Were it not for human presumption, we would all still speak the language of Adam, the treatise asserts. That language was Hebrew.

Now in paradise Adam explains to Dante that this is wrong. Language, being a human creation, was mutable from the very beginning. It never was static and fixed. The punishment for Babel was that people could no longer understand one another; it was not linguistic change as such. In this dramatic encounter with his authoritative interlocutor the mature Dante tactfully but forcefully corrects the mistaken views on language expounded by his younger self—a striking example of his evolving thinking incorporated into the fabric of the poem.

These issues—whether language is God-made or man-made, whether linguistic change is inherent in the nature of language or is a punishment for human sin—may seem to us merely academic. But the care with which Dante constructs and places his encounter with Adam alerts us to the fact that for him they were profoundly important. The encounter comes near the end of the poem, in canto xxvi of the *Paradiso*. The pilgrim protagonist is about to leave behind the world of human endeavour and achievement; the poet is close to completing his poem, the triumphant outcome of his own struggle with language to create his masterpiece. This is his final word on the nature of language, the fruit of a lifetime's meditation on the medium of his craft. His mature conviction, expressed through Adam, that language is of its essence man-made, not God-made, and that mutability is inherent in its very nature, provides a key to some of the issues which lie at the heart of his achievement.

The *De vulgari*—an investigation into the most suitable form of the vernacular for a practising poet to use—is written in Latin. The implications of this curious fact are worth pondering. The treatise opens with a brief but pregnant statement contrasting two different kinds of language: vernacular speech (what we call a "mother tongue") and a second-order language (a *locutio secundaria*), which is acquired by study and training and is essentially a language of culture.

Latin in the Middle Ages was just such a *locutio secundaria*. It was the language of higher education, of science, of philosophy, of theology. It was the language of public record: all the surviving documents about Dante's life and the Florentine commune are in Latin, as are all his letters. It was *the* language necessary for abstract thought, for exploring and expressing the speculative (higher) side of man's nature. There was no tradition of writing on these subjects in any vernacular language. The *De vulgari* is written in Latin precisely because it is a serious examination of a theoretical subject, intended for an elite audience of intellectuals and fellow poets. What strikes us as odd—that this subject, the art of writing well in the vernacular, should be discussed in Latin—might well have seemed unremarkable to Dante's contemporaries.

A *locutio secundaria* is acquired by study and effort, by training and practice, at a school or institute of higher learning, unlike the vernacular, which is picked up without conscious effort or rule learning as an infant and toddler at the knee of one's mother or nurse. All human beings have a natural language, a vernacular; only a small educated minority (in Dante's time, almost exclusively male) has a *locutio secundaria*, a language of culture. After sketching out this distinction, and noting that other cultures (the Greeks, for example) have had their own *locutio secundaria*, Dante makes a bold and unqualified statement. Of the two kinds of language, the vernacular is the nobler: *nobilior est vulgaris*. This is a radical, even scandalous, point of view.

The function of a *locutio secundaria* like Latin is that of preserving history and culture—the sayings and deeds of great men of the past—for the benefit of later generations. The language of culture gives access to the history of civilisation. The written record is preserved in a *locutio secundaria* precisely because of its stability—the very thing that sets it off from the vernacular. It is the mutability of natural languages, vernaculars, which makes the invention of a "secondary" language of culture necessary.

Dante's sensitivity to the fact that languages change through time, as well as geographically through space, is already a striking aspect of his thinking. His sensitivity to the second, as we have seen, is the fruit of his travels throughout Italy. He is able to report from experience that the inhabitants of Milan speak differently from the inhabitants of Verona, and the Neapolitans differently from their closely related neighbours in Gaeta. But there is more. Six hundred years before George Bernard Shaw's *Pygmalion* showed Professor Henry Higgins identifying with unerring accuracy, just from the way they talked, which part of London people had grown up in, Dante notes that within a single city the inhabitants of one street speak differently from those of another. Within Bologna the speech of Borgo San Felice differs from that of Strada Maggiore. The two streets now run out like the spokes of a wheel from the city centre in opposite directions; in Dante's time Strada Maggiore was within the city walls, while Borgo San Felice lay just outside them. Dante even recognises what modern linguists call idiolect when he comments that individual families have their own characteristic and distinctive ways of speaking not shared with neighbouring families.

The fact that languages change through time is asserted with equal confidence. If the inhabitants of Pavia of a thousand years ago were to return to their native city, he says, they would think it taken over by foreigners, so different would the speech of its modern inhabitants be from what their ancestors spoke. When he meets his great-great-grandfather Cacciaguida in paradise, his forebear speaks to him *non in questa moderna favella*, "not in this modern speech"—that is, not the way people speak now in Dante's time.

The issue of language change is always at the heart of the argument when the question of the relative value of Latin and Italian is considered. On this question Dante says different things—even apparently contradictory things—in different contexts. In the *Convivio*, written in these same early years of exile before he started writing the *Commedia*, his starting point is a more conventional and conservative one. Here he is writing in Italian, explicating and commenting on some of his own longer poems, and defending his use of the vernacular for a function (a learned commentary) normally reserved for Latin. Once again, and characteristically, he is breaking new ground, pushing at the linguistic barriers.

In a lengthy and rather defensive opening section, he sets out his reasons for choosing to write his commentary in Italian. Among them is his desire to reach an audience that would not otherwise have been able to read it and benefit from it. He provides an evocative list of such people: "princes, barons, knights and many other noble people, not only men but women," for there are many worthy men and women who are *non litterati*, who do not know Latin.

Yet here—arguing that to have used Latin for the commentary on his poems would have been inappropriate, since a superior language would have been at the service of an inferior one—Latin is said to be superior to Italian in three respects. It is nobler (*più nobile*), because immutable, unchanging; it has greater expressive power (it can deal easily with abstract concepts, whereas the vernacular struggles to express them); and it is more beautiful because it is governed by *arte* (rules, grammar) and not by *uso* (custom, usage).

In the *De vulgari*, by contrast, "nobler"—*nobilior est vulgaris*—correlates with quite different qualities: primacy in time (the vernacular existed before any language of culture); universality in place (all human beings in all ages and everywhere in the world have had some form of speech, a vernacular, but not all of them have a language of culture); and (a crucial argument) naturalness—the language of culture by contrast is *artificialis*, artificial, conventional, not a product of nature. The very quality which in one context is a sign of superiority (being a product of *arte* rather than of nature) is now a measure of inferiority. The intellectual ferment of these years that preceded his embarking on the *Commedia* is nowhere reflected more clearly than in the unresolved contradictions apparent in these passages from roughly contemporaneous works.

Dante never explicity addresses these contradictions. The contrast between the two different ways of conceptualising the relationship between the languages suggests that a seismic shift had occurred in his thinking—a shift which is never described or explained but which Adam's words in the *Paradiso* allow us to reconstruct. Proceeding with all due caution, we can attempt to formulate it as follows. Latin is immutable: this fact remains constant. In Dante's early thinking its unchanging nature emulates the quality of fixity that was there in the God-given language at the beginning. It is therefore closer to the ideal than the vernacular, whose mutability is a direct consequence of sin (the hubris of the attempt to build the Tower of Babel to reach heaven).

But if the notion of a God-given language is abandoned, and language was mutable from the very beginning, as Adam tells us, then mutability is no longer a marker of sinfulness and the fixity of Latin is no longer something which makes it closer to God. Its unchangeable nature no longer signifies superior value, but is rather something artificial imposed on it by man. Depending on which perspective one adopts, *arte* takes on very different meanings: skill, distinction, artistry, in the first view, or artifice, artificiality, conventionality in the second.

Dante's deepest creative instincts must have led him to his conclusion about the value of the vernacular, but the confident assertion *nobilior est vulgaris* sits oddly in a text where very traditional views about the language of Adam still provide the overarching theoretical framework of the argument—an argument that touches on such arcane questions as: what was the first word spoken by Adam? can we trust the biblical account which says Eve was the first speaker? (The answer to this second question, incidentally, is no. It would be irrational to think a woman spoke before a man.) It is deeply satisfying that in the *Commedia* Adam himself provides one missing piece in the puzzle.

Something Dante never discusses directly is the relationship between classical and medieval Latin. He lacks our modern awareness that by his time medieval Latin had become an impoverished and fossilised version of what was once a living language. He is aware that the three Romance languages he knows well—Italian, French and Provençal—derive from a common parent language (just as the Germanic languages and the Greek languages do), but it is clear that he does not identify that parent language with Latin. Indeed he seems to suggest exactly the opposite: that Latin as a *locutio secundaria* is something that men sat down and invented—a kind of Esperanto *avant la lettre*, though an immensely more successful version of it, devised at some unspecified point in human history precisely to fulfil the function of preserving culture in that large part of Europe where the romance languages are spoken. Dante was not alone in this (to modern eyes) highly eccentric view.

He says, for example, that Italian seems to be closer to Latin than to either French or Provençal, and he illustrates this by saying that the *inventores* ("devisers") of Latin relied more heavily on Italian, as reflected in their choice of *sic* to mean "yes," very close to Italian *sì*. We of course know that Italian *sì* derives from Latin *sic*—but only because we have the benefit of hindsight derived from the relatively recent discipline of historical linguistics. The view that Latin was the ancestor of Italian was first voiced by the early humanist Poggio Bracciolini a century after Dante died; and it was not until the pioneering work of the great philologists several centuries later that the true genealogical relationship between the languages was mapped in detail.

It is instructive to consider the case of Virgil: both what we know about him and what Dante thought about him. Virgil wrote in Latin, obviously, but for Dante Latin is a *locutio secundaria*, a second-order language of culture. Virgil was born in Mantua, so in Dante's view he grew up speaking the vernacular of Mantua; but that, as Dante himself insisted, would have been very different from the way Mantuans spoke in Dante's time, some thirteen hundred years later. He lived in Rome, so—we may think—may have adapted to that form of the spoken language, just as Dante, born in Florence, spent his later life in other parts of the country and may have adapted his speech patterns in part as a consequence. In the *Commedia*, Virgil is on one occasion addressed as: *tu . . . che parlavi mo lombardo* ("you . . . who were speaking lombard just now"). Dante the author is clearly showing him to be recognised as a speaker from northern Italy, just as Dante the character in the poem is frequently recognised as Tuscan or Florentine by his speech or accent.

What seems certain is that Dante would not have given the name Latin to the form of the vernacular Virgil spoke. He seems to assume that the linguistic picture (local varieties of language alongside an overarching Latin secondary language which was the same for everybody) was identical in Virgil's day to his own day, though the issue is not addressed directly and is somewhat clouded by related terminology. The generic term for Italians in the *Commedia* is *latini*. The term identifies anyone born in Italy (*terra latina* at *Inf.* xxvii 27 and *Inf.* xxviii 71, derived from Latium, modern Lazio, the area around Rome) and thus anyone Dante will be able to converse with easily. Encounters with a new group of shades sometimes begin with him enquiring if any of them are *latini*—i.e., Italians. The noun *latino* in the singular is a generic term for language or speech (e.g., at *Par.* xii 144 and *Par.* xvii 35). In medieval Latin in Italy the normal term for the Latin language is *gramatica* (the word is used in this sense in *De v. E.* I xi 7 and II vii 6).

The most perplexing question of all is what Dante thought the relationship was between how Virgil spoke and how he wrote. The modern answer to that question is that Virgil wrote an immensely more refined and polished version of the language he spoke, both of which we call Latin. But the modern reader will be struck by the fact that the solution Dante is proposing in the *De vulgari* for a poet aspiring to write well— that he should write a form of the language that is much more refined and polished than any actual spoken form of the vernacular—looks curiously similar to our historical understanding of Virgil's situation.

The language Dante is advocating and describing in the phase of his career when he wrote the *De vulgari* is, paradoxically, beginning to look very much like a *locutio secundaria*, a language as far removed from everyday colloquial vernacular speech as it is possible to imagine, whereas he had started out with the confident assumption that in writing of the vernacular he was treating a language utterly different in kind from Latin. One reason he broke off writing the treatise may well be that the internal contradictions of his position were beginning to become clear to him and were ultimately unresolvable.

The *De vulgari* is a fascinating work, but English poetry lovers who read it for the first time may find it disappointing, even disconcerting. Writing about writing poetry, Dante says nothing at all about the creative process, the inner workings of the poet's mind. There is none of the thrilling rhetoric of Shelley's "Defence of Poetry" with its eloquent claims for the status of poetry ("at once the centre and circumference of knowledge") and of poets ("the unacknowledged legislators of mankind"). There is nothing about the unique sensibility required to be a poet, and the involuntary nature of genuine poetic inspiration and composition ("the mind in creation is as a fading coal, which some invisible influence, like an inconstant wind, awakens to transitory brightness . . .").

Nor are we given any sense of what the process of composition is like, as we are so strikingly in the essays of, say, Seamus Heaney, when he talks of "the feeling of the writing experience . . . the almost muscular sensation that rewards successful original composition." Instead we have an argument that moves from the very general and schematic (the nature and history of language) to the minutely particular (the phonetic qualities of certain sounds which make them unsuitable for use in poetry). The treatise illuminates the way Dante thought about writing poetry when he was young—the thinking reflected in the poems of the *Vita nova*, for example—but it is only by knowing where he started that we will understand how fundamentally different is the language and poetry of the *Commedia*.

The *De vulgari* is abandoned unfinished—abandoned, indeed, in mid-sentence. The *Convivio* is also abandoned unfinished (only four of a planned fifteen books were written). The creative imperative takes over from the theorising impulse. Dante starts to write the *Commedia*, and he writes in the vernacular, not in Latin. In the light of the vastly ambitious new creative project, it seems, the earlier expository and explanatory ones had simply lost their interest for him. His thinking on language had evolved to a point where doing was more important than theorising, writing more important than talking about how to write. All the more so since his approach to language in the new work was to be something entirely and radically new.

Dante left no theoretical statement which systematically explains the thinking about language which lies behind the *Commedia*—nothing that does for the *Commedia* what the *De vulgari* does for the earlier poems. We have hints, as in the encounter with Adam; and we have the poem itself as it embodies that thinking. Dante is a poet in whom the writing of poetry is always accompanied by critical reflection on his art. When he reflects on his art in the *Commedia* he does so in two characteristically concrete ways: in scattered references to the arduous process of composition and the challenges it presents, and in the dramatic form of encounters with other poets. These encounters, some of the most moving in the poem, complete the sketch of early vernacular poetry already adumbrated in the treatise. There is a strong linguistic dimension to both these themes—the artist's struggle with his medium and his taking stock of the achievements of his predecessors—but the treatment is poetic and dramatic rather than expository and explanatory. We piece together our sense of what is at issue. The experience of reading the poem is our only guide.

What is distinctive about Dante's use of language in the *Commedia*? The language of the poem is often described as "plurilinguistic." The term was first used by Gianfranco Contini, who contrasted Dante's stylistic practice in the poem with the "monolinguistic" style of Petrarch, a poet born not quite forty years later, whose remarkable sonnets in praise of a lady called Laura are collected in his *Canzoniere*. The terms *plurilinguistic* and *monolinguistic* reflect the radically different approaches to language of the two poets in the creation of their masterpieces.

Petrarch's is a practice of exclusion, of rigorous selectivity. Nothing is admitted into his poems that is not exquisitely harmonious, musical, polished, refined (and, it goes without saying, decorous). We are close to the prescriptiveness of the *De vulgari*. By contrast Dante's practice in the *Commedia* is inclusive. Just as no aspect of human life is unworthy of scrutiny and representation, so no aspect of human language that has expressive potential is ruled inadmissible.

The point can be underlined neatly by comparing the body parts named in the two poets' poems. In the *Canzoniere* we read of Laura's hand (*la bella man*), her foot (*il bel piè*), her eyes, her hair: this is the sum total of details of her physical appearance. The poems are obsessively about her, yet she remains a numinous presence rather than a physical one. By contrast, in the *Commedia* the rich lexicon of body parts includes jaw, shins, belly, breasts, fingernails, guts, buttocks and buttock cleft, intestines, arse. Farting and shit are mentioned. The physicality of our embodied state, including its disfigurement and dismemberment in the punishments of hell, is recorded with relish, not squeamishness—linguistic relish.

Botticelli matches Dante's linguistic verve with his own graphic élan when he draws the devil who summoned his troops with an unorthodox signal: *ed elli avea del cul fatto trombetta* ("and he had made a trumpet of his arse"). To recoil with distaste, on the grounds that such words offend against good taste and linguistic decorum, is to fail to get the point.

Fig. 32   Botticelli: The devil's trumpet.

"Low" words are necessary to depict the brutal realities of hell. These in turn evoke the reality of the human moral degradation punished there. And when words from this low register are used in *Paradiso*, as they famously are on occasion, the effect is electrifying. Reveal everything you have seen, Cacciaguida tells Dante, *e lascia pur grattar dov'è la rogna* ("and let them scratch where the itch is"). Christ did not say to the apostles, Beatrice reminds him, *"Andate, e predicate al mondo ciance"* ("Go, and preach idle gossip to the world"). The person who usurps my place on earth, Saint Peter tells him, has turned the Holy See (built over Peter's tomb) into a *cloaca del sangue e de la puzza* (a "sewer of blood and stench"). We feel a frisson of shock at coming across these low words in the context of paradise.

The lower down in hell Dante travels, the harsher his language needs to be to do justice to the horror he experiences. As he nears the bottom, he describes this challenge to his linguistic resources:

> S'ïo avessi le rime aspre e chiocce,
>> come si converrebbe al tristo buco
>> sovra 'l qual pontan tutte l'altre rocce,
> io premerei di mio concetto il suco
>> più pienamente; ma perch' io non l'abbo,
>> non sanza tema a dicer mi conduco;
> ché non è impresa da pigliare a gabbo
>> discriver fondo a tutto l'universo,
>> né da lingua che chiami mamma o babbo. (*Inf.* xxxii 1–9)

> (If I had harsh and raucous rhymes, such as would be fitting for
>> the wretched hole on which all the other rocks press down,
>> I would squeeze out the juice of my thought more fully; but
>> since I do not, it is not without fear that I set about writing;
>> for describing the bottom of the whole universe is not an
>> undertaking to take on in jest, nor one for a tongue that calls
>> mummy or daddy.)

Yet even as he laments his inability to find the "harsh and raucous rhymes" needed for the task, his rhymes are strikingly harsh and raucous. The difficult rhymes on -*occe* and -*abbo*—each of them so difficult that they occur only once in the 14,233 lines of the poem—enact the very phonetic reality he says he despairs of achieving. The Russian poet Osip Mandelstam was struck by the auditory colouration of these lines, drawing attention to the physical sensations in the mouth and lips as the words *abbo, gabbo, babbo* are articulated, and inviting us to see Dante not, as he is so often seen, as the spokesman for a religious orthodoxy, but as someone delighting in and experimenting with the phonetic qualities and possibilities of language itself. Virtuoso rhyming is particularly prominent in the *Inferno* as Dante exploits the *rime aspre e chiocce* with at times pyrotechnic brilliance.

Another harsh rhyme used only once in the poem is *-egghia*. It occurs in a passage which shows low speech in its simplest and least controversial sense: language used to evoke the concrete practical realities of daily life in the kitchen or the stable, far removed from the elegant courtly pursuits of the higher social orders.

Dante and Virgil have reached the last subdivision of the eighth circle in hell, where various kinds of "falsifiers" are punished. The sinners are afflicted with different forms of disease; they lie on the ground or drag themselves along, unable to stand upright. The two described here are covered with leprous scabs which they scratch off in a frenzy of itchiness.

> Passo passo andavam sanza sermone,
>   guardando e ascoltando li ammalati,
>   che non potean levar le lor persone.
> Io vidi due sedere a sé poggiati,
>   com'a scaldar si poggia tegghia a tegghia,
>   dal capo al piè di schianze macolati;
> e non vidi già mai menare stregghia
>   a ragazzo aspettato dal segnorso,
>   né a colui che mal volontier vegghia,
> come ciascun menava spesso il morso
>   de l'unghie sopra sé per la gran rabbia
>   del pizzicor, che non ha piu soccorso;
> e sì traevan giù l'unghie la scabbia,
>   come coltel di scardova le scaglie
>   o d'altro pesce che più larghe l'abbia.   (*Inf.* xxix 70–84)

(Meanwhile we walked on without speaking, looking at and
    listening to the sick people, who could not stand upright. I
    saw two of them sitting leaning against one another back to
    back, as we prop one pan against another to heat them up,
    blotchy from head to foot with scabs; and I never saw a curry-
    comb wielded so furiously by a stable boy whose master was
    waiting for him, or by someone anxious to get to bed, as each

of them used his nails to bite into himself on account of the
great rage of the itchiness, which has no other relief; and their
fingernails dragged off the scabs, as a knife does the scales of
a bream or of some other fish which has bigger ones.)

Here the balanced pans set on the fire to heat, the energetic clean-
ing of a fish by scraping off its scales—the vividly recognizable depiction of familiar homely events—help to anchor the surreal reality of an
imagined otherworld. Dante is unmatched at evoking the daily domestic
activities of ordinary life with a compelling realism which makes the
horrors of hell believable.

A striking aspect of the *Commedia* is the high proportion of direct
speech it contains: well over half the lines in the poem are dialogue. Dialogue is intrinsically dramatic, and allows for demotic expressiveness
in the low style which Dante exploits with great verve. Usually these
exchanges are brief, but on one occasion in the depths of hell we witness
a vulgar brawl between two sinners who exchange insults at length in
what is in effect a *tenzone*. The minor poetic genre in the low register
used jocularly by Dante and his friend Forese Donati is now reprised in
the deadly serious context of eternal damnation.

The circle of the falsifiers includes liars (falsifiers of words) and counterfeiters (falsifiers of coinage). The two sinners who squabble are Sinon
of Troy, who famously lied about the Trojan horse, and Mastro Adamo
(Master Adam), who had been burnt at the stake in Florence in 1281 for
putting counterfeit florins into circulation—a particularly reprehensible
sin because it threatened the economic prosperity of the city. The gold
florin, stamped with the Florentine lily on one side and the city's patron
saint, John the Baptist, on the other, had been minted from 1252 onwards
and had quickly become the medieval equivalent of the American dollar
today, an internationally secure and trusted currency, acceptable even to
Saracens. No city had ever minted its own gold coins before. The florin
was a symbol both of sovereignty and of economic power. Each florin
contained twenty-four carats of pure gold: in Mastro Adamo's florins
three of those carats were base metal.

The counterfeiters are suffering from hydropsy, their bodies grotesquely disfigured, with enormously distended bellies and huge swollen lips. The liars suffer from a violent fever and are bathed in stinking sweat. Sinon takes it amiss when he is identified as "the false Greek Sinon of Troy." He reacts violently by striking Mastro Adamo's taut lute-shaped belly, which resounds like a drum. Mastro Adamo retaliates by striking Sinon across the face. There follows an almost ritualistic exchange of insults between the two sinners—an ancient Greek whose infamous role in the breaching of the walls of Troy is recounted in book II of the *Aeneid*, and an obscure Englishman of no particular renown, whose execution in Florence when Dante was an adolescent must have left a lasting impression on him. A more unlikely pairing of verbal sparring partners it would be hard to imagine—testimony to the daring of Dante's imagination, and a dramatic enactment of the afterlife as leveller across time as well as social class. Dante is transfixed listening to thirty lines of taunting, mesmerised by the explosive energy of the language in all its idiomatic and colloquial force.

Dante's experimenting with language in the 1290s had taken two forms. There was the *tenzone* with Forese, with its ebullient embracing of linguistic coarseness and harshness. And there were the poems known as the *rime petrose* ("stony poems"), written for a "stony" lady who is indifferent to his passion. Here the phonetic qualities of the words give a palpable sense of strenuous effort to match style to a hard, resistant subject matter. Together, it is now clear, these formed the indispensable stylistic apprenticeship for describing the depths of hell.

Another word often used to suggest the linguistic inclusiveness and multifariousness of the *Commedia* is *encyclopedic*. The poem is an "encyclopedia of styles." Where the earlier works aspire to be encyclopedic in their content—the *De vulgari* an encyclopedia of linguistic and poetic theory, the *Convivio* an encyclopedia of general philosophical and scientific interest—the *Commedia* is encyclopedic not only (and more comprehensively) in its content (every aspect of human life) but also in its language. Indeed the two are indivisible.

In the *Commedia* Dante draws not just on Italian itself at every register or stylistic level but on regional and dialect words, on foreign languages, and even on invented languages. Pluto, the infernal guardian of the fourth circle in hell, greets Virgil and Dante with the exclamatory and not easily intelligible (but clearly hostile) *"Pape Satàn, pape Satàn aleppe!"* Lower down in hell Nimrod, the giant who plotted the tower of Babel, shouts: *"Raphèl maì amècche zabì almi."* The meaning and the linguistic origins of these garbled and corrupted phrases, which incorporate elements of Hebrew, Greek and Latin, may test the ingenuity of readers, but their dramatic function in context is quite clear. They are meant to baffle, to intimidate, to repulse, to alienate.

Dante uses regional words both to advance the action and to place his characters, as when Virgil is recognised as coming from northern Italy because of his use of the word *istra*, "now" (*Inf.* xxvii 21). As though to mark the distance he has travelled since writing the *De vulgari*, he uses two Florentine words specifically rejected in the treatise as unsuitable for use in poetry: *manicar* ("to eat") at *Inf.* xxxiii 60 and *introcque* ("meanwhile") at *Inf.* xx 130. Machiavelli two centuries later, though himself a Florentine, still baulked at Dante's use of this second word in the *Commedia*, declaring it to be *goffo*, "clumsy." But *introcque* does provide a rhyme on *nocque*, a word otherwise not usable at the end of a line. This too is a rhyme used only once in the poem.

In *Purgatorio* xix Pope Adrian V, lying facedown on the ground with his hands bound behind his back on the terrace of the avaricious, identifies himself to Dante with ecclesiastical solemnity in Latin: *scias quod ego fui successor Petri* ("know that I was Peter's successor"). When he becomes aware that Dante is kneeling—the pilgrim has instinctively dropped to his knees out of respect in the presence of the pontiff—he switches linguistic register to the robustly colloquial, urging him to get up: *Drizza le gambe, lèvati sù, frate!* ("Straighten your legs, get up, brother!") The intimate tone of the admonishment underlines the distance that separates the world of the living from the afterlife, where distinctions of earthly rank, even those between pope and layman, no longer have any meaning. The switch from Latin with its formal subjunctive (*scias*) to the vernacular with its urgent and intimate imperatives (*drizza, lèvati*) shows

Dante alive to the dramatic effects of moving easily between languages and registers. He is showing not telling.

Dante's boldness in challenging comfortable linguistic expectations is a crucial component in one of the most moving scenes in the poem. In a remarkable bravura act he has a Provençal poet speak to Dante the character for eight lines in Provençal, lines which form the climax and conclusion to canto xxvi of *Purgatorio*. The episode shows Dante's glorious capacity to sidestep conventional expectations and to move with complete stylistic and linguistic freedom and confidence at any point in the poem.

Here in *Purgatorio* xxvi the lustful are punished in flames which occupy almost the whole of the flat surface on this last terrace on the mountain. Virgil, Statius and Dante make their way in single file around the extreme outer edge of the terrace, taking care to avoid the flames. Trapped in the fire—an obvious counterpart of the passion celebrated in their poetry—are two earlier vernacular love poets, an Italian (Guido Guinizzelli) and the poet from Provence (Arnaut Daniel). Two poets in the flames, three poets walking around the edge of the terrace. Other poets will be mentioned in the course of the canto; yet others will have their words echoed.

The sin of lust is represented in hell by a reader of poetry (Francesca), in purgatory by writers of love poems—the connection with literature seems inescapable. A stay on this terrace was an occupational hazard for poets of Dante's time, since love was a mandatory subject for any aspiring poet. It is precisely the relationship between the erotic impulse, however sublimated, rarefied or intellectualised, and lust, which this canto calls into question. The canto also brings to culmination other broader themes which have been developing over the length of the poem: what makes a poet great? what makes one poet better than another? what is the ultimate meaning and value of artistic achievement?

When the souls in the fire learn that Dante is a living man they fall silent in amazement. A famous simile compares their response to the reaction of the mountain dweller who comes to the city for the first time, an image no doubt drawn from Dante's firsthand experience of country bumpkins from the foothills of the Apennines coming to the thriving

metropolis of Florence. The visitor to the city is dumbstruck: an arresting image in a context that will be notable for its concern with speech
and degrees of skill in its use.

> Non altrimenti stupido si turba
>   lo montanaro, e rimirando ammuta,
>   quando rozzo e salvatico s'inurba, . . .   (*Purg.* xxvi 67–69)

> (Just as the mountain dweller is amazed and bewildered, and
>   gazing about him, is speechless, when rough and uncouth he
>   comes into the city, . . .)

There is a high degree of verbal inventiveness here. The verbs *ammuta*
and *s'inurba* are both words Dante coins. (The reflexive verb *inurbarsi*—"to
come into the city," literally "to encity oneself"—struck some copyists as
so odd that they amended it to a more conventional *entra in urba*, "enters
the city," losing the boldness and originality of Dante's word.)

One striking aspect of the way Dante writes in the *Commedia* is just
how inventive he is with language. His many neologisms (new words not
found in any other writers of the time, words almost certainly invented by
him) give an almost plastic sense of his shaping the language to his purposes. Both *ammuta* and *s'inurba* fall in the rhyme position: the demands of
the metrical form, far from being experienced as a constraint, seem on the
contrary to have acted as a spur to his creative impulse. The author of an
early commentary known as the *Ottimo* ("the Best"), one of the very few
commentators who had known Dante personally, relates that he heard
him state that the need to find a rhyme never forced him to say something
he had not intended to say, but that he made language do things it had not
done before, things that other writers were not able to do. A high proportion of Dante's neologisms are verbs and many of them fall in the rhyme
position. As Proust noted (though he was not talking about Dante): "The
tyranny of rhyme forces the poet to the discovery of his finest lines."

The mountain dweller at a loss for words, here evoked so strikingly,
contrasts with the eloquent soul who will now answer Dante's question.

There is a contrast also with Dante's own silence when, a little later, he too will find himself unable to speak. Dante falls silent after the revelation of Guinizzelli's identity—but his is a silence of a very different kind. It conveys deeply felt and complex emotions.

> son Guido Guinizzelli; e già mi purgo
> per ben dolermi prima ch'a lo stremo. (*Purg.* xxvi 92–93)

(I am Guido Guinizzelli; and I am already purifying myself
   because I grieved to good effect before the end.)

The simile which describes Dante's reaction to this revelation is not descriptive and realistic, but literary and allusive. We are expected to know the story told in Statius's *Thebaid* of King Lycurgus's grief and anger when his baby son was bitten by a snake and died of the wound. His careless nursemaid Hypsipyle was seized by soldiers and taken off to be put to death. Her sons came upon her unexpectedly as she was being taken away. They rushed forward, embraced her, and pulled her to safety. But none of this is explained by Dante. As we read this soaring simile, there is an almost palpable sense that we are approaching an emotional climax.

> Quali ne la tristizia di Ligurgo
>   si fer due figli a riveder la madre,
>   tal mi fec'io, ma non a tanto insurgo,
> quand'io odo nomar sé stesso il padre
>   mio e de li altri miei miglior che mai
>   rime d'amor usar dolci e leggiadre;
> e sanza udire e dir pensoso andai
>   lunga fiata rimirando lui,
>   né, per lo foco, in là più m'appressai. (*Purg.* xxvi 94–102)

(Just as on the occasion of Lycurgus's grief, the two sons did on
   seeing their mother again, so I did, but I do not rise to such

heights, when I hear the father of me and of others my betters who ever wrote sweet and graceful love poems say his name; and without hearing and speaking I walked on lost in thought for a long time gazing at him, nor, because of the fire, did I move any closer to him.)

On learning that he is talking to Guido Guinizzelli, Dante feels the same surge of emotions as the sons of Hypsipyle (shock, delight, dismay). But unlike them he does not act. His failure to step into the fire and embrace Guinizzelli is the last in a series of embraces or failures to embrace which mark out the action of *Purgatorio* and the meetings between its poets and artists (Casella and Dante, Sordello and Virgil, Statius and Virgil). For all Dante's feelings of affection and gratitude, Guinizzelli cannot draw him into the fire, let alone lead him out the other side.

There is a long pause as the two walk along in parallel, Dante gazing at Guinizzelli, unable to express the filial feelings that Dante the poet has clearly articulated. When Dante the character does manage to speak, voicing his admiration for Guinizzelli's poems, he will address the older poet deferentially, using the polite form *voi*. Guinizzelli implicitly and tactfully corrects him when he replies using the intimate form *tu*. He calls Dante *frate* ("brother"), echoing Virgil to Statius at a similar moment of high emotion between fellow poets.

When Dante has gazed long enough, he offers his services to Guinizzelli, who asks why, to judge by his words and looks, Dante feels affection for him. Dante replies:

> E io a lui: "Li dolci detti vostri,
>   che, quanto durerà l'uso moderno,
>   faranno cari ancora i loro incostri."   (*Purg.* xxvi 112–14)

(And I said to him: "Your sweet poems, which as long as modern usage lasts will make dear the very ink they are written with.")

Just as Oderisi da Gubbio had done on the terrace of pride, Guiniz-zelli deflects the compliment and points to a better artist:

"O frate," disse, "questi ch'io ti cerno
    col dito," e additò un spirto innanzi,
    "fu miglior fabbro del parlar materno."   (*Purg.* xxvi 115–17)

("O brother," he said, "the man I'm pointing out to you," and
    he pointed to a spirit ahead, "was a better craftsman of the
    mother tongue.")

Like Oderisi the illuminator, Guinizzelli has transcended all pride in his own earthly achievement as an artist. But the animus with which he elaborates the point is surprising. He becomes eloquent on the question of poets who are rightly admired and poets who have inflated reputations, vehemently voicing his belief in the objective nature of literary value. Poetic achievement is not a matter of opinion or whim, of taste or fashion. This attack on the fools who get it wrong is surprising in a soul who is supposedly beyond earthly rivalries—doubly so in the light of the parallel with canto xi, where Oderisi had concluded by denouncing the vanity of earthly fame.

Literary polemic erupts into the afterlife as Dante, through Guiniz-zelli, imposes his own pattern of meaning on recent literary history, naming the predecessors who have been overvalued and pointing to the one who should be honoured. This purgatorial encounter adds further detail and emphasis to the picture of the history of vernacular poetry which had begun to emerge in canto xxiv (and in so doing it corrects and amplifies Dante's first systematic attempt to map out the terrain of vernacular literature in the *De vulgari*). It rewrites the record, polemically asserting the true line of poetic succession.

More importantly, it introduces the *miglior fabbro* as the figure for whom Guinizzelli expresses the kind of admiration that Dante feels for Guinizzelli. The poetic perspective lengthens and broadens, temporally and geographically, as we are carried back to the Provençal tradition from which Italian lyric poetry took its origins, and which the closing lines of the canto will so memorably celebrate.

Arnaut Daniel is presented as the supreme master of vernacular literature, who surpassed all other writers, whether of verse or prose. His influence on Dante, already acknowledged in the *De vulgari* as profoundly important, must in retrospect have come to seem decisive, the thing that made it possible for him to write so effectively in the low style in the *Inferno*. Guinizzelli's influence had been equally decisive. The praise poems of the *Vita nova*, inspired by his example and always seen by Dante as a turning point in his own development as a poet, lead ultimately to the celebration of Beatrice in the *Paradiso*. So it is especially moving to find these two poets here together at the top of the mountain.

When Arnaut himself at last addresses Dante, in courteous response to the pilgrim's eager interest, he speaks Provençal. The narrative convention that all souls, even foreigners, speak Italian is, on this one occasion and to brilliant dramatic effect, abandoned. Everything in the canto has led to this moment, to Arnaut's unexpected speaking in his own voice.

The effortless switch into Provençal startles and delights the reader. It makes the figure of Arnaut seem remote and solitary, linguistically set apart. But at the same time it reinforces the idea of the modern vernacular tradition as a continuum, geographical and temporal, clearly set off from the literary heritage of antiquity. It sets the seal on the new stylistic ideal of the *Commedia*, which definitively abandons the theoretical position of the *De vulgari*, substituting for a rigorous selectivity within the "high" style a willingness to exploit all the expressive possibilities of human speech.

Guinizzelli asks Dante to say a Pater Noster for him when he reaches paradise, then disappears into the flames, like a fish going down through water to the bottom—the verbal equivalent of a cinematic dissolve.

> Poi forse per dar luogo altrui secondo
> > che presso avea, disparve per lo foco,
> > come per l'acqua il pesce andando al fondo.

Io mi feci al mostrato innanzi un poco,
   e dissi ch'al suo nome il mio disire
   apparecchiava grazïoso loco.   (*Purg.* xxvi 133–38)

(Then perhaps to make space for someone who was close by him,
   he disappeared into the fire, like a fish going down through
   water to the bottom. I moved forward a little towards the
   man who had been pointed out to me, and said that my desire
   prepared a welcoming place for his name.)

That man now addresses Dante:

El cominciò liberamente a dire:
   "Tan m'abellis vostre cortes deman,
   qu'ieu no me puesc ni voill a vos cobrire.
Ieu sui Arnaut, que plor e vau cantan;
   consiros vei la passada folor,
   e vei jausen lo joi qu'esper, denan.
Ara vos prec, per aquella valor,
   que vos guida al som de l'escalina,
   sovenha vos a temps de ma dolor!"
Poi s'ascose nel foco che li affina.   (*Purg.* xxvi 139–48)

(He began freely to speak: "Your courteous request so pleases
   me that I cannot nor would I wish to conceal myself from
   you. I am Arnaut, who weeps and goes singing; grieving I
   see my past folly, and I see rejoicing the joy I hope for before
   me. Now I beg you, by that goodness which guides you to the
   summit of the stair, remember my pain in good time." Then
   he hid in the fire that refines them.)

   Dante, in this ultimate act of homage to a waning poetic tradition,
has Arnaut speak words which seem both a distillation of the essence of
troubadour lyric and yet at the same time personal. His lines are a skill-

ful mosaic of poetic fragments from his own poems and those of others. *Ieu sui Arnaut* is a self-citation from his own most famous poem, here linked with the theme of weeping while speaking (as both Francesca and Ugolino had done). The themes of joy and suffering in love, and the vocabulary associated with them, are generically troubadour rather than distinctive to Arnaut. Yet the words do also stand in counterpoint to Arnaut's own poetry. *Joi* is almost a leitmotif in his poems, where it is characteristically associated with the lady's favour, sometimes even more explicitly with her bedchamber. Suffering is caused by her aloofness. Value belongs to her or (less frequently) to the poet or his words.

So everything here is recognizable, yet everything has taken on an opposite significance to what it had in the poems he wrote while he was alive. Those poems give a powerful sense of time as a dimension of human life, with the poet experiencing and expressing his passion in relation to the natural cycle of the seasons, in a physical world full of material objects. Here in purgatory time has been reduced to its essence. Arnaut, a ghostly figure in an insubstantial medium, is poised between past and future, folly and joy. *Folor* encompasses biography and literature, the lived experience and the poetry which grew out of it—the folly of being obsessed with an earthly love, the folly of turning his poetic talents to the celebration of such a love.

But Arnaut does not talk about poetry. Bonagiunta, who was anxious to understand what was new in Dante's way of writing poetry, had still been absorbed in his own practice as a poet, and where he fell short. Guinizzelli had brushed aside references to his own distinction as a poet, but he was still concerned to set the literary record straight. Arnaut, by contrast with these two, has transcended literature both as a topic for discussion and as a pretext for display. The most striking of all the ways in which his words here in purgatory contrast with his own poetry is the directness, the lack of artifice with which he expresses himself. He had been a poet whose technical virtuosity was inseparable from the difficulty of his poems. Here he seems consciously to renounce the hermetic manner.

The only ambiguity is in his final line, which can mean, as it has usually been glossed, "remember my suffering and pray for me." In this sense it is exactly symmetrical to Guinizzelli's closing request. It can also mean (and surely does mean) "remember my suffering and act on it, take heed, learn your lesson." These are the last words Dante hears from any soul in purgatory. Their ambiguity perfectly encapsulates the double aspect of his relationship to the penitent shades on the mountain. Indeed Arnaut's whole speech—Dante's leave-taking from sinful humanity—reminds us (in the rhyme words *folor-valor-dolor*) of the three constants of the purgatorial experience: human folly, God's goodness, which offers the possibility of redemption, and the suffering through which that redemption is achieved. God is more important than poetry.

If Arnaut's words invite us to look back, they also compel us to look forward. In the protective custody of Virgil and Statius (indeed, now sandwiched between them), and with their active and solicitous encouragement, Dante must pass through the fire, and in spite of his terror, he will emerge unscathed on the other side. Virgil and Statius, and the mention of Beatrice's name, bring him through. Guinizzelli and Arnaut, the revered vernacular masters, must be left behind, trapped in the fire, the penitential reality that has replaced the poetic metaphor for passion. The fire refines the poets as they had once refined the language. The artisan image of purifying and tempering a resistant medium, implicit in the verb *affina* ("refines") as it had been implicit in the noun *fabbro* ("craftsman"), but now transposed from the linguistic-artistic endeavor to the spiritual one, is the haunting image with which the canto closes.

Dante could not have written the *Commedia*—a work of epic ambition and form to stand alongside the great poems of the ancient world— without the example and help of the great classical poets. Their work nourishes and feeds his. The narrative line of *Purgatorio* xxvi explicitly and movingly enacts this literary-historical truth. There was nothing in the vernacular tradition which could serve him as a model. All the more startling then that instead of writing in Latin in direct emulation of them, with the solid support of established literary models, he felt able to take on this challenge using the humble language of his birthplace, the Florentine vernacular.

The challenge to the classical poets is explicitly formulated at one notable point in the *Inferno*, when Dante consciously takes on Lucan and Ovid in their descriptions of metamorphoses: *Taccia Lucano . . . / Taccia di Cadmo e d'Aretusa Ovidio . . .* ("Let Lucan fall silent . . . / Let Ovid fall silent about Cadmus and Arethusa"). Dante sets out to outdo them when he describes the monstrous transformations of the thieves in *Inferno* xxv. Men turn into serpents, serpents turn into men, or—and this climactic moment is where he trumps the classical poets—a serpent and a man meld together, then separate, each having turned into the other. This is a bravura act, as Dante is well aware, a show-stopping performance in competition with the greats.

When T. S. Eliot in 1925 added a dedication to the second English edition of *The Waste Land*—For Ezra Pound, *il miglior fabbro*—his graceful acknowledgement of his friend's contribution to the definitive shaping of his own poem was elegantly indicated in a single pregnant phrase borrowed from *Purgatorio* xxvi. Pound, notoriously, had subjected the whole of *The Waste Land* to a radical process of cutting and revision. The leaner, tauter poem that emerged from his ferocious but impeccably judicious subediting is the one that was published and the one we read today.

If we examine the autograph manuscripts of *The Waste Land*, we can see that the Arnaut Daniel episode played a definitive role in the gestation of the poem. The concluding line of the canto (*Poi s'ascose nel foco che li affina*) had from the earliest drafts been one of the "fragments I have shored against my ruins" with which Eliot's poem concludes. In early drafts there is a whole section called "Exequy," which Pound ruthlessly excised from the final version. The line *Sovegna vos al temps de mon dolor* [*sic*] had been used in this section. In the typescript it is cancelled and in its place Eliot adds in longhand the line *Consiros vei la pasada folor*. This line is then in its turn crossed out. Eliot seems to be haunted by Arnaut's speech, every phrase of which appears to have a special resonance for him.

Indeed he plundered Arnaut's speech for resonant phrases on many other occasions as well. *Ara vus prec* was the title of a small volume of poetry already published in 1919. The confident attack of *Stand on the highest pavement of the stair* echoes the *som de l'escalina*. In the "Ash Wednesday" sequence, he planned at one point to use the phrase *som de l'escalina* as a heading for one of the poems, and *jausen lo jorn* for another. In the event, he used only the phrase *sovegna vos*, which appears in "Ash Wednesday" iv.

Perhaps because Eliot was so reluctant to lose the Arnaut connection excised by Pound from *The Waste Land*, in the definitive version of the poem lines 145–48 of *Purgatorio* xxvi are cited in the notes to the text. (There had been no notes in the version published in *The Criterion* in October 1922 and in *The Dial* in November 1922, preceding the New York edition of December 1922.) According to Pound, it was the presence of the notes that provoked the attention of the reviewers.

The question of whether the notes were to be regarded as an integral part of the poem or as extraneous to it became a central issue for the New Critics, for whom it sparked the celebrated debate on authorial intention. The Arnaut Daniel episode in *Purgatorio* thus lies not just at the heart of one of the great poetic masterpieces of twentieth-century English literature but also at the heart of one of the major critical debates of the century. What Dante was doing in this canto in narrative terms— placing himself in relation both to his contemporaries and to the great poets of the past—is exactly what Eliot is doing in *The Waste Land* in a more elusive and allusive way.

It is worth pausing briefly to consider Eliot's views on Dante's language, since they are a standard point of reference for English poetry lovers. Eliot talks of a "universal" quality in Dante's Italian, by which he perhaps means that the Latin ancestry of the language, with its imperial and ecclesiastical cultural heritage, is clearly perceptible in it. In the opening lines of the poem (*Nel mezzo del cammin di nostra vita / mi ritrovai per una selva oscura, / che la diritta via era smarrita*), many English readers will recognise that *vita* is Latin *vita(m)*, *selva* is Latin *silva(m)*, *via* is Latin *via(m)*. But to come at the question from this angle, thought-provoking though it is, is not especially helpful for our purposes. Seamus Heaney is much closer to the mark when he talks of the "raucous and parochial energies" in Dante's language.

As a poet Heaney is in a situation in some sense precisely the reverse of Dante's. He has written illuminatingly about the predicament of an Ulster poet using standard English, forced at times to betray his sense of the local and "parochial" rightness of a word in the interests of being more widely understood. *My father wrought with a horse-plough* is amended to *My father worked with a horse-plough*, even though *wrought* was the word always used in the Ulster of Heaney's childhood for working with any kind of agricultural implement, and *wrought* is the word that comes to him naturally.

Heaney has a fine-tuned sense of standard English against which his own regional forms of speech can be measured. By contrast, there was in Dante's time no standard form of Italian. He chose to write in his native vernacular, but there was no accepted or received form of the vernacular to influence or guide his linguistic choices. He wrote in Tuscan, and because he wrote so well, so expressively and with such absolute mastery of his language, Tuscan *became* the standard form. This is what people mean when they talk of Dante "inventing" Italian.

In the *De vulgari* Dante had distinguished between no fewer than five varieties of Tuscan, as spoken in Florence, Pisa, Arezzo, Siena and Lucca. He had cited characteristic phrases from each of these regional varieties, and mentioned five poets, one from each city, whose poems fail to make the grade for a discerning reader. All are dismissed as "municipal"— that is, lacking in distinction and linguistic finesse. (The Florentine is none other than Brunetto Latini, the revered master and mentor we met among the sinners against nature in canto xv of the *Inferno*. Clearly, Dante admired him more for his statesmanlike qualities and educational role than for his talent as a poet.)

Dante's Italian in the *Commedia* is Tuscan—broadly speaking, Florentine, though some other Tuscan forms occur. Indeed the number and variety of forms available to him, in the absence of a "standard" language, is one of the advantages of the linguistic situation he found himself in. It made handling the metrical scheme easier than it might otherwise have been. (Translators do not have this advantage, nor do modern Italian poets, or certainly not to the same extent.) So in the space of two lines at *Inf.* iii 38–39, we find three forms of "they were" (*furon, fur, fuoro*), offering different possibilities for rhyming and syllable count. They are used when describing the fallen angels in the vestibule of hell: *quel cattivo coro / de li angeli che non* furon *ribelli / né* fur *fedeli a Dio, ma per sé* fuoro ("that wicked band of the angels who were not rebellious, and were not faithful to God, but were for themselves"). There are three more forms available, had he needed them, used elsewhere: *furo, furono* and *fuorono.* Similarly, the past tense "he lost" can be *perdè, perdette, perse,* or *perdeo.* All are used at different points, with no distinction in meaning or poetic effect; but they offer different possibilities for rhyming and for positioning in a hendecasyllable.

This variety in word form is matched by a similar variety in word choice. Thus "now" can be *ora, adesso, mo,* plus (for purposes of characterisation) the regional forms *issa* and *istra.* Lexical variety can be vertical as well as horizontal, so we have the possibilities *vecchio, veglio* and *sene* for "old man." The choice here is dictated by what is appropriate to context. Caron with his demonic energy in *Inferno* iii is *un vecchio, bianco per antico pelo* ("an old man, hair and beard white with age"). Cato in *Purgatorio* i is *un veglio solo, degno di tanta reverenza in vista* . . . ("a solitary old man, worthy of such great respect in his appearance . . ."). The French origin of the word *veglio* gives it a more elevated feel than *vecchio,* befitting the dignity of the guardian of purgatory, though the meaning and the Latin root of the words *vecchio* and *veglio* are identical. In paradise Saint Bernard, an even more venerable figure than Cato, is a *sene* (a true Latinism, which has not survived into modern Italian, but which gives us the adjectival form *senile*). There is huge linguistic potential and flexibility in this situation before the vernacular language has solidified into a standard form.

Having made the choice to write in the vernacular, Dante has extraordinary freedom in his linguistic choices. There is no particular sense of opposition to a received vernacular linguistic form or lexicon. He is uniquely alive to the expressive force and potential of the vernacular and it is this exhilarating feeling of freedom—of energy, of limitless expressive possibilities—that one responds to reading the poem. The idea of needing to forge a language from scratch is strongly and increasingly present when Dante calls on the muses for help and talks of the challenges to his linguistic resources.

It is difficult for us today to imagine the reality of a rich multilingual culture where no form of the vernacular had as yet been accepted as the standard or received form, and where Latin was the accepted medium for serious intellectual endeavour. But some sense of the confident ease with which Dante moved in this linguistic environment is given in a small poem in three languages that is almost certainly by him. The poem moves fluently between French, Latin and Italian. The *congedo* (the final short section where the poet takes leave of his poem) gives a taste of this jeu d'esprit:

> Chanson, or puez aler par tout le monde,
>> Namque locutus sum in lingua trina
>> Ut gravis mea spina
>> Si saccia per lo mondo. Ogn'uomo il senta:
>> Forse n'avrà pietà chi mi tormenta.

> (Song, now you can go throughout the whole world [French], for
> I have spoken in a trinal language so that my heavy suffer-
> ing [Latin] may be known throughout the world. Let every
> man hear it: perhaps the one who torments me will take pity
> [Italian].)

The ease with which Dante moves between Latin and Italian constitutes a distinctive aspect of the linguistic texture of the *Commedia*. When he quotes from or echoes the Scriptures, incorporating a Latin fragment into a vernacular linguistic environment, there is an intoxicating sense of a malleable linguistic medium which offers joyous possibilities for experimenting with words and rhythm. The first spoken words in the poem are those of the pilgrim lost in the dark wood when he calls on Virgil for help, though he does not yet know that it is Virgil he is talking to: "Miserere *di me," gridai a lui* ("'Take pity on me,' I shouted to him," *Inf.* i 65). His words echo the opening of Psalm 50 (*Miserere mei Deus secundum misericordiam tuam*: "Have mercy on me, O God, according to your steadfast love")—

the penitential psalm par excellence. The heartfelt cry implicitly establishes at the outset that Dante is to be identified with the biblical David, author and singer of the psalms. But *Miserere* ("take pity") is also the word used by Aeneas when he calls on the sybil for help in *Aeneid* vi 117.

Miserere is a Latin word, though one which would have been very familiar to Dante's readers from its use in the liturgy. Only by keeping it in Latin can he preserve the double allusiveness, to the Bible and to the *Aeneid*. But it is fitted here into a vernacular context: *Miserere di me*, where *di me* is Italian, and where the hybrid phrase forms a perfect first half of a 6, 10 hendecasyllable (see "The Hendecasyllable" on pp. 263–65). The Latin form *Miserere mei* would not have worked here metrically.

We find the same quotation from Psalm 50 at the end of the poem when, among the blessed in the Empyrean, the biblical Ruth is identified as the great-grandmother of David, *che per doglia / del fallo disse* "Miserere mei" (*Par.* xxxii 12) ("who grieving for his sin said '*Miserere mei*"). Here the Latin words, this time with no accommodation to the vernacular, are the last in the line (and conclude a perfect 4, 8, 10 hendecasyllable); and *mei* is a useful though not difficult rhyme. The fluidity of the language allows Dante to use this thematically crucial phrase in two different forms, forms which have equal poetic force but a different metrical character, at the beginning and the end of the hendecasyllable—and, perhaps not by chance, at the beginning and the end of his poem.

We have the opposite case—a line of Latin into which, for metrical reasons, Dante has inserted an exclamatory vernacular *oh!*—when in the earthly paradise Beatrice's arrival is heralded by angels quoting a line from Virgil (yes, with startling boldness, Dante has his Christian angels quote Virgil at this climactic point in the action): Manibus, *oh*, date lilia plenis ("Oh, give lilies with full hands"). An astute commentator suggests that the sharp intake of breath represented by the *oh!* might be taken to mark the very moment of Beatrice's appearance on the scene.

Dante's use of Latinisms as distinct from actual Latin words tends to be a characteristic marker of the high style in the poem. Latinisms are Italian words which still retain a strong sense of their Latin origin: they almost invariably denote abstract concepts rather than concrete objects, and are typically used in contexts elucidating philosophical, scientific, astronomical, or theological ideas. They become much more frequent in the *Paradiso*, where the encounters with the shades of the dead often focus less on narratives about lives lived on earth than on the explanation to the pilgrim of intellectually challenging ideas: the creation of the universe, the nature of time, the hierarchies of the angels, whether reparation can be made for broken vows, and so on. Beatrice, Dante's guide in this third realm, enlightens him on many issues such as these; she proves an eloquent spokesman for key aspects of scholastic theology. His teachers include also four doctors of the church who were to become saints (Thomas Aquinas, Bonaventure, Benedict and Bernard) and his examiners on the three theological virtues are, as we have seen, the three apostles Peter, James and John. Typical Latinisms are the scholastic terms *quiditate* and *sillogismo*: both occur in Dante's viva voce examination on faith conducted by Saint Peter. Significantly, *quiditate* is in the rhyme position (as *mei* had been). Using Latin words in rhyme is not something Dante did before the *Commedia*, and not something his contemporaries ever did.

There have always been those who found Dante's language problematic. Two hundred years after he died, Pietro Bembo, the arbiter of linguistic usage in the Renaissance and author of a book on vernacular speech called the *Prose della volgar lingua*, acknowledged Dante's stature as a poet but found his style defective. This was not just because of the occasional coarseness and impropriety but also because of the linguistic liberties Dante took. One thing Bembo singled out for criticism was precisely Dante's use of Latin words; but he also objected to his use of foreign words, archaic words, rough words (*rozze*), ugly, dirty words (*immonde e brutte*), harsh words (*durissime*), his mangling of pure, noble words (*pure e gentili*), and his indiscriminate making up and inventing of words (*senza alcuna scielta o regola, da sè formandone e fingendone, ha operato*). Bembo said that in its language the *Commedia* was like a beautiful field of corn choked with weeds and chaff.

For Bembo it was a question of fastidiousness and good taste, the need as he saw it to establish a standard form of the vernacular acceptable to polite courtly society. The qualities we as moderns tend to value are pre-

cisely those Bembo decried: inventiveness, inclusiveness, audacity, fresh-
ness, verbal energy, richness of lexical register, the breaking down of
divisions constructed through linguistic registers, willingness to exploit
all the qualities language offers. It seems safe to say that Dante's use of
language is an aspect of his poem that any modern reader is likely to find
dazzlingly original and inventive. His "uncensored access to every coffer
of the word-hoard" (the phrase is Heaney's, though he was not talking
about Dante when he used it) is the mark of his genius. The result is
not a linguistic hodgepodge. All these various linguistic elements always
serve an expressive and functional purpose, as we have seen with the
anguished *Miserere di me* of the opening canto. Interestingly, translators
of this phrase divide into two camps, those who preserve the Latin word
and those who render it in English as "take pity" or "have mercy." Far
from embodying a ragbag eclecticism (a fault not always avoided by translators), the *Commedia* reflects its author's unerring sensitivity to context
and narrative moment—the linguistic equivalent of perfect pitch. This
is no haphazardly assembled collection of linguistic items. Everything
is done with an impeccable sense of tone and precisely calculated effect.

The linguistic dimension of the *Commedia* achieves a special promi-
nence and is given a special twist in the last human beings Dante encounters at the end of each cantica. Arnaut Daniel is the last person who
speaks to him in purgatory. Adam is the last to speak to him in paradise.
The *Inferno* had ended, horribly, with speechlessness. At the very bottom of hell, in the last of the four sections of treachery, the one reserved
for betrayers of benefactors, Dante observed but was unable to speak to
sinners frozen beneath the surface of the ice. With this final group, not
even their heads stick out. The sinners are visible beneath Dante's feet,
frozen in the ice, trapped in the transparent medium like straws in glass
(*festuca in vetro*). Dante notes their various postures with clinical detachment and brisk efficiency: some are horizontal, some vertical (head up or
feet up), others bent over backwards so that their heads touch their feet.
The chilling spectacle evokes their loss of humanity. They are less than
human, less even than animals or plants, become simply specimens for
dispassionate observation.

The extinguishing of their capacity for language, the very thing that signifies and expresses their humanity, is a fitting measure of and punishment for their icy-heartedness, their lack of human empathy. Language, the tool for empathy and communication, for reaching out to one's fellow human beings, for being (in Aristotle's phrase) a "social animal," is finally extinguished at the bottom of hell. The point is all the more powerful for coming so soon after the emotional high point of Ugolino's speech in the previous canto, the last of the great operatic arias of the *Inferno*.

Whenever the subject of language comes to the fore in the *Commedia* the result is likely to be thought-provoking. Why is Dante so tough on the flatterers? Their misuse of language is harshly punished. They are immersed in a ditch full of human excrement (not animal dung: the point is made explicitly), echoing the reality of life in a medieval town, where the plumbing arrangements, such as they were, had sewage draining into an open ditch outside the city walls. This might seem unduly harsh treatment for simple verbal extravagance, even though it is self-serving.

Cristoforo Landino, the author of a lengthy commentary on the *Commedia* printed in 1481, offers an intriguing explanation for the punishment of the flatterers. Landino's large, handsome volume was the first edition of the poem printed in Florence (it had already been printed in Foligno, Venice, Mantua, Naples and Milan in the space of a few years). Landino explains that just as food nourishes the body and that part of it which is harmful and not productive of health is excreted as waste, so flattery is the unhealthy, harmful part of language. He sees the flatterers as wallowing in the filth that metaphorically represents their own words, their own sordid and self-serving misuse of language. Modern psychologists would call flattery an "instrumental" linguistic act, where language becomes a means of achieving a narrow personal goal, the overriding concern being one's own immediate self-interest, rather than a means of exploring truth in a disinterested way or expressing empathy with other human beings—or indeed with creating a work of art, where an element of inventiveness and play comes in.

The linguistic register of the *Paradiso* tends to be the high style. The expounding of complex philosophical and theological ideas plays a greater

Fig. 33 Botticelli: The flatterers (detail).

role than in the previous two cantiche, and as we have seen there is in consequence a higher proportion of Latinisms. But nonetheless Dante can, and frequently does, speak with great simplicity and directness, even when talking of profound and complex matters. Thus the opening lines lay out a basic principle which underlies the structure of the universe. The universe is ordered in terms of how much it is illuminated by God's light. That light is both a reflection of beatitude and its vehicle.

> La gloria di colui che tutto move
> > per l'universo penetra, e risplende
> > in una parte più e meno altrove.   (*Par.* i 1–3)

> (The glory of him who moves all things penetrates through the
> > universe, and shines more in some parts and less in others.)

God's presence is manifest throughout the cosmos: different parts of it shine with greater or lesser light according to their receptivity.

The other key principle that operates throughout the *Paradiso* is that beatitude consists in an act of the intellect, as Aquinas believed—as opposed to the mystical and Franciscan traditions, which emphasised the primacy of love. This principle is articulated by Beatrice when she describes the orders of the angels:

> e dei saper che tutti hanno diletto
>> quanto la sua veduta si profonda
>> nel vero in che si queta ogne intelletto.
> Quinci si può veder come si fonda
>> l'esser beato ne l'atto che vede,
>> non in quel ch'ama, che poscia seconda;   (*Par.* xxviii 109–11)

> (and you should know that all of them feel delight to the extent
>> that their seeing penetrates deeper into the truth in which
>> every intellect comes to rest. From this it can be seen how
>> beatitude is based in the act of seeing, not in the act of loving,
>> which follows from it;)

Seeing is understanding; love follows from understanding. The verb *vedere*, to see, is used more frequently than any other in *Paradiso*. The word *occhio* ("eye") is the most frequently used word in the poem (used 263 times). (The second most frequently used word is *mondo*, "world," trailing way behind at 143 occurrences.) The final cantos of the poem embody and enact this conception of beatitude, although they do so with an ardour that belies any modern notion that seeing and understanding are coolly rational in their operation, or are in any way at odds with the notions of intense desiring and joy.

Dante faces a new linguistic challenge in the *Paradiso*, the challenge of expressing what strictly speaking cannot be put into words—the ineffable. The difficulty is stated at the outset: *trasumanar significar per verba / non si poria* ("it is not possible to express in words the experience of

246 | READING DANTE

going beyond the human condition"). One can sense language straining even to state the problem: *per verba* is Latin (again in rhyme); *significar* is a biblical Latinism, meaning precisely "to put into words"; *trasumanar* is a verb Dante invented. Yet *trasumanar*—to transcend the human condition, to go beyond the limitations of what it is to be a human being—is what the pilgrim must do if he is to see the divinity. This is the ultimate goal of his journey; this the ultimate challenge to the writer.

The inexpressibility theme runs right through the final cantica, culminating in the last four cantos of the poem, where Dante enjoys first the vision of the heavenly hosts, and then, in the final canto, the vision of God. The pivotal moment at which he reaches the Empyrean—Heaven, as distinct from the heavens through which he has been passing in the previous twenty-nine cantos—is described in *Paradiso* xxx, a fine example of the language of the cantica: elevated but with no loss of drama, profound yet also simple, intellectually and theologically penetrating yet joyous. At this point the pilgrim emerges into eternity, leaving the created world, our human world of time and space, behind him. The experience of *trasumanar*, of going beyond the human, is finally accomplished and described in words, however far those words may fall short of the experience itself.

Paradiso xxx marks both an end and a beginning. It is the end of the physical journey, the moment of arrival at the goal towards which the pilgrim has been striving since he lost his way in the dark wood. From this point on, his progress is marked purely in terms of his ability to see and to understand. He travels forward in the intellectual sense only. But equally canto xxx marks a beginning: the beginning of Dante the character's final effort, as a living man, to penetrate and comprehend the mystery of God; and the beginning of Dante the poet's final strenuous effort, as an artist, to capture in words the experience of visionary understanding in which his journey culminates.

The experience of eternity unfolds as a single episode over these last four cantos of the poem, as Dante moves from understanding God through his angels and the blessed to understanding God directly, without the need of an intervening medium. *Paradiso* xxx is the canto in which he is initiated and acclimatized into this new world—the first stage in a crescendo of light and joy and ecstatic fervour, whose true climax is in the closing lines of the poem, where Dante's power to see and understand embraces the whole of creation through the creator.

The shape of the canto, like that of the whole poem, is from lesser to greater light, from lesser to greater understanding. But in this canto a qualitative change occurs. The pilgrim's power to see is transformed, and he begins to be able to experience the mystery of beatitude directly, instead of apprehending it imperfectly through his limited human faculties.

Following this transformation, he perceives a series of visions of mounting splendour and radiance. Each stage in the action is followed by a short speech from Beatrice, who explains what the vision signifies, and in what way Dante's sight is still defective. The pattern of the canto is vision followed by explanation, seeing followed by understanding, image followed by doctrine. The dramatic unfolding of the action in the central sequence gives us both dazzlingly beautiful images and profound theological truths.

Dante had had his first direct experience of God in *Paradiso* xxviii, when he saw a tiny but intensely bright point of light with nine concentric circles spinning dizzyingly around it: *da quel punto / depende il cielo e tutta la natura* ("from that point depend the heavens and all nature"). The point is God, the circles are the hierarchies of angels, each one responsible for the motion of one of the heavenly spheres circling the earth. The point and fiery circles are yet another prefiguring, in a form accessible to human understanding, of what he is to see in its true nature at the end of his journey.

Dante's repeated protestations that his powers are unequal to the task he has taken on are far from unself-conscious. Such protestations were a commonplace of medieval rhetoric, often no more than a routine compliment to a patron's generosity or a lady's beauty. This revitalisation of a hackneyed theme is entirely characteristic of his art, so deeply rooted in medieval rhetorical traditions, yet so vital and original. Here in paradise there is a chain of inadequacy. The visionary nature of his experience in the Empyrean makes it three stages removed from the words on the page. The human mind is unequal to the task of fully grasping what it momentarily experienced; memory cannot recall even what the mind did grasp at the time; words fall short even of what memory can recall.

Earlier in the poem Dante had tended to emphasise the limitations of his own command of language. Now towards the end it is on the first and second links in the chain that the emphasis falls: the limitations of any human being qua human being in the face of divinity.

The opening lines of the *Paradiso* had stated the inexpressibility theme and spelled out the links in the chain: the inadequacy of human language (4–6), the failure of memory (7–9), the limitations of the human mind (10–12). The theme is restated with particular insistence at the beginning of canto xxx (when Dante is initiated into eternity) and at the end of canto xxxiii (when the disparity between the experience and the language which describes it becomes so great that he simply stops writing). The whole of the final section of the poem is framed by these two statements, the first in relation to Beatrice, who now in the Empyrean is resplendent in her full glory as a blessed soul, the second in relation to God.

The action will build in intensity in an uninterrupted series of images and speeches right through the final cantos of the poem. Beatrice will be replaced by the medieval mystic Saint Bernard of Clairvaux as the poet's companion and guide as he approaches the Godhead. But for now she is still with him, his guide and companion at the key point where he transcends his human condition, when his capacity to see becomes capable of taking in eternity.

Noi siamo usciti fore / del maggior corpo al ciel ch'è pura luce ("We have emerged from the largest body to the heaven that is pure light"), she tells Dante as they emerge from the *primum mobile*, the largest body or circling sphere, to the Empyrean. The transition from *corpo* ("body") to *luce* ("light") is a crucial stage in the journey. But the light of the Empyrean is not the sensible light we know in our world. It is pure light or intellectual light:

luce intellettüal, piena d'amore;
   amor di vero ben, pien di letizia;
   letizia che trascende ogne dolzore.   (*Par.* xxx 40–42)

(intellectual light, full of love; love of true good, full of joy; joy
   that transcends every sweetness.)

The circular linked syntax and rhythm of the tercet echo the thing it describes. In its geometric perfection the circle, having no beginning and no end, was a traditional image for eternity.

The analogy with sensible light can help us understand the notion of intellectual light. Seeing requires three things (an eye, the object to be seen and light). Light acts as the intermediary between the organ of sight and the object, and makes possible the seeing of the latter by the former. In the same way understanding requires three things (a mind, the truth to be grasped and intellectual light). Intellectual light is the medium which makes the act of understanding, of grasping the truth, possible. Dante uses this notion of pure or intellectual light to represent what would otherwise be unrepresentable. It is the light of which the Empyrean is made. God is its source, Heaven its reflection.

Dante's sight must now be purified and elevated beyond its normal human capacities. Once he has been initiated into this light—*lumen gloriae*, the "light of glory"—he is potentially able to see God. The rest of the poem shows how his new powers are exercised and gain strength, and he gradually becomes more and more able to absorb the reality that is before him, to penetrate it deeper and deeper.

There are four stages in the process of acclimatisation: a powerful narrative energy runs through this central section of the canto. First a lightning flash that temporarily blinds him and marks the moment of his initiation to the *novella vista* ("new sight"—a new, transformed capacity to see): *così mi circunfulse luce viva* ("so a living light shone around me"). The Latinate verb is the very one used of Saint Paul on the road to Damascus. Dante, at this moment of transcending his human limitations as he approaches the Godhead, is a new Saint Paul. Then he sees a great river of light flowing between flowering banks: *e vidi lume in forma di rivera* ("and I saw light in the form of a river"), with jewel-like sparks shooting out of the river and into the flowers on the banks and then back into the river. Even as he gazes at it, this river of light turns into a circle: *mi parve / di sua lunghezza divenuta tonda* ("it seemed to me that from its length it had become round"). The change from length to circularity—from river to circle—represents the change from time to eternity. The circle in its unity, simplicity and perfection is a traditional symbol of those qualities in the creator.

Finally, as Dante's renewed capacity to see takes in the reality of what he is looking at, the circle itself is transformed. In a series of shifting images or visual analogies the true form of paradise is at last revealed. The circle becomes a hillside rising from a lake; then an amphitheatre, with the souls of the blessed seated in rising tiers around the arena at their feet which is the light of God. In a crescendo of light and joy and astonishment, the souls of the blessed and the angels are revealed in their true identity. The flowers and sparks along the riverbank had been *umbriferi prefazi* ("shadowy prefigurings") of their true reality: a magnificently evocative Latinism that shows how Dante could wrest expressive poetic force from his Latinate heritage. The amphitheatre then becomes metaphorically a rose—a rose with God as its centre, the souls of the blessed as its luminous petals.

The two threads running through the canto are seeing and light. The richness and variety and seeming inexhaustibility of the vocabulary associated with light contrasts with the insistence on the simple verb *to see*, culminating first in a dramatic failure to rhyme (*vidi,* "I saw," repeated three times in the rhyme position in lines 95, 97 and 99); and then, in the last of these lines, the directness, simplicity and urgency of the invocation to the source of light itself for help: *dammi virtù a dir com'ïo il vidi* ("give me the power to tell it as I saw it").

In lines of magisterial incisiveness and energy Dante concludes this central section of the canto with a second definition of intellectual light:

Lume è là sù che visibile face
  lo creatore a quella creatura
  che solo in lui vedere ha la sua pace.   (*Par.* xxx 100–102)

(There is a light on high which makes the creator visible to those
  of his creatures whose only peace lies in seeing him.)

Beatrice draws Dante into the rose and invites him to contemplate
the ranks of the blessed. Dante takes in the vast dimensions of the rose;
distance does not impede his seeing with perfect clarity even its further-
most outer edges. The rose is humanity, flowering in heaven in its fullness and beauty.

The rose image for paradise, with its poetic associations of beauty, per-
fume and luminousness, is Dante's invention. There is no known direct literary source, although there are biblical, patristic and liturgical texts where
the blessed are flowers and the Virgin Mary herself is a rose. Some readers
have suspected a connection with rose windows in medieval churches and
cathedrals. The beautiful ancient Basilica of San Zeno in Verona, for example, has a rose window that Dante will certainly have known.

There is a literary connection of a quite different kind that is hard
to overlook. The *Roman de la Rose*, we remember, is a secular poem
where the rose of the title symbolises sexual love; and we remember
too that Dante may well be the author of a late-thirteenth-century
translation of the *Roman* into Italian, where it bears the title *Il Fiore*
("*The Flower*"). The celestial rose of the blessed might be a counterpart
to and corrective of the erotic rose of the poet's youth—just as the failure to rhyme *Cristo* with anything but itself in *Paradiso* makes amends
for the morally dubious rhyming on the name of Christ in the *tenzone*
with Forese.

The elaboration of the rose image occupies the next two cantos.
Dante explores the rose by gazing at it. *Vola con li occhi per questo giar-
dino* ("Fly with your eyes through this garden"), Saint Bernard, who has
taken over from Beatrice without Dante's noticing it, urges him. Bernard

explains the seating arrangement of the blessed in the rose, pointing out figures from the Old and New Testaments, famous saints (Francis, Benedict, Augustine), the many children. Beatrice herself is now visible at the outer edge, in the third row from the top (the poet's usual precision doesn't fail him, even here). Most of the places in the rose are already occupied. Not much time remains in human history. The end of the world is not far away.

In the final canto of the *Paradiso*, Saint Bernard prays to the Virgin, asking her to grant Dante the vision of God. Dante's gaze penetrates deeper and deeper into the light. We no longer have the dazzling descriptions of a landscape we can visualise in all its luminosity and splendour, as in canto xxx, but something quite different. What Dante must now describe exceeds not just his speech but even his memory.

Bernard gestures to him to gaze up into the light, and Dante does so. But he can no longer find words to describe what he saw:

> Da quinci innanzi il mio veder fu maggio
> che 'l parlar mostra, ch'a tal vista cede,
> e cede la memoria a tanto oltraggio.   (*Par.* xxxiii 55–57)

> (From this point on my capacity to see was greater than words
> can show, which fail in the face of such seeing, and memory
> fails in the face of such excess.)

All he can do is attempt to convey the sense that remains in him now of what he experienced then. Three evocative comparisons remind us of analogous experiences in our world: things that leave some faint trace behind them in our consciousness even after they are gone and cannot be recaptured. A dream that one cannot recall on waking leaves a trace of the emotions experienced in it. Snow melting in sunlight retains a faint trace of an imprint on it. The oracles of the Sybil are lost on the winds that blow away the pages they were written on.

As Dante gazes into the divine light he has a perception of the unity of creation, a unity that underlies the complex, multifarious and fragmented experience of our daily living in the world. In a breathtaking counterbalancing image to the Sybil's pages scattered on the wind, he describes this moment of illumination as he gazes into the light:

> Nel suo profondo vidi che s'interna
>> legato con amore in un volume,
>> ciò che per l'universo si squaderna: (*Par.* xxxiii 85–87)

> (In its depths I saw gathered, bound with love in one volume,
>> what is scattered in gatherings through the universe:)

In this moment of visionary experience, the multifariousness and variety and plenitude of our experience of the world now make sense to him as a unity.

The justly famous image he uses to convey this sense of unity draws on an experience at the centre of a medieval writer's world. The gatherings which are the constituent parts of a medieval manuscript and which were copied by scribes and could circulate separately are stitched or glued together to form a complete volume. Each gathering contains a number of folios or pages; each page contains words. The twelfth-century mystic Hugh of Saint Victor had said that the whole universe is like a book written by God's finger. Human experience can be thought of as learning to read and understand that book, the world around us. What binds the constituent parts of the universe together, Dante's image tells us, is divine love. The bookbinding image takes us from the words on the page—our experience in living—to the mind of the author who wrote the book.

The language or languages Dante uses in the *Commedia*, in all their multiplicity, variety and richness—as rich and varied and multiform as the physical world he lived in—are brought into perfect unity in his poem, a single volume, by his creative poetic act. Human creativity is the grandchild of God. It is a sobering thought that in his lifetime Dante can never have seen a complete copy of the *Commedia* with all its parts bound together to form one volume. *Inferno* and *Purgatorio* were released separately upon completion and circulated independently. *Paradiso* was finished not long before he died. It was left to his son Jacopo to assemble a complete copy of the poem after his father's death, and take it to Florence.

Dante's perception of the oneness of the universe is followed by a vision of the three-personed Christian God, the Trinity. The image he uses to capture this vision is as far removed as it is possible to be from the personalised God—a stern old man with a beard—as represented in, for example, Michelangelo's Sistine ceiling painting of God creating Adam. The Godhead as Dante sees it is perceived as a geometric figure, as three superimposed, differently coloured, yet connected circles reflecting back at one another like rainbows. Dante, perhaps deliberately, has described something that, strictly speaking, it would be impossible to draw, or even to visualise.

The second of the three circles bears our human likeness. Like a geometer trying to square the circle, Dante tries to understand this ultimate mystery of faith. There is another lightning flash which illuminates it. In what are almost the final lines of the poem he has an intuition, though he cannot remember it, of the way the human image is fitted to the circle—that is of the principle of the union of the divine and human natures in Christ. Then his imagination fails, as his intellect and will rotate, turned by the love that moves the heavens: *l'amor che move il sole e l'altre stelle.*

This summary of the final cantos of the *Paradiso* perforce loses the subtlety of presentation, the imaginative power, and the quality of Dante's poetic language: the vitality, the simultaneous limpidity and profundity, the brilliance of the images, the energised and lapidary quality of so many lines. In an earlier passage Dante had explained the need to accommodate to human limitations when talking of the divine. The need to talk to human beings in terms they can understand means, as he puts it, "giving God hands and feet," painting angels in churches with human faces so that human beings can connect, however imperfectly, with a reality that is ultimately beyond their capacity fully to comprehend.

Per questo la Scrittura condescende
  a vostra facultate, e piedi e mano
  attribuisce a Dio, e altro intende;
e Santa Chiesa con aspetto umano
  Gabrïel e Michel vi rappresenta, . . .   (*Par.* iv 40–48)

(This is why Scripture condescends to your capacities, and attributes feet and hands to God, and means something else; and
Holy Church represents Gabriel and Michael to you with a
human face . . .)

Dante's writing in the vernacular should be understood in this broader
context of the struggle to make divine realities intelligible to human
beings with their very real human limitations.

So why did Dante write the poem in Italian? One commonsense (and
perfectly sensible) answer is: to reach a wider audience. By adopting the
vernacular, the familiar, immediate, intimate language of daily life, he
is emulating the *sermo humilis* ("humble speech") of the Gospels, which
were read in Latin in his time, but in a simple, direct Latin far removed
from the rhetorical elaboration of the great classical authors. There is
a famous anecdote about Saint Jerome, the translator of the Bible into
Latin, being reproached in a dream for the pleasure he takes in the style
of classical writers. *Ciceronianus es, non Cristianus*, he is told: you are a
Ciceronian, not a Christian. That is, you care more for stylistic elegance
and refinement than for the truth of the message the words convey. The
Gospels have a message for all of humanity, not just for an educated elite.
So does the *Commedia*.

A truer answer to the question of why Dante wrote the poem in Italian is likely to be that he became aware that his command of the vernacular was more complete than his command of his *locutio secundaria*,
and closer to the source of his creative energies. He was a competent
writer of Latin prose, within the limitations imposed by his time and
his scholastic training. But his Italian was more alive, more expressive,

more instinctive, more varied and more original than anything he could do in Latin. To follow his creative instinct he had to jettison all the theoretical framework inherited from antiquity and his medieval predecessors about hierarchies of languages and stylistic levels within them and their appropriateness to different genres and subjects. It is a measure of his genius that he was able to do this. He could not have written with the same energy and power and marvellous fertility of invention had he written in Latin.

Dante's creative activity as a poet in its linguistic dimension seems best described by the words *seismic* or *volcanic*. After him, the linguistic terrain in Italy was radically and definitively altered. Like Adam in the Garden of Eden inventing the language he spoke by exercising his innate language faculty, Dante "invents" Italian by showing its full expressive and poetic potential in a single work which encompasses everything it means to be human. As we have seen, there was no standard or received form of Italian in existence at this time, any more than there was a received or standard form of English. But whereas in England geographical and cultural features conspired to make the eventual dominance of southern English centred on London and the court and a literary culture seem almost inevitable, with Italian the situation was far more problematic, since the geographical fragmentation went hand in hand with strong and competing local cultural traditions. Dante wrote a masterpiece which established Tuscan as the acknowledged (though never uncontested) norm for the language. The question of whether it really was the best and most appropriate form for writers to use and for Italians to speak continued to be debated robustly for centuries. Dialect cultures in Italy (Milanese, Roman, Venetian) had thriving literary exponents and vigorous local traditions until quite recently.

Why did Dante call his poem the *Commedia*? The most satisfactory answer to this perennial question is that the title reflects the linguistic inclusiveness of its language. (A less sophisticated answer, though not untrue, is that it is a comedy because it starts badly, in hell, and ends well, in heaven.) Comedy is no longer a genre which required the use of a single linguistic register (the middle register, as in traditional rhetorical theory), or even two linguistic registers (middle and low), as the *De vulgari* already allows. (The missing fourth book of the *De vulgari*, which was to deal with comedy, is as great a loss to medievalists as Aristotle's lost work on the same subject—the second book of the *Poetics*—is to classicists.) Now in his masterpiece it has become a genre that embraces all aspects of language which have expressive potential, with nothing excluded a priori as unsuitable. "Uncensored access to every coffer in the word-hoard" is the mark of its greatness.

The *Commedia* was an eruption into the field of vernacular poetry, subverting and overturning preconceived notions, systems, hierarchies. Dante created a new poetic form, the *terza rima*, and he created the language which made the new metrical scheme take on concrete form, a language which could be as earthily concrete or sublimely elevated as the context required. He produced a masterpiece in which the language was already fully formed, already showed everything it could do, how it could be used at all stylistic levels and registers with matchless expressive force. Hundreds of lines incised on the national memory bear witness to that lapidary power.

Here are some of the ones we have already seen. Florence is corrupted by *La gente nuova e i sùbiti guadagni* (*Inf.* xvi 73) ("the new people and the quick profits"). Dante loathed businessmen and bankers. Piccarda tells Dante why souls in the lowest sphere of heaven are content with their lot: *E 'n la sua volontade è nostra pace* (*Par.* iii, 85) ("And in His will is our peace"). Francesca draws a veil over what happened between her and Paolo: *quel giorno più non vi leggemmo avante* (*Inf.* v 138) ("That day we read no further"). Ugolino is equally reticent about his final hours: *Poscia, più che 'l dolor, poté 'l digiuno* (*Inf.* xxxiii 75) ("Then hunger was more powerful than sorrow").

Here are some other lines of particular rhythmic or expressive power. The souls in purgatory cleansing themselves of the stains of sin are *purgando la caligine del mondo* (*Purg.* xi 30) ("purging the mist of the world"). Dante walks along in tandem with Guinizzelli *lunga fiata rimirando lui* (*Purg.* xxvi 101) ("for a long time gazing at him"). Cacciaguida describes his death in the Crusades: *e venni dal martiro a questa pace* (*Par.* xv 148) ("and I came from martyrdom to this peace"). Manfred's appearance is striking: *biondo era e bello e di gentile aspetto* ("fair-haired he was, and handsome and noble-looking"). His bones should by rights still lie where they fell on the field of battle, *sotto la guardia de la grave mora* (*Purg.* iii 129) ("under the guardianship of the heavy cairn"). Pia de' Tolomei's life and death can be summed up in a line: *Siena mi fé, disfecemi Maremma* ("Siena made me, Maremma unmade me"). Oderisi turns eagerly towards Dante and his eagerness is reflected in the syntax and the urgent rhythm of the line: *e videmi e conobbemi e chiamava* (*Purg.* xi 76) ("and he saw me and recognised me and called out").

Dante seems able to do anything he wants with Italian. With effortless ease he modulates between lines where almost every syllable is a separate word to lines with as few as three words. Ten words, or even eleven, are fitted easily to the eleven metrical syllables: *lo mondo è cieco, e tu vien ben da lui* (*Purg.* xvi 66) ("the world is blind, and you certainly come from the world"); *che questa è in via e quella è già a riva* (*Purg.* xxv 54) ("for this is in mid-journey and the other has already arrived"). Lines with just three words can have massive poetic impact: *maravigliando diventaro smorte* (*Purg.* ii 69); ("in wonderment they became pale"); *sillogizzò invidiosi veri* (*Par.* x 138) ("with syllogistic argument he proved unwelcome truths"). In the *De vulgari* Dante had mentioned a long word that in itself constitutes a hendecasyllable (*sovramagnificentissimamente*), and reminded his readers that there is an even longer word (too long for poetry): *honorificabilitudinitate* (which has twelve syllables, and thirteen in oblique cases in Latin). The same word, obviously a novelty item, is mentioned by Shakespeare in *Love's Labour's Lost*, and seems to have had the same currency in medieval and early modern times as modern *floccinaucinihilipilification*, which, as most English-speaking children know, is the longest word in English.

Fitting the syntax to the metre seems as effortless as fitting the words to the hendecasyllable. The matching of syntax to tercet is strikingly frictionless: it seems inevitable and preordained. A sentence almost invariably ends at the end of a line, usually at the end of a tercet. The last line of a tercet is often the strongest, the final rhyme of the three locking the meaning into place. Single tercets often have a lapidary quality. When strung together, as they are when a series or list of examples is given, they are like perfect beads on a string. Here is one from the list of examples of pride punished in *Purgatorio* xii:

> Mostrava ancor lo duro pavimento
>   come Almeon a sua madre fé caro
>   parer lo sventurato addornamento.   (*Purg.* xii 49–51)

> (And now the rocky pavement showed how Alcmeon made his
>   mother think it a heavy price to pay for the unlucky necklace.)

The self-contained perfection of single tercets can be illustrated from across the poem. There are countless tercets which stand as perfect examples of the form. Here is one, chosen at random:

> Chiamavi 'l cielo e 'ntorno vi si gira,
>   mostrandovi le sue bellezze etterne,
>   e l'occhio vostro pur a terra mira;   (*Purg.* xiv 148–50)

> (The heavens call you and circle around you, showing you their
>   eternal beauty, and yet your eyes still gaze at the earth;)

Dante becomes more confident in his mastery of his metre as the poem progresses. Increasingly, tercets are linked into larger syntactic structures, though there is still almost always a clear division between the single tercets which comprise a longer unit. Tercets linked together in this way tend to be clearly marked-off parts of a larger structure, syntactically and conceptually distinct components which build to a larger whole. When Dante gets going, the magnificent sweep of linked tercets seems an unstoppable flow. But although the impetus and momentum is similar, nothing could be rhythmically further from the grand flow of Miltonic blank verse in *Paradise Lost*, with its constant enjambement and sentences ending mid-line.

Here is Beatrice berating Dante in *Purgatorio* xxx in the earthly paradise. He has not seen her for ten years. We might have expected a moment
of joyous reunion. But instead she takes him fiercely to task, explaining
to the angels who accompany her how he abandoned her after her death.
At this climactic moment he is reminded (we are reminded) of how far
he strayed from the true path, how dire was the moral and spiritual condition into which he sank, how necessary this visit to the afterlife was if
he was to be saved from the dark wood in which he found himself at the
beginning of the poem.

Beatrice explains to the angels that his natural gifts—both those due
to propitious stellar influences (first tercet) and those given him directly
by God (second tercet)—singled him out as a young man of extraordinary promise (third tercet):

> Non pur per ovra de le rote magne,
>> che drizzan ciascun seme ad alcun fine
>> secondo che le stelle son compagne,
> ma per larghezza di grazie divine,
>> che sì alti vapori hanno a lor piova,
>> che nostre viste là non van vicine,
> questi fu tal ne la sua vita nova
>> virtualmente, ch'ogne abito destro
>> fatto averebbe in lui mirabil prova.   (*Purg.* xxx 109–117)

> (Not only through the working of the great wheels, which direct
>> every seed to its end according as the stars accompany it, but
>> through abundance of divine grace, which rains down from
>> such lofty vapours that our sight falls far short of it, this man
>> in his youth was such in his natural potential that every good
>> disposition would have had a marvellous outcome in him.)

The linked sequence echoes the three-part structuring of a syllogistic
argument, building to an unarguable conclusion. But alas, the young
man went astray after her death:

Quando di carne a spirito era salita,
  e bellezza e virtù cresciuta m'era,
  fu' io a lui men cara e men gradita;
e volse i passi suoi per via non vera,
  imagini di ben seguendo false,
  che nulla promession rendono intera.   (*Purg.* xxx 127–32)

(When I had risen from flesh to spirit, and my beauty and virtue
  had increased, I was less dear to him and less pleasing; and he
  turned his steps along a path that was not true, following false
  images of good, which never fully deliver what they promise.)

These are the merest, briefest hints of what Dante can do with *terza rima*. To quote Seamus Heaney on the language of poetry one last time: "Poetry is language in orbit . . . it runs on its own energy circuit. And the energy coursing in the circuit is generated and flows between the words and the metre, the metre and the line, the line and the stanza . . ." Dante created a new poetic form, the *terza rima*, and he created the language to go with it. The language he fashioned flows into and fills with seemingly effortless ease and grace the metrical scheme he invented. The two are a perfect match. The *Commedia* is perhaps the greatest example in Western civilisation of human making by a craftsman *col nome che più dura e più onora* ("the name that lasts longest and brings most honour"): a wordsmith, a craftsman using language, a maker with words — a poet.

EXCURSUS ON METRE

A. THE HENDECASYLLABLE

Every line of the *Commedia* is a hendecasyllable—that is, it has (must have)
eleven syllables, with the exception of a small number of lines where the
final word is a *parola tronca*, with an accent on the final syllable (here
the line will have ten syllables), or a *parola sdrucciola*, with an accent on
the antepenultimate syllable (and here the line will have twelve syllables).
Both these exceptions are used very sparingly. In the 14,233 lines of the
poem, there are thirty-two ten-syllable lines—for example, *Purg.* iv 72
(asterisks mark the accentuated syllables): che mal non se*ppe carreggiar*
Feto*n; and just seventeen twelve-syllable lines—for example, *Inf.* xxiv 66:
a parole forma*r disconvene*vole. These ten-syllable and twelve-syllable
lines are still technically hendecasyllables (see below).
Lines that appear to have more than eleven syllables, as many of them
do at first glance, prove to have exactly eleven when the principles
of what can loosely be called elision (the technical term is sinaloepha) are taken into account. Sinaloepha is mandatory between vowels
across word divisions, except in certain specific circumstances. Thus
the phrase *"selva oscura"* has four syllables, not five: sel¹va_o²scu³ra⁴,
even though the metrical calculation does not affect the pronunci-
ation of the words (both the *a* of *selva* and the *o* of *oscura* are pho-
netically fully articulated when the line is read aloud). Elision in the
normal English sense where a sound is suppressed is always indicated

by an apostrophe, as in *la notte ch'i' passai con tanta pieta*, where *che io* is elided to become *ch'i'*. Dante's use of sinaloepha is one of the most telling aspects of his metrical mastery. Thus a line like *biondo era e bello e di gentile aspetto* has four cases of sinaloepha, meaning that fifteen syllables scan as eleven.

Accentual stresses in the line are also crucial. There must always be a stress on the tenth syllable—this is the fundamental rule. (This rule accounts for the admissibility of the ten- and twelve-syllable lines described in the first paragraph.) There will be a second stress on either the sixth or the fourth syllable, and where the second stress is on the fourth syllable, there will be another stress on the seventh or eighth syllable.

These "three canonical patterns," as they are sometimes called (6, 10; 4, 7, 10; 4, 8, 10), account for over 99.7 percent of the 14,233 lines of the poem. There is only a tiny handful of exceptions. (Dante scholars continue to debate how these apparently anomalous lines are to be read.) We do not know Dante's views on the stresses on the sixth or fourth syllable, and we cannot even be certain that he thought in terms of three basic types of hendecasyllable. The types were theorised only in the sixteenth century in his *Prose della volgar lingua* by Pietro Bembo, who based his analysis on Petrarch's much more regular metrical practice.

In accordance with the principles just described, almost every line of the poem will fall naturally into two halves: a slightly longer half followed by a slightly shorter half (the 6-10 pattern, conventionally termed *a maiore*), or a slightly shorter followed by a slightly longer half (4-7-10 or 4-8-10, conventionally termed *a minore*). There will usually be a slight natural sense pause or caesura separating the two halves.

The hendecasyllable is thus fundamentally different in its governing principles and its rhythmic structure from the English iambic pentameter, which it superficially resembles in length. Compare Gray's "Elegy Written in a Country Churchyard" as a classic example of iambic pentameter:

> The curfew tolls the knell of parting day,
> The lowing herd wind slowly o'er the lea,

The ploughman homeward plods his weary way,
And leaves the world to darkness and to me.

The first two lines of the *Commedia* illustrate the *a maiore* and *a minore* patterns (the asterisks mark the accented syllables):

Nel mezzo del cammi*n // di nostra vi*ta [6, 10]
mi ritrova*i // per una se*lva_oscu*ra [4, 8, 10].

(Diphthongs like the -*ai* of *ritrovai* are normally elided and count as one syllable.) The seemingly endless and effortless variety of modulation and rhythmic effect Dante produces within this tightly controlled scheme is one of the miracles of the poem.

The entire text of the *Commedia* marked up for metrical analysis can be consulted online at www.italianverse.reading.ac.uk. This invaluable resource is the work of David Robey. Readers interested in hearing the poem read aloud can go to www.princeton.edu/dante, where Lino Pertile reads the whole text. Alternatively, they can turn to the readings on CD made by a collection of Italian actors, including the incomparable Romolo Valli (for details, see p. 288.)

B. THE INVENTION OF THE *TERZA RIMA*

We can only speculate about how Dante came to invent the *terza rima*. Two generations before Dante, Giacomo da Lentini, an Italian poet working at the court of Frederick II in Palermo, invented the sonnet, and the form immediately became popular. The structure of the sonnet as it was used by Italian poets up to and beyond Petrarch and the Renaissance consists of a pair of quatrains (the octave), followed by a pair of tercets (the sestet). One set of rhyme sounds is used in the quatrains (commonly in the pattern *abba* or *abab*, repeated); a new set is introduced in the tercets. The varying possibilities for the arrangement of the rhymes in the tercets allow for an element of experiment and subtle variation, which Dante and his contemporary poets exploited to the full. Here are the patterns used by Cavalcanti and Dante in their sonnets: *cdc cdc*; *cde cde*; *cde edc*; *cdc cdd*; *cdd dcc*; *cde dce*; *cdc dcd*. The last one is already potentially close to the *terza rima*.

Shakespeare's sonnets, more familiar to English readers, crucially alter this structure, replacing two quatrains and two tercets [4+4+3+3] with three quatrains and a couplet [4+4+4+2]. This structure, with its clinching couplet, feels very different both in its organisation and its rhythm.

A plausible explanation for Dante's invention of the *terza rima* sees it as a fruitful cross between the tercet of the sonnet and the four-line metrical unit of the *serventese*, a more extended verse form that had been imported into Italy from Provence. The *serventese* was commonly used for narrative, discursive and satirical rather than lyric poems. One form of the *serventese* popular in Italy used a four-line unit with a relatively undemanding rhyme scheme (*aaab bbbc*), where a shorter fourth line created a link through rhyme to the following unit. Against the sonnet's mandatory fourteen lines, the *serventese* could be as long as the poet pleased. Dante certainly wrote at least one *serventese*, though it no longer survives. It was a poem, he tells us in the *Vita nova*, in which he listed the names of all the attractive young ladies in Florence, and in which, no matter how he rearranged the material, Beatrice's name always ended up in ninth position. Nine is of course three times three, and thus doubly significant as Beatrice's number.

Dante wrote many sonnets, and he may have written a sonnet sequence. If, as many people believe, he is the author of *Il Fiore* ("The Flower")—a late-thirteenth-century Italian translation of the *Roman de la Rose* into a sonnet sequence—then he had worked with the tercet as an element in an extended narrative structure, albeit still embedded within the sonnet form. The sonnets of the *Fiore* all follow the pattern *cdc dcd* in their tercets, with no variation or experimentation at all: this pattern, as noted above, is already potentially close to the *terza rima*. All that remained to do was to eliminate the quatrains, liberate the tercets from the larger metrical structure, and devise the linking rhyme scheme.

GLOSSARY

ALLEGORY A technique of composition and interpretation by which a work is deemed to have more than a single meaning.

ANTE-PURGATORY A steep, rocky region at the base of the mountain of purgatory where those who repented only at the end of their lives must wait to begin the process of purgation. There Dante finds the excommunicates (who must wait there thirty times the length of their excommunication), the lazy, those who died a violent death and repented in extremis, and princes whose secular responsibilities distracted them from a proper sense of their spiritual duties.

ARTE ("art") In the context of medieval politics, the primary meaning of *arte* is "guild": thus the Palagio dell'Arte della Lana (now the home of the Società Dantesca Italiana in Florence) is the Wool Guild Hall. More broadly, *arte* is any skill or expertise acquired by study and training; an artist is one who is skilled at making things.

BARGELLO The seat of government in the Florentine commune before the building of Palazzo Vecchio. Also known as Palazzo della Podestà. Now a national museum.

CANTO The name of each of the one hundred sections into which the *Commedia* is divided.

CANTICA ("canticle") The name given to each of the three major sections of the poem, *Inferno*, *Purgatorio* and *Paradiso*.

CERCHIA ANTICA ("ancient circle") The old Roman walls of Florence, still the city walls in the early Middle Ages at the time of Dante's great-great-grandfather Cacciaguida. They were subsequently vastly expanded, first in 1258 and then in 1284–1333. See map on p. 12.

COMUNE ("commune") The normal term in medieval times for the independent city-states or city-republics of central Italy, which valued and defended their autonomy in the face of threats from both papacy and empire. In modern Italian, the Comune is the central administrative body of any city.

DOLCE STIL NOVO ("sweet new style") The term used in *Purgatorio* xxiv by Bonagiunta da Lucca, an earlier Tuscan poet, to describe Dante's style in his lyric poetry. The two adjectives suggest stylistic refinement (*dolce*) and thematic innovation (*novo*): in both respects Dante is said by Bonagiunta to have marked a break with his vernacular precursors.

EARTHLY PARADISE The place where Adam and Eve lived before they were expelled for eating from the Tree of Knowledge; also known as the Garden of Eden.

EDITIO PRINCEPS ("first edition") The first printed edition of any given book. These editions (and indeed all early editions) are of great interest to scholars, since they often enable us to reconstruct lost manuscripts on which they were based.

EMPYREAN The name for where God and the blessed reside, beyond time and space.

FIGURALISM A technique of biblical interpretation that establishes a network of meaningful links between characters and episodes in the Old and New Testaments. This kind of "theological" allegory is distinguished from poetic allegory by the fact that both literal and secondary meaning are believed to be historically true (in "poetic" allegory, the literal meaning is fictional).

INTERTEXTUALITY A term used to signify the many ways in which one literary work echoes, or is inescapably linked to, another literary work. The two great "intertexts" of the *Commedia* are the *Aeneid* and the Bible, but there are countless other connections with works of classical and medieval literature.

LIMBO (literally, "edge") The name of the first circle of Dante's hell—

that is, its outer edge—where the virtuous pagans who lived before the coming of Christ, including the great poets and philosophers of the classical world, are found.

MANUSCRIPT A handwritten copy of a work. Before the invention of printing in the mid-fifteenth century, all books were manuscripts. No two manuscripts are identical, so where there is no autograph copy (that is, no copy in the author's own hand), editors are faced with the problem of reconstructing medieval texts from varied and sometimes conflicting testimony.

MIGLIOR FABBRO ("better craftsman") The term used by Guido Guinizzelli in *Purgatorio* xxvi to acknowledge the superior artistry of the Provençal poet Arnaut Daniel; the phrase was famously used by T. S. Eliot when he dedicated *The Waste Land* to Ezra Pound.

NEOPLATONIC The adjective is applied to works and ideas touched by the strong renewal of interest in Plato's thought in fifteenth-century Florence, inspired in particular by the philosopher and humanist Marsilio Ficino, who translated and commented on all Plato's extant works. Cristoforo Landino's commentary on the *Commedia* is Neoplatonic in its interpretation of the poem, highlighting as it does the idea of the upward movement of the human soul to God as it frees itself from the domination of the senses.

PODESTÀ ("Chief magistrate") To avoid partisanship, the post was normally held by an outsider, not by a Florentine.

POPOLO ("people") In the context of medieval Florentine politics, *popolo* usually refers not to the whole population of the city, but to that part of it whose interests were in conflict with those of the powerful families (*magnati*, "magnates" or more simply *grandi*, "the big guys") who historically had controlled the commune. The *popolo* was made up of some members of the major guilds (*popolo grasso*, "fat" or "prosperous people") and the minor guilds (*popolo minuto*, "little people"). The admission of the *popolo* to full participation in the political process in the closing decades of the thirteenth century was bitterly and bloodily contested.

PRIMUM MOBILE ("first mover") The ninth heavenly sphere, which imparts motion to all the nesting spheres enclosed within it.

PRIOR The name given to the six elected officials who served a two-month term of office as head of the commune.

QUADERNO ("gathering") In medieval bookmaking, a gathering was the name for a number of pages folded and stitched together, usually in groups of 3, 4, 5 or 6 (creating 6, 8, 10 or 12 leaves, and twice that many pages if we count recto and verso separately). The gatherings are then stitched or glued together to form a codex or manuscript. In a striking image at the end of the poem, Dante uses the verb *squadernarsi* ("to be dispersed in separate gatherings") for the multifariousness of experience in the universe, which in his final moment of vision he sees bound in a single volume by divine love. In modern Italian a *quaderno* is a notebook.

SCRIPTORIUM Originally the room in a monastery dedicated to the copying of manuscripts; subsequently the name given in towns to commercial premises devoted to copying texts.

SERMO HUMILIS ("humble speech") The term is used for the simple, direct Latin of the Bible, as contrasted with the elaborate rhetoric of classical writers like Cicero.

SESTIERE Medieval Florence was divided into six districts or quarters. One prior came from each *sestiere*.

SPIRITI MAGNI ("great souls") The term used of the virtuous pagans in Limbo, including the great poets and philosophers of the ancient world.

STELLE FISSE ("fixed stars") The stars, including the constellations of the zodiac. They are "fixed" in that their position in relation to one another never changes, unlike the planets, whose orbits can be tracked across the sky at night. In Dante's cosmos, the "fixed stars" form an eighth or "crystalline" sphere inside which the seven planetary spheres are nested. This eighth sphere is in turn enclosed by the *primum mobile* ("first mover"), the ninth sphere, which imparts motion to all those below. See Fig. 28 on p. 161.

TENZONE ("conflict" or "quarrel") In literature, a dispute conducted in verse, usually in the form of an exchange of sonnets.

TERZA RIMA The metre of the poem, consisting of an interlinking series of tercets, where the middle rhyme of one tercet becomes the first and third rhymes of the following one (so *aba bcb cdc ded* . . .). See the "Excursus on Metre" on pp. 263–66 for a full account.

TERZINA ("tercet") The three-line unit of which the *terza rima* is composed.

TORRE DELLA CASTAGNA The tower where the priors were sequestered during their two-month term of office to keep them safe from intimidation and violence. Still standing in Florence today.

UBI SUNT? ("where are they?") A traditional motif in medieval literature, mourning the passing of time and the disappearance of once–familiar things; often echoed in later writers as well, as in the French poet Villon's phrase *où sont les neiges d'antan?*, translated by Dante Gabriel Rossetti as "where are the snows of yesteryear?" (quoted, in French, by Maggie Smith in *Downton Abbey*, no less).

VULGARE ("vernacular") The spoken language one learns instinctively and spontaneously as a child by imitating one's parents and family; no schooling or study is involved. Whereas in the modern world education normally takes place in one's vernacular—one's so-called mother tongue—in medieval times the language of any kind of advanced study was not the vernacular but Latin (*gramatica*).

1250 Death of Emperor Frederick II; for sixty years there will be no crowned Holy Roman Emperor, and there will be no effective incumbent in Dante's lifetime.

1260 Battle of Montaperti. The Sienese Ghibellines, in alliance with the Florentine Ghibellines led by Farinata degli Uberti, defeat the Florentine Guelfs and expel them from the city.

1265 Dante is born in Florence.

1266 Battle of Benevento. Manfred, the illegitimate son of Frederick II, is killed and imperial hopes in the Italian peninsula die; the Guelfs return to power in Florence.

> *c. 1283* → Dante establishes himself as a leading love poet in Florence.

1289 Battle of Campaldino. Dante serves with the Florentine Guelf forces against the Ghibelline city of Arezzo.

> *c. 1292* Dante assembles an anthology of his poems with linking narrative to form the *Vita nova*, in celebration of his love for Beatrice, a Florentine girl who had died two years earlier.

> *c. 1293* → Dante embarks on the study of philosophy; he goes on to write poems on philosophical themes.

1293 The Ordinances of Justice mark a radical move towards a more democratic political system in Florence: more than seventy powerful elite families are excluded from eligibility for office and the right to vote, while major (and later minor) guild members now become eligible.

1294 Boniface VIII becomes pope, following the abdication of the hermit pope Celestine V.

1295 Dante enters political life in the commune of Florence, having enrolled in the guild of physicians and apothecaries; in the following years, he serves on several councils; the Guelfs split into two factions, which will become known as Blacks and Whites.

1300 *June 15–August 15*: Dante serves as one of the six priors who exercise executive power under the Gonfaloniere di Giustizia, or Standard-Bearer of Justice. Guido Cavalcanti is sent into exile and dies later in the summer.

> *1300 Easter*: the fictional date of Dante's journey to the realms of the afterlife as it will be described in the *Commedia*.

1301 *October*: Dante is absent from Florence when the Black Guelfs, whose leaders had recently been exiled, stage a coup and return to power (he is probably on a mission representing the commune at the papal curia in Rome).

1302 *January 27*: in his absence, Dante is fined, excluded from public office and banished from Tuscany on a fabricated charge of corruption.

March 10: the sentence is confirmed; if Dante falls into the commune's power, he will be burnt at the stake.

December: Boniface proclaims the supreme authority of the church in temporal affairs in the bull *Unam sanctam*.

1303   *October*: death of Boniface.
       Election of Benedict XI, who dies the following year.

1304   Dante becomes a "party on his own," abandoning his allegiance
       to his fellow White Guelf exiles; in the following years, he trav-
       els extensively all over Italy.

> *c. 1304–c. 1308* Dante writes the *De vulgari eloquentia*, his
> treatise on vernacular speech, and the *Convivio*, which is
> to provide an extensive prose commentary on his philo-
> sophical poems (both works remain unfinished).

1305   Election of Pope Clement V, a Frenchman who never comes to
       Rome; the papacy is subsequently established in Avignon.

1308   Henry of Luxembourg is chosen by the imperial electors, and has
       Clement's backing.

> *c. 1308* Dante starts the *Commedia*, which he works on
> until shortly before his death.

1309   *January*: Henry is crowned as Emperor Henry VII at Aix-
       la-Chapelle (Aachen in German, Aquisgrana in Italian).

1310   *October*: Henry VII embarks on his Italian campaign. Dante writes
       an open letter in Latin to the rulers and people of Italy, urging
       them to welcome the emperor, who will bring peace and justice.

       Pope Boniface is posthumously brought to trial by Philip the
       Fair of France; the charges include nepotism, usury, sorcery,
       heresy and atheism.

1311   *January*: Henry VII is crowned in Milan.

       March 31: Dante writes to the Florentines, urging them to recog-
       nise Henry.

       April 17: Dante writes to the emperor, urging him to act against
       Florence, "the viper that turns against the vitals of her mother."

1312   *June*: Henry VII is crowned in Rome, but (because of papal opposition) not in St. Peter's.

1313   *April*: Henry declares all men subject to the emperor's authority.

   June: Clement's bull *Pastoralis cura* rejects imperial claims to overlordship.

   August: Henry VII dies; the imperial electors fail to reach agreement on a successor.

1314   at the very earliest and possibly much later: Dante writes the *Monarchia*.

1315   *June*: an amnesty is offered to the Florentine exiles, provided they acknowledge their guilt; Dante rejects the offer.

   October: Dante's exile from Florence is reconfirmed for life and is now extended to his children (his punishment if captured will be decapitation); his later years are spent in Verona at the court of Can Grande della Scala and in Ravenna at the court of Guido Novello da Polenta.

   c. 1320 Dante writes the *Questio* and the *Egloge*.

1321   Dante dies at Ravenna.

   c. 1325 Dante's son Jacopo takes a complete copy of the *Commedia* to Florence, where it immediately becomes popular and is widely copied.

   c. 1327 The Dominican Guido Vernani writes the *De reprobatione Monarchiae*, a savage attack on Dante's political treatise. He does not name Dante, but refers to him as "the vessel of the Devil."

1329   According to Boccaccio, the *Monarchia* is publicly burnt as a heretical text in Bologna, but a plan to burn Dante's bones with his treatise is foiled.

1335   The *Commedia* is banned by the Dominican order in Tuscany.

1336   The oldest securely dated surviving copy of the poem dates from 1336.

1472   The *editio princeps* of the *Commedia* is published at Foligno in April; other editions follow in the same year at Mantua and Venice. A few years later, editions with commentaries are printed in Venice, Milan and Florence.

1554   The *Monarchia* is placed on the Vatican's Index of prohibited books, from which it is removed only in the twentieth century.

1559   The *editio princeps* of the *Monarchia* is published in Basle.

A BASIC DANTE BIBLIOGRAPHY CONSISTS OF SOME FIFTY THOUSAND items. A new book or scholarly article on Dante is published almost every day. More than a generation ago, scholars were already talking of the dismay they felt in the face of these facts. What I offer here is a highly selective bibliography, mostly in English, designed to enable readers to explore the various themes developed in each chapter by consulting resources that are readily available and that, wherever possible, incorporate the findings of the most recent research. The list also includes some classic studies that any Dante enthusiast will want to read. The bibliography is organised by chapter, followed by a general section, some recommended translations of Dante's works into English, and a list of electronic resources.

CHAPTER 1

Guido da Pisa's Latin commentary on the *Inferno* is available in an English edition: Guido da Pisa's *Expositiones et Glose super Comediam Dantis or Commentary on Dante's Inferno*, ed., with notes and an introduction, Vincenzo Cioffari (Albany: State University of New York Press, 1974). All the early commentaries on the poem can be consulted online, and line by line, at the invaluable Dartmouth Dante Project (DDP) Web site (http://dante.dartmouth.edu).

On merchant life in medieval Europe, Peter Spufford's *Power and Profit: The Merchant in Medieval Europe* (London: Thames and Hudson, 2002) is authoritative, richly illustrated and unmatched in its wealth of detail.

On the buildings and city architecture of medieval Florence, Richard Goy's *Florence: The City and its Architecture* (London: Phaidon, 2002) is a good starting point. On Arnolfo di Cambio and his contribution to the architecture and sculpture of late-thirteenth-century Italy, there is no study in English to match the splendid exhibition catalogue *Arnolfo: Alle origini del Rinascimento fiorentino*, ed. Enrica Neri Lusanna (Florence: Polistampa, 2005).

A magisterial account of Florence in Dante's time is given in the opening chapters of John M. Najemy's *A History of Florence, 1200–1575* (Oxford: Blackwell Publishing Ltd, 2006). A good English translation of Compagni is *Dino Compagni's Chronicle of Florence*, trans., with an introduction and notes, Daniel E. Bornstein (Philadelphia: University of Pennsylvania Press, 1986). Daniel Waley's *The Italian City Republics* (London: Weidenfeld and Nicholson, 1969) gives a comprehensive overview of medieval Italian communes, with a helpful account of the Guelfs and Ghibellines (pp. 200–218).

Herbert L. Kessler and Johanna Zacharias, *Rome 1300: On the Path of the Pilgrim* (New Haven: Yale University Press, 2000), is about the first Jubilee. *Bonifacio VIII e il suo tempo. Anno 1300 il primo Giubileo*, ed. Marina Righetti Tosti-Croce (Milan: Electa, 2000), is the catalogue of an exhibition to mark the 2000 Jubilee in Rome.

On medieval political thought, Antony Black's *Political Thought in Europe 1250–1450* (Cambridge: Cambridge University Press, 1992) offers a useful overview. Nicolai Rubinstein's "The Beginnings of Political Thought in Florence," in *Journal of the Warburg and Courtauld Institutes* 5 (1942): 198–227, is a more narrowly focused study.

Dante's sonnets to Forese Donati and Forese's to Dante can be found, with an ample commentary, in Kenelm Foster and Patrick Boyde, *Dante's Lyric Poetry* (Oxford: Oxford University Press, 1967); vol. 1, pp. 148–55: texts of the sonnets and translation; vol. 2, pp. 242–53: commentary. Piero Boitani's *Dante's Poetry of the Donati* (Leeds: Maney Publishing, 2007) examines the role of this extended Florentine family in the

Commedia. Anthony Cassell, "Mostrando con le poppe il petto" (*Purg. xxiii 102*), in *Dante Studies* 96 (1978): 75–81, cites the sumptuary laws introduced in 1310 by the newly appointed bishop of Florence that prohibit women's dress from leaving uncovered any part of the torso, on pain of excommunication.

Erich Auerbach's *Mimesis: The Representation of Reality in Western Literature,* trans. W. Task (New York: Doubleday Anchor, 1957), contains a classic account of Farinata and Cavalcante in *Inferno* x.

CHAPTER 2

T. S. R. Boase's *Boniface the Eighth, 1294–1303* (London: Constable, 1933) is an exhaustive biography of the pope Dante loathed, including a full account of the charges brought against Boniface in his posthumous trial and the testimony against him (ch. 14: "Trial Without Verdict," pp. 353–79). See also *Boniface VIII en procès: Articles d'accusation e dépositions des témoins (1303–1311),* ed., with introduction and notes, Jean Coste (Rome: Fondazione Camillo Caetani—L'Erma di Bretschneider, 1995). This weighty volume (almost one thousand pages) also prints the invective against Boniface of another medieval Italian poet, Jacopone da Todi (pp. 65–69). The design for the façade of the new cathedral in Florence with Arnolfo di Cambio's statue of Boniface in pride of place is discussed in *Arnolfo: Alle origini del Rinascimento fiorentino,* cited above. A reconstructed model of the façade, with the statue of Boniface on the third tier to the left of the main entrance, is on display in the Museo dell'Opera del Duomo in Florence, along with the statue itself.

On the Celestine affair, Valerio Gigliotti (University of Turin), "Celestine V According to Dante: Law and Literature" (paper delivered at the 45th International Congress on Medieval Studies, Kalamazoo, Michigan, 2010, publication forthcoming), analyses the legal debate surrounding Celestine's abdication. B. McGinn, "Angel Pope and Papal Antichrist," in *Church History* 47 (1978): 155–73, puts the episode in a broader context.

Daniel Waley, *The Papal State in the Thirteenth Century* (London: Macmillan, 1961). William M. Bowsky, *Henry VII in Italy: The Conflict of Empire and City-State, 1310–1313* (Lincoln: University of Nebraska Press, 1960). Kenelm Foster, "The Canto of the Damned Popes, *Inferno XIX*," in *The Two Dantes and Other Studies* (London: Darton, Longman and Todd, 1977), expertly places Dante's condemnation of Boniface against the wider background of papal intrigues and misconduct in the thirteenth century.

CHAPTER 3

The *Codice diplomatico dantesco,* ed. R. Piattoli (Florence: Gonnelli, 1940), prints all the surviving documentary evidence about Dante's life. Stephen Bemrose's *A New Life of Dante* (Exeter: University of Exeter Press, 2000) gives a sober and reliable account of the secure facts. Giovanni Boccaccio's *Life of Dante*, trans. Philip Wicksteed (London: Oneworld Classics, Ltd., 2009), is more fanciful. This small volume also contains Leonardo Bruni's *Life of Dante* as an appendix, and short excerpts concerning Dante from Giovanni Villani's *Chronicle.*

All Dante's surviving letters can be read in Paget Toynbee, *The Letters of Dante* (Oxford: Clarendon Press, 1920). Dante Alighieri, *Four Political Letters*, trans. and with a commentary by Claire E. Honess (London: Modern Humanities Research Association, 2007), offers a version of the political letters in less antiquated English. Giancarlo Savino reconstructs the autograph of the *Commedia* in *L'Autografo virtuale della "Commedia,"* (Florence: Società Dantesca Italiana, 2000).

Charles T. Davis's *"Dante's Italy and Other Essays* (Philadelphia: University of Pennsylvania Press, 1984) is a collection of essays on many aspects of Dante's world, including "Education in Dante's Florence," "Dante's Vision of History," and "Brunetto Latini and Dante." The scholars who have called into question Brunetto's homosexuality are: André Pézard, *Dante sous la pluie de feu (Enfer, chant XV)* (Paris: J. Vrin, 1950); Richard Kay, *Dante's Swift and Strong: Essays on Inferno XV* (Lawrence: Regents Press of Kansas, 1978); Peter Armour, "Dante's Brunetto: The Paternal

Patarine?" in *Italian Studies* 38 (1983): 1–38. John M. Najemy, "Brunetto Latini's 'Politica,'" in *Dante Studies* 112 (1994): 33–51, examines Brunetto's political thought in relation to the turbulent Florentine background. The bibliography on the allegory of the *Commedia* is vast, and I list here just a few key items. A seminal essay by Erich Auerbach entitled "Figura," first published in German in 1938, is available in *Scenes from the Drama of European Literature*, trans. R. Mannheim (New York: Meridian, 1959), pp. 11–76. Johan Chydenius, "The Typological Problem in Dante: A Study in the History of Medieval Ideas," in *Commentationes humanarum litterarum* (Societas Scientiarum Fennica) 25, no. 1 (1958): 1–159, is another fundamental contribution; as is Robert Hollander, *Allegory in Dante's Commedia* (Princeton, NJ.: Princeton University Press, 1969). The Charles Singleton quotation cited on p. 82 is to be found in "The Irreducible Dove," in *Comparative Literature* 9 (1957): 129–35.

On the figurative side, Peter Breiger, Millard Meiss, Charles S. Singleton, *Illuminated Manuscripts of the Divine Comedy* (Princeton, NJ; Princeton University Press, 1969), remains a fundamental work of reference. Sandro Botticelli, *The Drawings for Dante's Divine Comedy* (London: Royal Academy of Arts, 2000) is a handsome volume that reproduces all the surviving drawings. The connection between the figurative arts and the punishments in Dante's hell is explored in Anthony K. Cassell's *Dante's Fearful Art of Justice* (Toronto: University of Toronto Press, 1984).

High-quality digitised images of five early manuscripts of the *Commedia*, showing the characteristic layout of the poem—including ms. Trivulziano 1080, which gives a good idea of what the autograph might have looked like—are to be found on the DVD Dante Alighieri, *Commedia*, ed. Prue Shaw (Florence and Birmingham: Sismel-SDE, 2010). The Società Dantesca Italiana Web site (http://www.dantesca.it) lists all the known surviving manuscripts of the poem, and gives a complete digitised image record of a small number of them.

William Anderson, *Dante the Maker* (London: Routledge and Kegan Paul, 1980).

CHAPTER 4

The Translations of Ezra Pound, with an Introduction by Hugh Kenner (London: Faber and Faber, 1963), contains all of Pound's Cavalcanti translations, including "Donna me prega."

Dante's concept of nobility as consisting of innate intellectual capacity and sensitivity, and not wealth or family connections, is explored in Book IV of the *Convivio*, and in his poem "Le dolci rime d'amor, ch'i solia"; the Foster-Boyde commentary on this poem (Foster and Boyde, *Dante's Lyric Poetry*, cited heretofore: text and translation, vol. 1, pp. 128–39; commentary, vol. 2, pp. 210–28) is particularly helpful.

Estela V. Welldon's *Playing with Dynamite* (London: Karnak, 2011) develops the idea of interposing thought between impulse and action as the key to treating compulsive sexual offenders in the context of forensic dynamic psychotherapy.

Patrick Boyde, *Human Vices and Human Worth in Dante's Comedy* (Cambridge: Cambridge University Press, 2000), analyses the ethical values reflected in the *Commedia* in relation to the classical, Christian and courtly ethical systems, and concludes with an assessment of Dante's Ulysses seen against this background.

CHAPTER 5

Charles T. Davis's *Dante and the Idea of Rome* (Oxford: Oxford University Press, 1957) is the classic study of this subject.

Alan C. Charity, *Events and Their Afterlife: The Dialectics of Christian Typology in the Bible and Dante* (Cambridge: Cambridge University Press, 1987).

CHAPTER 6

The Wolf Man's trinitarian obsession is cited by Tom McCarthy in "Letting Rip: The primal scene, the veil and Excreta in Joyce and Freud (originally delivered at the International James Joyce Symposium, Dublin, 2004; published in *Hypermedia Joyce Studies* 5, 2005). The Tom

Phillips lithographs can be found in *Dante's Inferno: the first part of the Divine Comedy of Dante Alighieri*, trans., and illus. Tom Phillips (London: Thames & Hudson, 1985).

Saint Augustine, *The Trinity*, trans. Stephen McKenna, C.SS.R. (Washington, D.C.: Catholic University of America Press, 1963). Augustine's meditation on the trinitarian nature of the human mind occupies books 9, 10 and 11; book 10, chapters 11 and 12, focuses on memory, understanding and will.

A fuller and more nuanced account of Dante's ideas about creation is to be found in Patrick Boyde's *Dante Philomythes: Man in the Cosmos* (Cambridge: Cambridge University Press, 1981).

Honorius of Autun on syllogisms lurking in the Bible is quoted by G. Cremascoli, "Allegoria e dialettica: sul travaglio dell' esegesi biblica al tempo di Dante," in *Dante e la Bibbia*, ed. G. Barblan, (Florence: Olschki, 1988), p. 165.

V. H. Hopper, *Medieval Number Symbolism* (New York: Columbia University Press, 1938).

Ernst Robert Curtius, *European Literature and the Latin Middle Ages*, trans. Willard R. Trask, from the German (New York: Pantheon Books, 1953).

Jacques Le Goff, *The Birth of Purgatory*, trans. Arthur Goldhammer (Aldershot, England: Scolar Press, 1984).

Marc Cogan, *The Design in the Wax: The Structure of the Divine Comedy and Its Meaning* (Notre Dame, IN: University of Notre Dame Press, 1999).

David Robey's entries ("Hendecasyllable" and "Terza rima") in the *Dante Encyclopedia*, ed. Richard Lansing (London: Routledge, 2010), expand on the account given in this chapter and in the "Excursus on Metre" (pp. 263–66), and are especially informative on Dante's rhymes and on the relationship between syntax and metre in the *Commedia*.

CHAPTER 7

Tullio de Mauro, the distinguished historian of the Italian language who for a time served as his country's Minister for Education, reminded us of the two key facts about Dante's Italian cited here on p. 205 in a lecture he gave at University College London some years ago.

Some examples of the terminology for Latin and Italian in Dante's usage cited on pp. 216–17: the word *latini* for Italians is used at *Inf.* xxii. 65, *Inf.* xxvii 33, *Inf.* xxix 88, *Inf.* xxix 91, *Purg.* vii 16, *Purg.* xi 58, *Purg.* xiii 92; the word *latino* for language is used at *Par.* xii 144 and *Par.* xvii 35; the word *gramatica*, meaning Latin, is used in the *De vulgari* at I xi 7 and II vii 6.

The trilingual poem cited on p. 239 is no. 18 in the *edizione nazionale* of Dante's *Rime*, ed. Domenico De Robertis (Florence: Le Lettere, 2002) pp. 252–55.

Robert Durling, "The Audience(s) of the De vulgari eloquentia and the Petrose," in *Dante Studies* 110 (1992): 25–35, argues that the *De vulgari* and the *Convivio* remained unfinished because of Dante's ambivalence towards his public and his inability to establish to his own satisfaction either the nature of his true audience or the attitude he wished to take towards it.

Erich Auerbach, *"Sermo humilis,"* in *Literary Language & its Public in Late Latin Antiquity and in the Middle Ages*, trans. Ralph Manheim (London: Routledge & Kegan Paul, 1965).

Modern poets cited in this chapter: Osip Mandelstam, "Conversation About Dante," trans. Clarence Brown and Robert Hughes, in *Journey to Armenia & Conversation About Dante* (London: Notting Hill Editions, 2011); T. S. Eliot, *Dante* (London: Faber and Faber, 1965). The various quotations from Seamus Heaney come from Dennis O'Driscoll, *Stepping Stones: Interviews with Seamus Heaney* (London: Faber and Faber, 2008); and Seamus Heaney, *Finders Keepers: Selected Prose 1971–2001* (London: Faber and Faber, 2002). Heaney's translation of *Inf.* ii, 127–32 is in section VI of the poem *Station Island*, in Seamus Heaney, *Station Island* (London: Faber and Faber, 1984).

Peter Dronke's essays on *Paradiso* xxx ("Symbolism and Structure in *Paradiso* 30" in *Romance Philology* 43 [1989]: 29–48) and *Paradiso* xxxiii ("The Conclusion of Dante's *Commedia*," in *Italian Studies* 49 [1994]:

pp. 21–39) reflect the author's unrivalled knowledge of the medieval Latin sources and his sensitivity to poetic effect. Dronke argues that the principal inspiration behind Dante's rose was probably more verbal than visual. John Ahern, "Binding the Book: Hermeneutics and Manuscript Production in *Paradiso 33*" in *Publications of the Modern Language Association* 97 (1982): 800–809, discusses the implications of the volume-gatherings-pages-binding image at the end of the poem in relation to medieval bookmaking.

An overview of the history of the Italian language is given in Bruno Migliorini, *The Italian Language*; abridged, recast and revised by T. Gwynfor Griffith (London: Faber and Faber, 1984).

GENERAL

Dante Encyclopedia, ed. Richard Lansing (London: Routledge, 2010).

The Catholic Encyclopedia, ed. Charles G. Herbermann et al. (New York: Robert Apppleton, 1906). A version is available online.

John A. Scott, *Understanding Dante* (Notre Dame, IN: University of Notre Dame, 2004), offers a comprehensive, authoritative, judicious and up-to-date overview of Dante's life and works.

Useful collections of essays on different aspects of Dante's work and the *Commedia* include:

Cambridge Companion to Dante, ed. Rachel Jacoff (Cambridge: Cambridge University Press, 1993).

Dante: Contemporary Perspectives, ed. Amilcare A. Iannucci (Toronto: University of Toronto Press, 1997).

Dante Now: Current Trends in Dante Studies, ed. Theodore J. Cachey (Notre Dame, IN: University of Notre Dame Press, 1995).

The Mind of Dante, ed. U. Limentani (Cambridge: Cambridge University Press, Cambridge, 1965).

Dante: A Collection of Critical Essays, ed. J. Freccero (Englewood Cliffs, NJ: Prentice Hall, 1965).

The World of Dante: Essays on Dante and his Times, ed. Cecil Grayson, for the Oxford Dante Society (Oxford: Clarendon Press, 1980).

Dante in Context, ed. Z. G. Barański and L. Pertile (Cambridge: Cambridge University Press, forthcoming).

The California Lectura Dantis volumes offer readings in English of each canto of the poem (the quality is variable, but some are very good): *Inferno: A Canto-by-Canto Commentary*, ed. Allen Mandelbaum, Anthony Oldcorn, Charles Ross (Berkeley: University of California Press, 1998); *Purgatorio: A Canto-by-Canto Commentary*, ed. Allen Mandelbaum, Anthony Oldcorn, Charles Ross (Berkeley: University of California Press, 2008). *Cambridge Readings in Dante's Comedy*, ed. Kenelm Foster and Patrick Boyde (Cambridge: Cambridge University Press, 1981), has readings of ten cantos from across the poem.

Dante in English, ed. Eric Griffiths and Matthew Reynolds (London: Penguin Books, 2005), is a collection of translations into English of passages from Dante, and passages from English poets influenced by Dante, from Chaucer to the present.

The entire text of the *Commedia* read aloud by Lino Pertile can be heard on the Internet at the Princeton Dante Project Web site (http://etcweb.princeton.edu/dante/). Recordings of every canto read by distinguished Italian actors are available on CD: Antologia sonora. Collana diretta da Nanni De Stefani: *Letture, Divina Comedia: Inferno; Purgatorio; Paradiso*.

ENGLISH TRANSLATIONS OF DANTE'S WORKS

Two recent translations of the *Commedia* are outstanding. Robert Durling and Robert Hollander are distinguished American Dante scholars whose translations are the crowning achievement of a lifetime of devotion to their author.

The Divine Comedy of Dante Alighieri, ed. and trans. Robert M. Durling, with an introduction and notes by Ronald L. Martinez and Robert M. Durling (New York: Oxford University Press, 1996 [*Inferno*]; 2003 [*Purgatorio*], 2011 [*Paradiso*]). This is a prose translation, which follows the original text line by line, and is supported by ample but not overwhelmingly detailed scholarly notes. Supplementary short essays on some issues are a valuable additional feature for readers keen to pursue certain questions.

Dante, *The Inferno*, trans. Robert Hollander and Jean Hollander (New York: Anchor Books, 2002); *Purgatorio* (New York: Anchor Books 2004); *Paradiso* (New York: Doubleday, 2006). This is a slightly more poetic version of the *Commedia* (Jean Hollander is a poet), still closely linked to the facing Italian text, but taking occasional liberties in the name of a more natural or poetic-sounding English. Each canto is prefaced by a summary of its content (very helpful for those new to the poem). The notes are lively and informal but reflect a profound scholarly knowledge of the text.

Kenelm Foster and Patrick Boyde, *Dante's Lyric Poetry* (Oxford: Oxford University Press, 1967). It is difficult to imagine this translation and commentary being superseded in English.

The "Fiore" and the "Detto d'Amore": A Late 13th-Century Italian Translation of the "Roman de la Rose," Attributable to Dante, trans., with introduction and notes, Santa Casciani and Christopher Kleinhenz (Notre Dame, IN: University of Notre Dame Press, 2000).

The New Life of Dante Alighieri, trans. Dante Gabriel Rossetti (London: Ellis and Elvey, 1905). The old-fashioned language of this translation seems oddly suited to what the translator terms the "exquisite and intimate beauties" of this strange little book. A more up-to-date and very readable version is *Dante's Vita Nuova*, trans., and with an essay, Mark Musa (Bloomington: Indiana University Press, 1973), which usefully includes the texts of the poems in Italian and English.

Dante, *The Banquet*, trans., with an introduction and notes, Christopher Ryan (Saratoga, CA: Anma Libri, 1989).

Dante, *De vulgari eloquentia*, ed. and trans. Steven Botterill (Cambridge: Cambridge University Press, 1996). Easily the best version in English of this difficult text.

Dantis Alagherii Epistolae: The Letters of Dante, ed. Paget Toynbee, Emended Text with introduction, notes, and indices, and appendix on the Cursus (Oxford: Clarendon Press, 1920).

Dante, *Monarchia*, ed. and trans. Prue Shaw (Cambridge: Cambridge

University Press, 1995). The English text only (*Monarchy*) is available in paperback in the series Cambridge Texts in the History of Political Thought (Cambridge: Cambridge University Press, 1996).

The Temple Classics volume *A Translation of the Latin Works of Dante Alighieri*, trans. A. G. F. Howell and P. H. Wicksteed (London: J. M. Dent, 1904), contains a version of the *Questio de aqua et terra* by Philip Wicksteed.

Translations of all Dante's works into English are available online at the Princeton Dante Project Web site (where the translation is helpfully printed alongside the original text) and at danteonline.it.

ELECTRONIC RESOURCES

The Dartmouth Dante Project: as noted earlier, this invaluable resource contains all the early commentaries on the *Commedia* and many later ones.

The Princeton Dante Project is the single most comprehensive and reliable Dante Web site. It offers the Petrocchi Italian text of the poem, the Hollander translation, texts and translations of all the minor works, ample historical and interpretative notes, and links to the Dartmouth Dante Project and to other Dante sites worldwide.

The Web site of the Società Dantesca Italiana can be found at www.danteonline.it. It is another invaluable resource for scholars and general readers alike. As well as listing all surviving manuscripts, it maintains a bibliography of scholarly works on Dante in all languages, which is regularly updated.

Dante Alighieri, *Commedia*, ed. by Prue Shaw (Florence and Birmingham: Sismel-SDE, 2010). This DVD contains superb quality digitised colour images of five of the most important early manuscripts, reproduced in their entirety; an introductory essay offers an overview of the problems facing an editor of the poem. Allowing for the paradox that one is using an electronic medium to do so, the images give the reader unmediated access to the experience of reading the poem as Dante's contemporaries would have read it.

ACKNOWLEDGEMENTS

I WOULD LIKE TO THANK THOSE FRIENDS AND FAMILY MEMBERS WHO READ ALL
or parts of the book and made constructive suggestions: John Dickie, Claerwen James, Judy Davies, Peter Marsh, Jill Golden, Michael Hollingworth
and Giulio Lepschy. Any remaining infelicities are, it goes without saying,
my own. I would also like to thank other friends and colleagues with whom
I discussed particular points of interest or who gave invaluable practical
help: Rosetta Migliorini Fissi, Giancarlo Breschi, Silvia Gavuzzo Stewart,
Adam Beresford, Elizabeth Mozzillo Howell and Professor John Najemy.

The edition from which the Italian text is cited is Dante Alighieri, *La
Commedia secondo l'antica vulgata*, a cura di Giorgio Petrocchi, vol. VII in
Le opere di Dante Alighieri (Milan: Edizione Nazionale a cura della Società
Dantesca Italiana, 1966–67; 2nd ed., Florence: Le Lettere, 1994).

Translations from Italian and Latin are my own throughout, though
the work of other translators was helpful. The lines from the *Roman de la
Rose* cited in chapter 3 are from Guillaume de Lorris and Jean de Meung,
The Romance of the Rose, trans. Charles Dahlberg, 3rd ed. (Princeton, NJ:
Princeton University Press, 1995). The quotation from Cicero's *De amicitia*
used as an epigraph to chapter 1 is from the translation by E. S. Shuckburg.
The quotation from Osip Mandelstam used as an epigraph to chapter 5 is
from the translation of his *Conversation about Dante* by Clarence Brown and
Robert Hughes.

Other epigraphs and quotations:

Excerpt from "Dedication" ("What is poetry that does not save /
Nations or people"] from *Collected Poems 1931–1987* by Czeslaw Milosz.

Copyright © 1988 by Czeslaw Milosz Royalties, Inc. Reprinted by permission of HarperCollins Publishers.

Excerpt from T. S. Eliot's "Little Gidding" from *Four Quartets*, reprinted by kind permission of Faber and Faber Ltd.

Excerpt from "An Arundel Tomb" from *The Complete Poems of Philip Larkin*, by Philip Larkin, edited by Archie Burnett. Copyright © 2012 by The Estate of Philip Larkin. Reprinted by permission of Farrar, Straus and Giroux, LLC and Faber and Faber Ltd.

Excerpt from William Faulkner's *Requiem for a Nun* reprinted by permission of Random House.

Excerpt from Richard Feynman, *The Character of Physical Law*. Copyright © 1967 Massachusetts Institute of Technology, by permission of the MIT Press.

Excerpts from W. H. Auden, "In Memory of W. B. Yeats," used as epigraphs to chapters 2 and 5, by permission of Random House. The lines "Time . . . worships language and forgives / Everyone by whom it lives" are included in the version of the poem that appears in the Vintage edition of *Selected Poems, Expanded Edition* by W. H. Auden, edited by Edward Mendelson.

The Auden quotation used as an epigraph to chapter 7 is an excerpt from *Poets at Work* by Charles D. Abbott, W. H. Auden, and Karl Shapiro. Copyright 1948 by Harcourt, Inc. and renewed 1976 by Henry David Abbott, Karl Shapiro, and Rudolf Arnheim. Reprinted by permission of Houghton Mifflin Harcourt Publishing Company. All rights reserved.

Excerpt from "Station Island" from *Opened Ground: Selected Poems 1966–1996* by Seamus Heaney. Copyright © 1998 by Seamus Heaney. Excerpt from "The Redress of Poetry" from *The Redress of Poetry* by Seamus Heaney. Copyright © 1995 by Seamus Heaney. Reprinted by permission of Farrar, Straus and Giroux, LLC and Faber and Faber Ltd.

Finally, I would like to thank the Cambridge University Press for their permission to reproduce the chronology ("Principal Events in Dante's Life") published in the Cambridge University Press edition of my English translation of the *Monarchia* (*Monarchy*, Cambridge Texts in the History of Political Thought, CUP, 1996).

MAPS AND DIAGRAMS

The maps of Florence (Figs. 4 and 7) are adapted and simplified from Paget Toynbee's *A Dictionary of Proper Names and Notable Matters in the Works of Dante,* revised by Charles S. Singleton (Oxford: Clarendon Press, 1968). Fig. 7 also incorporates details from John M. Najemy, *A History of Florence, 1200–1575* (Oxford: Blackwell Publishing Ltd., 2006), p. 8. The diagram of Dante's cosmos (Fig. 2) is adapted from Toynbee's *Dictionary.* The map of central Italy (Fig. 5) is loosely based on a map in Daniel Waley, *The Italian City Republics* (London: Weidenfeld and Nicholson, 1969), p. 213.

The diagrams of purgatory and paradise (Figs. 26 and 28) adapt and simplify those in Anna Maria Chiavacci Leonardi's commentary on the *Commedia*: Dante Alighieri, *Commedia,* con il commento di Anna Maria Chiavacci Leonardi (Bologna: Zanichelli; *Purgatorio,* 2000; *Paradiso,* 2001). All the maps and diagrams are by Claerwen James.

ILLUSTRATIONS

Fig. 1. Botticelli's drawing illustrating the plan of Dante's hell (ms. Reg. lat. 1896, f. 101r). By kind permission of the Biblioteca Apostolica Vaticana.

Fig. 3. Guido Cavalcanti cornered by revellers outside the baptistery: a manuscript illustration to Boccaccio's *Decameron,* 6, 9 (ms. Ital. 63, f. 243v). By kind permission of the Bibliothèque nationale de France. RMN.

Fig. 6.   The baptistery in a fourteenth-century fresco in the Loggia del Bigallo, Florence. © 2013 Photo Scala, Florence.

Fig. 8.   A detail of Botticelli's drawing for *Inferno* xix: Dante talks to Pope Nicholas III. By kind permission of the Kupferstichkabinett, Gemäldegalerie—Staatliche Museen zu Berlin. BPK.

Fig. 9.   Surviving fragment of Giotto's fresco of Boniface preaching the Jubilee in 1300, basilica of St. John Lateran, Rome. Akg-images.

Fig. 10.   Arnolfo di Cambio's statue of Boniface made for the façade of the new cathedral in Florence, 1300; now in the Museo dell'Opera del Duomo. The Art Archive.

Fig. 11.   The document in the Florentine State Archive recording the death sentence imposed on Dante and other White Guelfs in March 1302 (*Libro del chiodo*, p. 15). Su concessione del Ministero per i Beni e le Attività Culturali; divieto di ulteriori riproduzioni o duplicazioni con qualsiasi mezzo.

Fig. 12.   F.10r containing the opening of *Inferno* x in ms. Triv. 1080 of the Archivio Storico Civico Biblioteca Trivulziana; copyright@Comune di Milano—tutti i diritti di legge riservati.

Fig. 13.   Jonah emerges from the belly of the sea monster as Christ Pantocrator in a mosaic which decorates the pulpit in the cathedral in Ravello, 1272. © 2013 Photo Scala, Florence.

Fig. 14.   The opening image in British Library ms. Egerton 943: the poet as dreamer. By kind permission of the British Library.

Fig. 15.   Pope Innocent III dreams of Saint Francis holding up the Lateran church in a fresco in the basilica of St. Francis in Assisi. The Art Archive.

Fig. 16.   The opening image in the Budapest University Library copy of the *Commedia* (ELTE University Library Cod. Ital. 1, f. 1r): the poet in a trance. By kind permission of the Eötvös Loránd University Library.

Fig. 17.   The opening image in the Holkham Hall manuscript (ms. Holkham Misc. 48, p. 1) now in the Bodleian Library: the poet in a trance. By kind permission of the Bodleian Libraries, the University of Oxford.

Fig. 18.   The opening image in ms. Vat. Lat. 4776, fol. 1r: the poet as creative writer. By kind permission of the Biblioteca Apostolica Vaticana.

Fig. 19.   The opening image in ms. Triv. 1080 of the Archivio Storico Civico Biblioteca Trivulziana: Dante and Virgil walk through the initial capital letter to enter the world of the poem. Copyright@Comune di Milano—tutti i diritti di legge riservati.

Fig. 20.   Dante and Virgil observe the metamorphoses of the thieves in the Chantilly manuscript of the *Commedia*. By kind permission of the library of the Musée Condé, Chantilly. RMN.

Fig. 21.   Dante and Virgil with the simoniacs in the Holkham Hall manuscript (ms. Holkham Misc. 48, p. 28). By kind permission of the Bodleian Libraries, the University of Oxford.

Fig. 22.   A detail of Botticelli's drawing for *Inferno* xxiv: Dante scrambles up over the rocks with help from Virgil. By kind permission of the Kupferstichkabinett, Gemäldegalerie—Staatliche Museen zu Berlin. BPK.

Fig. 23.   A detail of Botticelli's drawing for *Purgatorio* xii: Dante feels for the missing *P* on his forehead. By kind permission of the Kupferstichkabinett, Gemäldegalerie—Staatliche Museen zu Berlin. BPK.

Fig. 24.   A detail of Botticelli's drawing for *Purgatorio* x: Dante and Virgil deep in conversation. By kind permission of the Kupferstichkabinett, Gemäldegalerie—Staatliche Museen zu Berlin. BPK.

Fig. 25.   Diagram of Dante's purgatory showing how all the seven deadly sins derive from love gone wrong; from an early printed edition of the *Commedia* published by Aldo Manuzio in Venice in 1515, now held in the Biblioteca Nazionale Braidense in Milan. By kind permission of the Ministero per i Beni e le Attività Culturali; divieto di ulteriore riproduzione o duplicazione con qualsiasi mezzo.

Fig. 27.   A detail of Botticelli's drawing for *Inferno* xxvii: Dante and Virgil look down on the counsellors of fraud. By kind permission of the Kupferstichkabinett, Gemäldegalerie—Staatliche Museen zu Berlin. BPK.

Fig. 30.   A column of text from ms. Triv. 1080 in the Archivio Storico Civico Biblioteca Trivulziana. Copyright@Comune di Milano—tutti i diritti di legge riservati.

Fig. 31.   A detail of Botticelli's drawing for *Paradiso* xxvi: Dante talks to Adam. By kind permission of the Kupferstichkabinett, Gemäldegalerie—Staatliche Museen zu Berlin. BPK.

Fig. 32.   A detail of Botticelli's drawing for *Inferno* xxi: the devil's unorthodox trumpet call to summon his troops. By kind permission of the Kupferstichkabinett, Gemäldegalerie—Staatliche Museen zu Berlin. BPK.

Fig. 33.   A detail of Botticelli's drawing for *Inferno* xviii: the flatterers immersed in human excrement. By kind permission of the Kupferstichkabinett, Gemäldegalerie—Staatliche Museen zu Berlin. BPK.

Page 261.   A detail of Botticelli's drawing for *Paradiso* xxix: Dante. By kind permission of the Kupferstichkabinett, Gemäldegalerie—Staatliche Museen zu Berlin. BPK.

INDEX

Page numbers in *italics* refer to illustrations.

Virgil's journey with, xxix, 4–5, 27, 30,
32, 33, 43, 44, 47, 49, 57, 74, 86, 86, 90,
101, 103, 113, 117, 118, 121, 122, 136,
142, 145, 147, 155, 160–64, 166–70, 185,
186, 222, 225, 226, 234, 239
visionary experience of, 83, 87, 88,
117, 182, 246–53, 254
Dante (poet, author of the *Commedia*),
xvi, xxiii
afterlife's mapping by, 146–47
artistic struggle of, 6, 87, 135, 144,
218, 219, 221, 239, 245–46, 248, 253
artistic trajectory of, 6, 79, 95, 106,
128–29, 136, 141, 143, 211, 246
Beatrice's relationship with, xx, 41,
78, 92, 93
biographical information about,
67–74, 92–94, 95, 96, 212; *see also*
Commedia, autobiographical elements of
birth of, 67
Boccaccio's story about, 82
Boccaccio's veneration of, xxi, 94
censorship of, xx, 96–97
children of, 69, 93, 94; *see also* Dante,
Jacopo di; Dante, Pietro di
critical reflection by, 218–19
death of, 95
death warrant for, 66, 69, 70, 96
exile of, xv, xxiii, 27–28, 30, 42, 52,
53, 55, 62, 69, 70–71, 70, 92–93, 94,
134, 140–41
father of, 76
friends of, xv, xxii, xxiv, 6–10, 13, 17,
23, 29, 31–34, 37, 39, 163–65, 201
Giotto's acquaintance with, 200
illustrations of, 84, 84, 85, 85, 86, 86
imagination of, xiii, xiv, 77, 85, 87, 97,
202, 224
imperial beliefs of, xxv
Latini's influence on, 75, 76
letters of, xxv, 69–72, 93, 144, 184–85,
212
love life of, 93–94

manuscripts of, 72–74
military service of, 21
moral universe of, xiv, xxii, 1–2, 6,
49, 76, 81, 95–96, 106, 109, 113–14,
129–30, 131, 195
philosophical concerns of, xvi–xvii,
2, 42
philosophical studies of, xxii–xxiii,
106–7, 118–19
poetic evolution of, 6, 37, 41–43,
72–74, 93, 95, 100, 106, 107–8, 116,
141, 143, 144, 169, 171, 207, 209, 214,
218, 225, 231, 251, 256, 257, 268
poetic mentors of, xv, xxiv, 37, 100,
201, 231
poetic skill of, xiii–xiv, xv, xvii, xxi,
37, 39, 41, 96, 97, 137, 200, 207, 256,
257, 261, 264, 268
political activities of, xv, xxv, 4, 6, 13,
17–18, 23, 39, 42, 62, 68–69, 72, 95, 96
political views of, xxv, 61–62, 69, 88,
141, 142, 144; *see also* *Commedia*,
political vision in; *Monarchia*
psychological crisis of, 3–4, 6, 30, 32,
33, 88, 118–19, 260
religious beliefs of, 1, 2, 3, 27, 34, 39,
116–17, 127, 178, 179–80, 203
Roman de la Rose translated by, 251,
266
scientific knowledge of, xvi–xvii, 1,
88
as scribe, 108
self-citation by, 165
sculpture of, 65
temperament of, 71, 96, 114
vernacular use by, xvii, xx, 39, 42, 97,
206–19, 224, 225, 231, 234–35, 236,
237, 238, 239, 240, 255–56, 258, 261
wife of, 20, 93–94
youthful poetry of, 8–9, 33–34, 37,
41, 42, 101, 105, 106, 116, 163, 165,
218, 224, 251, 266; *see also* *Vita nova*
David, King, xxiii, 141, 198, 240
Dawkins, Richard, 179

Peter, Saint, xxviii, 60, 116, 172, 177,
    209, 220
  basilica of, 10, 65
Peter of Spain, xxvii, 119
Petrarch, 72, 219, 264, 265
Philip III (the Bold), King of France,
    xxii, xxvi, 55
Philip IV (the Fair), King of France, xxii,
    xxvi, 52, 55, 64
Phillips, Tom, 176
philosophy:
  Dante's study of, xxii–xxiii, 106–7,
    118–19
  use of Latin in, 212
  see also scholasticism
Phlegethon River, xxix
physics, 180
Piazza Signoria, 28
Picasso, Pablo, 67
Piers Plowman (Langland), 82
pilgrimages, 10–11, 128
Pilgrim's Progress, The (Bunyan), 78–79
Pillars of Hercules, 123, 127
Pisa, 92
Pistoia, 15, 69
planets, *see* heavenly spheres
Plato, 2, 179, 269
Pluto, xxvii, 225
Poetics (Aristotle), 257
poetry:
  allegory in, 79–80
  artistic reputations in, 200–201, 230
  Commedia's discussions of, 167–70,
    219, 226–34
  correspondence in, *see tenzone*
  Dante's evolution in, 6, 37, 41–43,
    72–74, 93, 95, 100, 106, 107–8, 116,
    141, 143, 144, 169, 171, 207, 209, 214,
    218, 225, 231, 251, 256, 257, 268
  Dante's influences in, xv, xxiv,
    xxviii–xxix, 37, 78, 100, 201, 231
  Dante's language choice in, 205,
    208; *see also* vernacular, Dante's
    use of

Dante's mastery of, xiii–xiv, xv, xvii,
    xxi, 37, 39, 41, 96, 97, 137, 200, 207,
    256, 257, 261, 264, 268
  Dante's writing about, 217–18
  Heaney's thoughts on, 151, 261
  intertextuality in, 171–72
  love's relationship to, 100, 116
  rhythmic patterns in, 202
  rivalry in, 29, 30, 39
  sea-voyage metaphor for, 128–29
  Statius and Virgil's conversation
    about, 167–70
  talent in, 30, 34
  of young Dante, 8–9, 33–34, 37, 41,
    42, 101, 105, 106, 116, 163, 165, 218,
    224, 251, 266; *see also Vita Nova*
  see also Commedia, poetic structures in
poetry, vernacular:
  of Arnaut Daniel, xx, 226, 231, 233
  of Cavalcanti, 8–10, 100, 116, 200, 201
  Commedia's history of, 230–34
  Dante's mastery of, xxi, 39, 257
  Dante's views on, 207, 208
  of Guinizzelli, xx, xxiv, 100, 101, 108,
    116, 200, 226, 231
  Italian tradition in, 99–101, 105, 208,
    226, 231
  see also vernacular
Polynices, 121
Pompey, xxii, 148
Ponte Vecchio, xxvi, 35
Pontius Pilate, xxvii
Pope, Alexander, 175
Porta di San Piero, 20, 21
Poujet, Bernard du, xx, 97
Pound, Ezra, 60, 100, 171, 209, 235, 236,
    269
power, 41–65
  art and, xv, 62–63, 65
  France's corruption by, 51–57
  Holy Roman Empire's struggle for,
    57–60
  papacy's perversion by, 43–51, 57, 60,
    153

PRUE SHAW received her education at the universities of Sydney, Florence and Oxford. Her years in Florence studying for her *dottorato* gave her an abiding love of the city and its great poet. She taught Italian language and literature at the universities of Cambridge (where she was a Fellow of New Hall) and London. She is an emeritus Reader in Italian at University College London.

She is the editor of the *edizione nazionale* of Dante's medieval Latin treatise *Monarchia* (the *edizione nazionale* is the official critical text of the poet's works published by the Società Dantesca Italiana). She is the only non-Italian to have achieved the distinction of being asked to edit a text in this prestigious series.

Her translation of the *Monarchia* into English is used on the Princeton Dante Project Web site (www.princeton.edu/dante/) and the Società Dantesca Italiana Web site (www.danteonline.it.) In 2000, she acted as consultant to the Royal Academy for their exhibition "Botticelli's Dante: The Drawings for the *Divine Comedy*."

Prue Shaw lives in Cambridge, England. Details of her other publications can be found on her Web site: www.prueshaw.com.

Printed in the USA
CPSIA information can be obtained
at www.ICGtesting.com
CBHW020331060824
12762CB00008B/198